To brother Yale:
"May the source
be with you.

Warren

Outsourcing Information Security

For a complete listing of the *Artech House Computer Security Series,*
turn to the back of this book.

Outsourcing Information Security

C. Warren Axelrod

Artech House
Boston • London
www.artechhouse.com

Library of Congress Cataloging-in-Publication Data
A catalog record for this book is available from the Library of Congress

British Library Cataloguing in Publication Data
A catalog record for this book is available from the British Library.

Cover design by Igor Valdman

© 2004 ARTECH HOUSE, INC.
685 Canton Street
Norwood, MA 02062

International Standard Book Number: 1-58053-531-3

10 9 8 7 6 5 4 3 2 1

To my own in-house support team: Judy, David, and Elizabeth

Contents

Foreword

In the current knowledge age, business thrives on the confidentiality, integrity, and availability of information. Information provides the nervous system in which business operates. The task to secure business information is simpler in a closed environment. However, our knowledge age is also one of outsourcing business processes and services to reduce cost and streamline the organization.

In addition to those who are already taking advantage of outsourcing, many other organizations are just beginning to consider the idea. The question frequently asked, after how much money will be saved, is: How safe of a proposition is it to send mission-critical code and information (e.g., intellectual property, regulated data, private data) to another business entity? Organizations are keen to understand how they can ensure the security of their code, data, compliance requirements, and intellectual property while still taking advantage of the cost benefits.

The answer is that outsourcing is as secure as you make it. There are multiple levels of security—both from a process perspective and a technology perspective—which companies can put in place to secure their business relationships, their data, and their intellectual property.

As companies allow business partners to access and process an increasing amount of proprietary data, applications, and intellectual capital, they are realizing that not only must they get their business partners to commit to formalized security measures and policies, but companies must also take steps to protect themselves in the event that their business partners have a security breach.

With the current political turmoil and focus, this is particularly imperative today in offshore vendor relationships. Certainly business partner security breaches anywhere can be devastating, but the publicity given to offshore outsourcing makes a security breach offshore a potential customer, reputation, and regulatory disaster.

While organizations need to address security in their business partner relationships, it is imperative to not go to the extreme and impose draconian controls that inhibit these relationships when it is unwarranted. The risk to information varies depending on the nature of the information. Not all business partner relationships warrant the same level of risk controls because the information and the nature of the relationships vary significantly.

The bottom line is that risk and business partner relationships vary and that controls should be appropriate for the circumstances. Companies are only as secure as their weakest link; in forming outsourcing relationships, keep the following in mind:

- Don't assume that "marquee clients" always equate to good security partners.

- Don't assume that IT service providers, even prestigious domestic ones, will be good security partners.

- Ensure that business partners commit to formalized security measures or policies, but companies also must take steps to protect themselves in the event that their business partners have a security breach. Lax business partner or vendor security can negate a company's entire investment in information security.

- Companies embarking on offshore outsourcing relationships should use new relationships as a catalyst to formalize all their business partner security processes.

This book provides valuable insight for organizations seeking an approach to securing business partner relationships and will be a valuable tool for anyone involved in outsourcing relationships, including information security and IT managers, IT executives, and senior management in the organization. The risk that organizations face in outsourcing extends to many parts of the business and could significantly impact operations and reputations. The approach and knowledge contained herein is a commendable work to present this to all interested parties.

By writing this book, Warren Axelrod specifically shows his experience to provide an approach that will secure outsourcing relationships but is not steeped in technology. While technology is important, Dr. Axelrod provides a very balanced risk-based approach to these relationships, an approach in which the benefits of the relationship are balanced with risks and exposures that it introduces.

The risk is clear. Business reputations can be affected by business partners—companies are only as trustworthy as the least reputable firms with which they deal. Therefore, one security breach with one business partner cannot only negate a company's entire investment in information security, but it can also damage the reputation and viability of a company. If companies cannot trust their business partners and vendors, they should not be doing business with them. In the case of IT outsourcing, companies may be better off internally supporting their IT systems than risking their support or development to third-party providers, at home or abroad.

Michael Rasmussen, CISSP
Principal Analyst, Information Risk/Compliance Management
Forrester Research, Inc.
September 2004

Preface

The idea for this book formed in 2001—a time when information technology (IT) outsourcing was not at all the object of controversy, as it became in the politically charged atmosphere of the United States in 2004. In fact outsourcing, particularly offshore IT outsourcing, was seen as a boon and as having "saved the day" with its contribution to preventing a computer meltdown during the calendar change from 1999 to 2000—known variously as "Year 2000," "Y2K," or the "Millennium date changeover."

The book concept began when a colleague, Russell Dean Vines, a leading author in the information security space, asked if I would write a book as one in a series on security, which a publisher had asked him to put together. We agreed that my book would address security aspects of IT outsourcing. This was appropriate for me since I have worked for IT outsourcing companies for more than two thirds of my career and have specialized in information security since 1996, earning a CISSP and CISM along the way.[1]

As luck would have it, Russ's publisher decided to cancel the series. However, I was fortunate to have Artech House accept the proposal a short time later. And the rest, as they say, is history.

---

1. The Certificate for Information Systems Security Professionals (CISSP) is awarded by the International Information Systems Security Certification Consortium (ISC)[2] to those who can demonstrate proficiency in the ten areas contained in the "body of knowledge." The Certified Information Security Manager (CISM) is granted by the Information Systems Audit and Control Association (ISACA) to those who have had substantial practical experience managing an information security function and who can demonstrate a required level of knowledge.

The Time Was Right

Looking into security aspects of outsourcing seemed timely because increasing concerns were being voiced during the Y2K remediation period that foreign outsourcers might be stealing intellectual property embodied in computer programs or injecting damaging code into computer programs for financial or political gain. But, as Dan Verton points out in his revealing book, there was no known evidence then or in the years that have followed that any such malfeasance has occurred [1].

In addition, lawmakers and regulators—in Europe and other countries, such as the United Kingdom, Canada, and New Zealand, and later in the United States—were increasingly reflecting the public's concerns about identity theft.[2] In the United States, federal and state legislators in general, and regulators in the financial and health services industries in particular, voiced major concerns that mirrored their constituents' fears about the stealing of individuals' personal information by those with evil intent. The regulators have already instituted extensive guidelines as to how to protect customers' information as well as that being handled by service providers, especially when such information may be farmed out for processing abroad. The European Union is particularly aggressive in this area.

The Intent of the Book

The goal of this book is to heighten your awareness of the many complex and confusing issues that you need to identify, quantify (where possible), and analyze, if you are to make the right outsourcing decisions while ensuring that security matters have been fully addressed and accounted for. The content is not intended to be all-encompassing, nor is it by any means the last word on the subject. The goal is to bring to your attention, as it did to mine during the research and writing processes, many items not typically included in analyses but that, in some cases, change the whole basis of an outsourcing decision.

The central theme of the book is that organizations must understand and consider what costs and benefits are incurred and gained, respectively, at the intersection of the two most dynamic, difficult, and controversial areas of information technology today, namely, outsourcing and security. If we look at these areas in a two-by-two table (see Table P.1), we see the full scope of the issues at hand.

2. On November 15, 2001, I testified before Congress on cyber security. However, the congressmen at the hearing expressed much greater concern over the growing identity theft issue than they did about the prospect of terrorists attacking through cyberspace.

Table P.1
The Intersections of Outsourcing and Security

	The Outsourcing	The Security
...of Outsourcing	Subcontracted IT services	Secure IT services
...of Security	Subcontracted security services	Secure security services

Now we will consider each box within the table to understand how it plays within the overall concept.

The Outsourcing of Outsourcing

This refers to when an outsourcer subcontracts one or more IT services to another service provider. The ultimate customer of the outsourcer may not even be aware that this is occurring. But increasingly that question is being asked, since the only way, for example, to be able to vouch for the protection of customer information is to know every pair of hands that has touched it or eyes that have viewed it. While this issue is not a major focus of the book, an organization must take it into account and include due diligence for providers to providers, to whatever depth is necessary to ensure that every relevant point of contact has been checked.

The Security of Security

Also, a lesser focus of the book, this subject relates to the security posture of managed security services. In the physical world, it is a matter of ensuring that security guards do not have criminal records. In the electronic world, it might include a check as to how secure a particular manufacturer's firewalls might be, that is, whether it has any known vulnerability. In a real sense, the security of security is the greatest risk of all, since so much reliance is placed on managed security service providers (MSSPs). If they are corrupted—by design or by accident—the basic premise of security is thwarted.

The Outsourcing of Security

Here we are dealing with, for the most part, MSSPs. Appendix A includes an extensive list of the types of security service available in the marketplace.

This is really a subset of general outsourcing, but it is a category that must be looked at most carefully. It somehow combines both the above categories.

The security services provider may well use a third party to check on the backgrounds of its staff, or third parties may supply software and "signatures" to facilitate the provider's work. Consequently, there is reason for concern as to how effective these once-removed services or subcontractors might be. This area is addressed throughout the book. It is frequently offered as a more extreme security situation relative to regular outsourcing, even critical services. Any risks that relate to these services can put many of an organization's activities at greater risk.

The Security of Outsourcing

This subject represents the main focus of the book. It is the general case and, as such, is subjected to all the concerns of the other entries in the table. It emphasizes the security issues that must be accounted for when making a decision to outsource and when selecting a particular outsourcer. Many of these issues are direct and specific to the provider of the services. But to the extent that the service provider relies on other providers for ancillary services, including security services, then due consideration must also be given to the security postures of these indirect service providers.

These dependencies, which have evolved over time, are on the verge of potentially spiraling out of control. New technologies, in the form of Web services and grid computing, bring with them the specter of large numbers of remote providers, many of whom may not be known to the user of the services. In order to deal bravely with this "new world," the analyst must be aware of the issues and how to address them. Such is the foundation that this book attempts to provide.

The Structure of the Book

Chapter 1 introduces our subject by defining the scope of the treatment of the joint topics of outsourcing and security. It gives a definition of IT outsourcing and traces the history of the recent rapid growth of such services. More detailed and extensive histories of both outsourcing and information security are provided in Appendices B and C, respectively.

While it is true that there are many new outsourcing and security issues and circumstances, many of these have been addressed in some form or another in earlier times. We can take some of these lessons from the past and apply them to the present and future. While appearances might be different, surprisingly much is fundamentally the same. Deciphering the similarities and differences makes for a much richer approach to current problems and many of the solutions can be tailored from past successes.

In Chapter 2, we lay out the range of information security risks that are confronted daily, whether an activity is outsourced or not. Threats can come from internal and external sources. Vulnerabilities arise in many areas with many causes. It is hard enough to protect against threats and manage vulnerabilities for one's own organization. How much more difficult it is to deal with threats and vulnerabilities as they impact third parties and in turn affect the security health of the customer of the services.

In Chapter 3, we look at the risks of outsourcing. The purpose is not to discourage organizations from engaging third parties; rather it is to ensure that the responsible parties have considered the risks, accounted for them, and after going through the process, are more comfortable in their decision. Awareness is important here. However, even when one thinks one knows all the risks, many of them remain obscure—they are difficult or impossible to measure, yet their impact can be enormous. This makes for some interesting subjective tradeoffs. Clearly some decisions will be reversed—in either direction—by allowing for these risk factors, but that is not a bad thing. It is far better to know what one is getting into than to proceed blindly and find out later when bad things actually happen.[3]

In Chapter 4, we get into greater detail and describe the categories of costs and benefits. We differentiate between tangible and intangible, direct and indirect, and objective and subjective costs and benefits as they relate to outsourcing. We provide examples of these costs and benefits, relating the categories specifically to risk and security areas.

Chapter 5 describes how the costs and benefits relate to the Request for Information (RFI) and Request for Proposal (RFP) processes. The analysis is done in the context of the status and viability of the outsourcing company, which is a major consideration in the decision.

In Chapter 6, we look at the evaluation process that takes place once the information has been collected and sorted. We consider issues that need to be addressed, what should be included in the analysis, and the relative importance of various items.

---

3. I am reminded of an industry newspaper report some 20 years ago of a major early player in the computer industry, which purportedly decided it would withdraw from the computer business based on a spreadsheet analysis that was later shown to contain a major error. Had the correct analysis been done, it would have projected that this particular company would have become a very profitable player in the business, as contrasted with the losing scenario portrayed by the incorrect analysis. Errors of commission and omission can equally lead to the wrong decisions. The goal here is to broaden the base of factors to be included in an analysis to improve its accuracy and lead to better decisions. The reader is encouraged to add factors of his or her own that I may have omitted and to check from many different angles to ensure accuracy in the analysis.

Chapter 7 delves into the specific security considerations that affect the outsourcing decision and how they should be handled. It is here that we take each of the categories usually ascribed to the field of security, map them to aspects of the outsourcing decision process, and describe what influence they might have. This is the crux of the book.

Finally, in Chapter 8, I summarize the full flow of the outsourcing evaluation and decision processes.

At the end of the book are three appendices. Appendix A is particularly important as it evaluates the various candidate security services that might be performed by a third party and shows their specific advantages and disadvantages.

Appendices B and C contain histories of outsourcing and information security, respectively. These provide the backdrop against which to view the current state of the art.

Reference

[1]   Verton, D., *Black Ice: The Invisible Threat of Cyber-Terrorism,* New York: McGraw-Hill/Osborne, 2003, p. 37.

Acknowledgments

There have been many contributors to this book, some of whom were not even aware of their participation. They include work colleagues, the staff and members of various industry and professional associations, with whom I worked on joint projects, and professionals in the information security field, with whom I discussed various topics.

Perhaps my most significant interactions were with the staff and members of the Banking Industry Technology Secretariat, or BITS, as it is better known. BITS is the information technology arm of the Financial Services Roundtable (FSR) and is an industry association run by a dynamic group of high-energy individuals led by CEO Cathy Allen. BITS staff, who made great strides in pushing the envelope on reducing the risks related to IT outsourcing, include Faith Boettger, John Carlson, and Margaret Prior, and former staffers Peggy Lipps (now at the Bank of America) and Laura Lundine. BITS members, myself included, created two of what I consider to be the definitive publications on the topic of IT outsourcing. One is the report "BITS Framework: Managing Technology Risk for Information Technology (IT) Service Providers," *Banking Industry Technology Secretariat, Financial Services Roundtable,* Washington, D.C., November 2003, http://www.bitsinfo.org, and the other is the "Expectations Matrix," *Banking Industry Technology Secretariat, Financial Services Roundtable,* Washington, D.C., January 2004, http://www.bitsinfo.org, a rigorous questionnaire that financial institutions are encouraged to use as a basis for their due-diligence efforts.

I also worked on a number of committees and working groups of the Securities Industry Association (SIA) and received a different perspective from SIA staffers Don Kittel, Art Trager, and John Panchery.

It was through BITS that several of its members became involved in reviewing work done at Carnegie Mellon University's Software Engineering Institute relating to selecting and engaging MSSPs. My collaboration with Julia Allen and Carol Sledge was very rewarding and helpful in clarifying my thoughts. The report that resulted from the research, *Outsourcing Managed Security Services,* Network Systems Survivability Program, Carnegie Mellon University, Pittsburgh, PA, Software Engineering Institute, January 2003; http://www.fedcirc.com, is well worth the reader's attention.

I am grateful to Mike Rasmussen and Steve Hunt of the Giga Information Group, which was acquired by the Forrester Research Group. Both of these gentlemen are leaders in the areas of security and outsourcing, and it was most helpful to learn from them.

Priscilla Tate, executive director of Technology Managers Forum (TMF), helped by facilitating discussions on the topic at TMF meetings.

And I must not forget the guidance and learning that I obtained from colleagues at work, including Charlie Carroll at the AXA Group; Jim Finnigan, Ted Gerbracht, and John Kirkwood at Credit Suisse First Boston; Mike Gergel, Jeff Kemp, Eliot Wagner, and Tom Whitman at Pershing; and Eric Guerrino and Sharon Kaufman at The Bank of New York. Each provided their own insights into security issues and outsourcing, which helped greatly in my formulating ideas. However, I take full responsibility for any errors or omissions in the content of the book.

The team at Artech House, namely, Tim Pitts and, particularly, Tiina Ruonamaa, the project editor, deserve a tremendous amount of credit for their patience and persistence mixed with encouragement. I have no doubt that this project would not have come to a conclusion without their prodding me to keep going at each step of the way.

And last, but certainly not least, I thank my family, particularly my wife Judy, for their patience, support, and encouragement to get it finished. The burden falls disproportionately heavily on those who are the closest. They suffer all the anguish and pain without having the satisfaction of creation that occurs when a book takes shape.

1

Outsourcing and Information Security

Modern societies can be distinguished from earlier, more primitive peoples by the degree of specialization, and the consequent interdependencies, that we find today. Early human society largely consisted of generalists endowed with and trained in the relatively few skills and capabilities necessary for survival. Today's developed societies are so complex that we see specialties beget subspecialties to the nth degree. And while there is always a small minority of "outbackers," who could probably survive independently, the majority of us need a complex support system of specialists to provide the goods and services that we need to lead our everyday lives.

Outsourcing is, in broad terms, the provision of certain goods or services by third-party specialists in direct or indirect exchange for money. A more detailed derivation of outsourcing and related concepts can be found in William Safire's humorous article [1].

Each of us typically outsources services hundreds if not thousands of times each day. Someone delivers the morning newspaper to our home. We buy a cup of coffee and a doughnut before taking a bus or train, or we have fuel put into our cars and drive to our offices, where we enter a heated, cooled, cleaned, and protected environment. In each case, someone else is providing a product or service to us, either directly or through intermediaries.

It is the miracle of our developed economies that such systems of interdependent service and product suppliers can be coordinated to function as well as they do. Today, for the most part, others meet our very many personal and business needs. Goods and services are available when and where we need them at a cost that is usually less than that of our making them or performing them ourselves, even if we have the ability, time, or materials to do so, which we often do not.

First ... Some Definitions

The term "outsourcing" is used extensively to describe many types of services provided by third parties. We shall focus on the outsourcing of IT services and address physical or human services only to the extent that they affect IT. In particular, we examine the types of outsourcing that have been facilitated by advances over the past half century in telecommunications and computer systems. IT outsourcing has become a business with revenues in the multibillions of dollars per year and exhibiting double-digit growth.

Less commonly used is the term "insourcing," by which we mean outsourcing that is done internally within the sphere of control of the organization, most likely by a separate division or subsidiary. The insourced service is assumed to be provided with a formal service level agreement (SLA) in place. The pricing of the service may or may not be at the market, but it should be competitive so that the "customer" can select the service that offers the most benefit at the lowest cost.

A hybrid of outsourcing and insourcing, whereby the responsibility for providing the services is shared in some manner between internal and external groups, is termed "cosourcing" or, to use Safire's term, "intersourcing" [1].

We will be concentrating primarily on risk factors relating to logical security (i.e., relating to IT). We will also address risk factors of physical security, to the extent that they affect the decision to outsource IT services, including managed security services. We will analyze how to determine whether or not to use outsourced services and how to evaluate particular services and to select providers. We will determine which services are suitable for outsourcing and the attributes of service providers, such as size, financial health, operational excellence, staffing, longevity, and location, that are required to meet such responsibilities. Outsourcing is a choice and should be based on informed analysis.

Second ... A Clarification

Considerable confusion and contradiction exist in the literature regarding the definitions of outsourcing and IT outsourcing. To some extent, outsourcing has become the *mot du jour* and is applied to situations that are not strictly outsourcing arrangements.

In "Outsourcing: Evolving Toward Trust," Sweet et al. define IT outsourcing as "...the transfer of IT services or business processes from one company to another" [2]. The authors note that, while outsourcing is related to service contracting, there are important differences between the two. In the case of service contracting, the purchaser, or client, of the services retains ownership of and responsibility for the services subject to the agreement, and the client specifies what is to be done by the service provider and how it is to be achieved. In contrast, with outsourcing the service provider generally takes on the additional responsibility for determining the manner in which requirements are met. The authors describe business process outsourcing as the assumption of even broader responsibilities by the service provider, allowing, for example, the service provider to redesign processes and apply new and existing technologies in different ways.

Differentiating outsourcing from other types of third-party services by the degree of control and responsibility taken on by the provider is a convenient way to limit the scope of our investigation. However, it should still be recognized that the line between outsourcing and other types of third-party services is fuzzy, especially as we see providers offering both types of service or combinations of the two. For our purposes, we shall define IT outsourcing as third-party computer-based services that involve some measure of third-party management and control of the overall processes.

Y2K as a Turning Point

At the turn of the millennium, the markets for IT and business process outsourcing, internal information security activities, and outsourcing of information security projects and managed security services were all sanguine. Expectations were high. The demand for services relating to Y2K computer application and system program remediation came at a particularly good time for the U.S. economy, which was experiencing a prolonged expansion and could readily absorb the hundreds of billions of dollars that were purportedly spent on the Y2K effort.[1]

The Y2K remediation effort in the United States pushed well beyond the resource limits of domestic consulting companies and their customers, both of which turned to third-party programming and testing services, at home and abroad, to fill the gap. The urgent and enormous Y2K requirements expanded dramatically the use of outsourcing and consulting, especially offshore IT outsourcing in countries such as India and Ireland.

1. In fact, the side effects of Y2K, such as the replacement of older computer equipment and software with new, had a very positive impact on the economy, particularly the technology sector.

Once the use of outsourcing had been established under the pressure of the immutable Y2K deadline, it became much easier and comfortable to continue using such services once the crisis had passed. The Y2K outsourcing push was less cost-driven than it was based on the need to engage adequate resources to get the job done within a short lead time. Subsequently, lower costs have become a driving force for outsourcing, particularly after the substantially lower costs of the offshore resources had been experienced firsthand.

A number of organizations outsourced their information technology and business process operations because they did not wish to undergo the huge internal effort anticipated for Y2K systems remediation. In general, the primary business of these companies was financial services, air transportation, or health services, for instance, and not IT or business processing. These companies determined that they did not want the aggravation, burden, and risk, as well as the cost, of making their own systems Y2K compliant. These organizations were mostly smaller companies, although a number of medium and large organizations took the same path. These organizations moved their computer and network operations, and sometimes their operational functions, to outsourcers with the expectation of defraying risk and cost. Outsourcers were generally more easily able to attract the requisite resources and bear the necessary expenses as they could spread the costs over a number of customers and realize substantial economies of scale.

During my personal involvement with both Y2K-related outsourcing and the ramping up of offshore outsourcing prior to, during, and after the turn of the millennium, I witnessed both the general use of outsourcing to meet the surge in Y2K technology requirements and the reliance on offshore resources. The latter was usually through intermediary contracting companies. I also saw a number of new customers, including relatively large firms, deciding that they did not want the problems of the Y2K remediation for their back-office systems, seek third-party service providers to solve that problem.

We then entered a period of retrenchment in 2001 and 2002, which followed the bursting of the dot-com bubble and the ensuing collapse of the many companies dependent on the "new economy." The emphasis on cost cutting, combined with the need to remain competitive globally through leveraging advanced technology, led to the increased substitution of offshore IT services for domestic resources. This trend will undoubtedly increase over the coming years as the infrastructure to facilitate such services is improved continually and the comfort level in using offshore services increases through positive experiences.

In the volatile political climate of 2004, concerns have been raised about moving domestic jobs abroad, particularly skilled technology jobs, and about the resulting unemployment among certain segments of the working population in the United States and other developed countries.[2] In this book, we will not address these emotionally charged political issues—issues that can change, either by becoming more or less significant, in the wink of an eye. I will merely observe that similar services, which are now considered a threat to jobs, were considered a lifesaver during the years of Y2K remediation, when the economies of the United States and other countries were booming and the demand for programmers far exceeded the supply. The supply now exceeds demand in these same areas of expertise—and this excess demand is being filled by an abundance of newly minted offshore staff.

The Post Y2K Outsourcing Speed Bump

The euphoria and high expectations of the early twenty-first century were soon dampened by the demise or desperate merger and acquisition of a number of outsourcing firms.

In some cases, the problems encountered were due directly to the lack of customers and shortfalls in revenues from the serious decline of dot-com and telecommunications companies. In other cases, failure was the result of flawed business models. In particular, expectations that information security would be the next big thing following Y2K were not realized to the level anticipated, perhaps because they were based more on hope than reality.

Consulting firms and IT service providers had amassed substantial teams of skilled IT workers and were counting on employing them profitably and in large numbers once the Y2K work had dissipated. These firms anticipated that the development, support, and operation of systems for e-commerce would be a profitable mainstay, but this did not happen. Therefore, high-powered technology teams were dismantled, along with development, testing, and operational facilities. The ratcheting down of these capabilities led to a particularly poor job market for U.S.-based IT professionals in the post-2000 period.

Those who were directly involved in Y2K remediation and contingency planning, as well as those of us who staffed the Cyber National Information Center,[3] understood that retaining the monitoring, reporting, and emergency

---

2. In the 2003–2004 period, articles in the computer press have been predominantly negative, with reports of failures of outsourcing, both domestic and global, given much more play than success stories.

3. The Cyber National Information Center was a group within the umbrella National Coordination Center (NCC). The President's Council on Year 2000 Conversion created the NCC, which was headed by John Koskinen. It was comprised of representatives of government agencies and the private sector. Information on incidents was reported from around the globe and entered into a system, which notified everyone in the NCC of problem areas. The information system was the basis of the regular reports presented to the country and the world.

response capabilities established for Y2K would make sense. Some $50 million was reportedly spent on building a federal government data gathering and communications center that monitored the status of millions of critical computer systems and communications networks. Regrettably, that facility and the related public-private cooperative infrastructures were dismantled. The individuals assigned to the Information Center at the millennium returned to their day-to-day roles and responsibilities. Yet that facility and its supporting systems and staff would have been extremely valuable during many crises of the new millennium, including the distributed denial of service (DDoS) attacks in 2000, the Code Red and Nimda computer worms of 2001, the SQL Slammer and Sobig attacks in 2003, the MyDoom virus early in 2004, the terrorist attacks of September 11, 2001, and the anthrax and ricin incidents.

Some of us who had been involved in Y2K preparation and contingency planning kept going with the national effort relating to critical infrastructure protection but, following the change of administration in Washington in 2001, most of these efforts were in a hiatus. No clear direction was seen until the September 11 attacks of that year accelerated the formation of the Department of Homeland Security. "The National Strategy for Critical Infrastructure Assurance" was launched in September 2002. Plans were put in place to effectively rebuild the Information Coordination Center along Y2K lines, and new life was breathed into many of the initiatives that had been spelled out in the May 1998 Presidential Decision Directive (PDD) 63 on Critical Infrastructure Protection and reiterated in the National Strategy.

On January 28, 2004, the National Cyber Security Division of the Department of Homeland Security announced the formation of the National Cyber Alert System as the initial step in building the capabilities, established for Y2K, that remain relevant for protecting against cyber attacks.

Shaky Managed Security Services Providers

The dramatic failures of some high-profile managed security services providers left prospective customers gun-shy. In some cases, customers had to scramble to maintain their network availability as some service providers closed down without prior notice [3].

These business failures, combined with a regulatory environment requiring more stringent due diligence, may well have put a considerable crimp into this market for a year or two. However, the pendulum appears to be swinging back—at least to the point where firms are reconsidering engaging security service providers, albeit after much more comprehensive due diligence efforts.[4]

---

4. There have been a number of industry efforts in the banking sector, in particular, with respect to coming up with questionnaires and evaluation methods for third-party information

Perhaps the need for such services is so great that the hurdles just have to be overcome. Interestingly, even though there may be some cautious return to outsourcing of security services, customers are approaching the process soberly, with "due diligence" as their mantra.

A Prognosis

In the August 2000 issue of *Information Security* [4], an article on managed security service providers appeared to be optimistic, arguing that, with appropriate evaluations and precautionary measures, firms could once again rely on third parties to operate various security services with measured confidence.

The future for outsourcing as a whole, and as a percentage of IT spending, remains favorable. In a survey by CAP Gemini, published in the July 8, 2002, issue of *InfoWorld,* 250 executives at 120 financial institutions expected outsourcing to rise from 29% of the IT budget in 2002 to 31% in 2004. In the April 29, 2002, edition of *InformationWeek,* three major IT outsourcing companies (IBM, EDS, and Keane) were reported to have shown substantial growth in outsourcing revenues, while revenues in other areas actually fell. For managed security services, the growth rate is running at about 35 percent per year compounded with an expectation of $16.5 billion by 2004, according to IDC.

The first recession of the new century began in 2001. During this time, we saw a large outflow of programming and system development work from the United States, in particular, to such countries as India, Ireland, Singapore, and, increasingly, China. The main motivator has been not so much the limitations in appropriately skilled domestic resources, as was the case for Y2K, because an excess of qualified domestic technology applicants has resulted from the downturn in the economy. Rather, the outflow was motivated by potential cost savings, as the daily rates for skilled programmers and systems analysts in these countries were a small fraction of rates in the United States and other developed countries.

The quality of the work outsourced to these countries is often comparable to, and sometimes better than, that obtainable from local practitioners. Furthermore, the experience level of the outsourcing labor pool has increased over the years. The local time differences, often greater than eight hours, may be considered an inconvenience in terms of personal communications, but that same time shift allows for virtually around-the-clock work and support.

technology (IT) service providers. For example, the Banking Industry Technology Secretariat (BITS) has developed extensive guidelines for evaluating both domestic and foreign-based IT service providers.

Consequently, the major barriers to offshore outsourcing of skill, knowledge, experience, ability, and communications have become much less significant than in the past. Furthermore, offshore project managers are usually more than willing to accommodate the time differences and be available for late evening or early morning voice and video conference calls, which they consider a small price to pay for the economic benefits of the relationship.

Not that everything is positive in such arrangements. Management control by the customer is more difficult and requires extra effort in the coordination of tasks, people, and other resources. There are structural and cultural differences that might lead to misunderstandings. Also, risks may be associated with the political volatility of some countries. All these issues must be accounted for and mitigated against, usually through the provision by the customer of domestic backup resources (including knowledge and skills), retention of up-to-date copies of design documents and program source code, and other methods.

Nevertheless, the critical mass of management and technical expertise is increasingly being applied to both domestic and offshore IT outsourcing, both of which are expected to grow in absolute terms and as a percentage of IT expenditures. The outsourcing of IT seems to be here to stay.

The Information Security Market

With the rapid increase in the number of information security software–related threats and vulnerabilities, as well as recent major incidents in the physical arena, one would expect that the market for information security (especially network-orientated cyber security) would flourish. In reality, we are seeing almost the opposite. Many information security software, equipment, and services vendors are struggling to survive. Stronger companies, which happen to be in the right market segment (such as antivirus software) or in a different business altogether (such as systems integration), are gobbling up their weaker competitors.

The service provider model is not proving to be as lucrative as initially expected due to notable failures and bankruptcies [3]. Furthermore, the already low security budgets of client companies seem to be cut back even further despite the pressing need to establish more secure environments. In difficult economic times, we often consider security (like insurance) to be discretionary in the short term and put it off or forego it completely. Management's risk preferences look to the costs of the additional protection versus the expense hit to the bottom line, and executives frequently seem more willing to take a chance that something bad will not happen. If they are lucky, nothing happens. But a number of high-profile incidents, both in the form of external attacks and internal misdeeds, have brought such judgment into question as reputation-ruining headlines appear in the press.

Why is it that, at a time when the risks and dangers of purposeful attacks and willful destruction are everywhere, the security response is so measured? In order to try to understand the forces that have led to this quandary, we shall look into several areas. In the next chapter, we shall examine the risks that currently prevail and against which we want to protect.

References

[1]   Safire, W., "On Language: Outsource ... And the Urge to Insource," *The New York Times Magazine,* March 26, 2004, p. 30.

[2]   Sweet, B., et al., "Outsourcing: Evolving Toward Trust," *CSC Consulting,* May 21, 2001, http://www.csc.com.

[3]   Berinato, S., "Security Outsourcing: Exposed!" *CIO Magazine,* August 1, 2001, http://www.cio.com.

[4]   James, N., "(Still) At Your Service," *Information Security,* Vol. 5, No. 8, August 2002, pp. 48–57.

2

Information Security Risks

There are two sides to security risks—threats and vulnerabilities. It is not until a threat meets a vulnerability that a security incident occurs. Threats will always be out there, somewhere. They can be discouraged through deterrence mechanisms, such as the possibility of punishment or retaliation, or they can be avoided by not engaging in activities that are threatened. Protective and defensive measures can be installed that will attempt to prevent attacks or ward off an attack when it occurs. Or vulnerabilities can be fixed so that an attacker penetrating defenses cannot perpetrate damage. In what follows, we shall list the more common IT-related threats and vulnerabilities and indicate how outsourcing affects them and how they affect outsourcing.

Threats

That the greatest threats to an organization reside within the organization itself is a commonly held belief by information security professionals and, by the press, although reporters emphasize external threats.

From Internal Sources

A number of categories of insiders present threats to the integrity and availability of an organization's computer networks and systems and to the confidentiality of the information that traverse over them and resides in them, respectively.

The Disgruntled Employee

The typical disgruntled employee might have been fired or still be on staff and is often from the IT department. He or she has all the qualities needed for wreaking havoc—intimate knowledge of the firm's computer applications, networks, systems, and procedures; physical access to the premises; logical access to applications and systems; and the desire to do harm.[1]

The Insider

The insider is an employee, contractor, or consultant who is very familiar with the organization's applications, systems, and procedures and who is able to use that knowledge for personal gain, through fraud, embezzlement, money laundering, and other methods.

The Opportunist

The opportunist is either an insider or an outsider who comes across a flaw or "hole" in a computer application or system, often by chance, and, rather than reporting the flaw to the appropriate authorities, decides to exploit it for personal gain.

The opportunist is just as guilty of committing a crime as someone who intentionally gains illegal entry into a system. Because of the risks relating to opportunism, many computer systems display a message or banner screen, as a deterrent, stating that information available through the system is proprietary or confidential. This notice might also state that the organization will take action—disciplinary and/or legal—should anyone steal or misuse the information that they are able to access.

Inadvertent Destroyer

The inadvertent destroyer is probably responsible for much computer system compromise and damage. Such a person can be an employee or contractor with legitimate access to various systems, or a customer who is entitled to access applications and information and to perform a variety of tasks. He or she might also be a support person or an administrator who is unfamiliar with a system and its nuances.

The inadvertent destroyer might be following normal procedures and then, either accidentally or mistakenly, issue a command or series of commands

---

1. There have been cases where an employee has been fired and the guards, particularly those on nights and weekends, not have been informed. The ex-employee will come to the facility, pretend to have lost his or her ID card and, because the guard knows him or her, be allowed onto the premises. If the ex-employee's system access has not been terminated, he or she has free reign of the systems. The company may not wish to pursue the matter as it would publicly disclose deficiencies in its controls.

outside the range of standard operations. The new command(s) might trigger inappropriate system responses or cause the system to fail. Since the culprit did not intend to intrude or cause an error, he or she is likely to report the incident, request official assistance, or simply not repeat the action, as opposed to exploiting it, which the opportunist would do. Such situations might come to light only if they create a severe error or breakdown.

The main concern for the organization is a reduction in confidence, because the system has exhibited a vulnerability that might be exploited by less well-intentioned individuals.

From External Sources

A number of types of individuals having very different motivations will attack or try to infiltrate an organization's networks and computer systems.

The Hacker (aka the Cracker)[2]

In the public's mind, the hacker—an evildoer who attacks systems—poses the greatest threat. Such a person might deface Web sites, steal credit card numbers (and sell them, hold them for ransom, or use them fraudulently), or put smart-aleck remarks on workstation screens. The hacker generally does damage to the system, commits fraud, and creates a publicity nightmare for affected organizations. To some extent, this notoriety is a result of the hyped reporting of an enthralled press.

The hacker has been generally depicted as a teenager playing with his computer in his bedroom, as shown in the movie *War Games*. The problem with this movie is that the hacker is made into a hero by saving the day and preventing the destruction of the world—a possibility that he created himself.

2. Some people feel very strongly about what they consider the misuse of the term "hacker." Originally, this term applied to a very bright, competent computer programmer and/or systems expert who would try to break into systems to reveal their deficiencies and vulnerabilities. The purpose of these ventures was to point out weaknesses in the systems so that the systems' builders could repair them and produce better quality work. The vindictive, destructive fellow, who is intent on breaking a system for the fun of it and to show his peers how smart he is, was termed a "cracker." Today, common usage is to apply the word "hacker" to anyone attempting to break into a system. Just to make things more complicated, the term "ethical hacker" arose to distinguish between the good guys or "white hats" and the bad ones, the "black hats." The distinction is fuzzy and difficult to deal with in real situations. The question arises as to whether or not one should hire a "reformed hacker," or a firm that employs such, to do one's security work. In this case, the person may be a known renegade, and may even have served jail time, but someone who has apparently seen the light and now only works on the right side of the law.

Too often this image of the playful prankster, who just happens to be smart or lucky enough to intrude into a supposedly well-protected computer system, prevails. Such a portrayal masks the criminal aspect of the deed. The crime of hacking is just as insidious and despicable as physically breaking into a building and smashing computer equipment or stealing secret files.

The Thief

While the hacker is interested in kicks and may be characterized by the teenager in his room, a more serious group of individuals intends to steal money or other valuable assets. This type of attacker is often well funded, highly committed to success, and not easily deterred or discouraged. The thief's unassisted exploits are likely to be less frequent and less successful than those that feature collusion with current or former internal staff, because inside knowledge of the systems, their vulnerabilities, and their most lucrative assets is extremely helpful.

The thief differs from the opportunist only in that he is actively searching for a "hole" in the system, versus just coming across one by chance. The persistence of this type of perpetrator works against an organization's defenses. Mostly the thief wants to leave as little evidence of the intrusion and missing assets as possible so as not to activate pursuit and capture. Such behavior contrasts with that of the hacker who wants his exploits to be noticed and publicized widely and who may, in some circumstances, notify authorities and the press of his being responsible for the attack.

The Virus Creator and Distributor

Computer viruses or worms that spawn across the Internet in a matter of hours or, more recently, in minutes, are opportunistic, undirected forms of attack. The person who generates the virus (or worm or Trojan horse) cannot be sure whom it will infect and who will spread the virus to others.

Individuals develop and spread viruses for a variety of reasons, such as to claim success to peers or to do damage for its own sake. The virus creator never knows for sure what the impact might be and, when caught, he often appears genuinely surprised that he was successful. The original Morris worm is a case in point—it was much more successful than its creator Robert T. Morris had anticipated [1]. There are perhaps hundreds, even thousands, of new viruses created every day and very few ever make it into "the wild." Of those that do, very few spread globally and cause significant damage and cost.

Although the numbers are not known, one might expect that those hackers who have specific intentions and targets are much more successful than virus creators, since, even if specific targets are not sought out in advance, the general category of victims, such as banks, can be selected and targeted.

Organizations have different policies regarding employee activities. Some organizations restrict e-mail and Internet access, some screen incoming and outgoing e-mails, some restrict access to certain Web sites, some allow standalone modems, and so on. When an organization engages a third party to provide IT services, their security standards and controls are almost certainly different (either better or worse) than those of the outsourcing company. These differences generally increase the risk of hacking of the combined organizations.

The Spy

The industrial or national spy can be dangerous to the credibility and viability of an organization. Such a person, or group of individuals, attempts to steal secrets about networks, systems, operations, and data. Such information can lead to subsequent acts of theft or terrorism or can be used for direct financial or military gain, often through the selling of secrets to other interested parties.

The spy has been profiled as a male in his twenties or thirties, usually from Eastern Europe or Russia, well funded by competing companies or opposing governments, and highly sophisticated in the use of expensive technologies. This image differs from that of the hacker as a teenager or student with too much time on his hands.

While there are potential spies within one's own organization and country, the possibility of providing access to spies increases dramatically when functions are outsourced to other companies. This is of special concern in countries where segments of the population are either equivocal or opposed to the client organization's own regime and sympathetic to other opposing philosophies.

The Cyber Terrorist

The cyber terrorist might be a combination spy and thief, but his motivation is generally destruction of, or major damage to, the "enemy." His methods are very specific and are aimed against well-defined targets. He may be acting alone, but is more likely to be part of a group. The nation state or terrorist group for which he works pays for his activities and is likely to be well funded itself.

Instances of cyber terrorism include events such as when Chinese hackers broke into and defaced U.S. government Web sites in protest of the deaths of a group of students on a boat that was inadvertently capsized by an American submarine. Another example is the bombing of the Chinese embassy in Kosovo, which activated a spate of cyber attacks against U.S. sites. During the Bosnian war, the United States itself blocked telecommunications using hacking techniques—or "cyber warfare," as such hacking is now known.

Because cyber terrorism involves specific targets, the organizations that are potential targets should understand their exposure, which may be due to their preeminence, popularity, or importance. Furthermore, they need take appropriate countermeasures.

Following the attack on the World Trade Center in 2001, it has become much more evident that the critical infrastructures that support a modern economy—such as energy, telecommunications, and transportation—are highly interdependent and very vulnerable to attack, even an indirect attack.[3]

This fact is understood by nations with a desire to destroy U.S. political and economic systems. Ongoing evidence exists of scans being done on crucial systems in the infrastructure, which is clearly the type of research that can precede terrorist attacks.

The fact that cyber terrorism has not become more prevalent to date is just a matter of preparedness and opportunity. Clearly, cyber terrorism is strongly indicated to become a preferred method as time goes by because it can be activated remotely from outside the target country.

Outsourcing to third parties, both at home and abroad, might inadvertently provide potential terrorists access to vulnerable infrastructure systems and networks.

Review of Threats

As can be seen from the above descriptions, threats of attack can come from sources that are internal or external, amateur or professional, motivated by personal gain or political cause, supported on a shoestring or well funded, and so on. From a protection point of view, the source of an attack may or may not result in a different defense. Ideally, an organization will build defenses that can meet all types of attack, but this is neither physically or economically feasible. Some middle-of-the-road approach is often taken, with everyday attacks being thwarted through regular methods, and with the more sophisticated and damaging attacks being addressed according to their risk and the availability of cost-effective countermeasures.[4]

---

3. The recognition of critical infrastructure interdependencies and the importance of protecting the critical infrastructure began in the United States in the early 1960s as a result of the Cuban missile crisis. However, the recent national plans and strategies emanated from the Presidential Decision Directive No. 63 (PDD-63) issued in May 1998 and escalated as Y2K approached. For an overview of initiatives relating to critical infrastructure and a description of the interdependencies, see [2].

4. Whereas it might seem reasonable to determine the level of security through economic risk analysis, laws and regulations reflect the risk appetites of legislators and regulators, which reflect those of their constituents. Hence, certain threats, such as identity theft, are given greater prominence in laws and regulations because of the relative influence of individual voters versus corporate lobbies. The cost of protecting against such threats may well be much higher than the benefits perceived from the corporate standpoint, or even for society as a whole. However, the potential for very expensive and damaging actions by regulators, for example, will generally favor compliance at any cost. Of course, the cost is eventually borne by customers and taxpayers.

When an organization has reached what is considered an acceptable level of defense, then it must ensure that its business partners, particularly third-party service providers, match or exceed that standard. Otherwise, the quality of protection is diminished by having less well-protected business partners introduce vulnerabilities into the overall infrastructure of the organization.

Vulnerabilities

A threat can do actual damage only if it comes up against vulnerable systems, processes, and procedures. There are many forms of vulnerability, ranging from technical to human, which need to be identified, evaluated, and mitigated.

Computer Systems and Networks

Modern computer systems and networks have all the characteristics that make for vulnerability. They are, among other things, generally accessible, ubiquitous, complex, written for features rather than security, and dependent on human beings, particularly in the handling of nonstandard situations.

The esoteric knowledge of computers and access to them, which were for a long time in the hands of a few specialists, are now broadly available. Millions of individuals around the world have been trained in application development, system programming, technical support, customer assistance, and system administration. Such skills are readily acquired by an educated population, easily transferable, and largely independent of location. These computer-savvy individuals, along with the hundreds of millions who have become proficient with PCs, have created a huge body of technical knowledge that can be used either productively or destructively. Add to that the global access provided by the Internet and you have a formula for malicious activities with far-reaching consequences.

Adding another dimension to the already difficult problem, outsourcing requires the management and control of computer experts across additional organizations. By entering into an outsourcing partnership, one organization automatically exposes its networks and systems to a new set of individuals, many of whom will have high levels of expertise and some of whom might have evil intentions. However vulnerable an organization might be from the misdeeds of its own internal staff, it is much more so when it links up with other entities.

Software Development

Expectations about the capabilities of computer systems have always run ahead of the technology needed to manage and control them. This has created a culture in which, for the most part, application functionality precedes quality and security. The fact of the matter is that applications and systems software have not in general been built to be secure, and as a result they usually contain many bugs or holes—vulnerabilities that can be exploited by evildoers.

Pressure from critics and customers has resulted in an emphasis on security, as in a recent pronouncement by Bill Gates that security is now the number one priority at Microsoft. However, it still remains to be seen whether this new concern with security is a knee-jerk reaction or a long-term commitment.[5]

Another area of concern regarding software, either commercial or home-grown, is the chance that someone will purposely inject malicious or exploitable code into a program. There have been several instances of computer viruses being put into shrink-wrapped software, intentionally or unintentionally, without the knowledge of the manufacturer. Concern has been frequently expressed in regard to software developed or modified in foreign countries, where activist groups might be determined to undermine the recipient of the software.

When organizations partner in an outsourcing arrangement, the likelihood of significant differences in cultures, attitudes, and standards of excellence is high, particularly when it comes to security requirements. Objective standards are needed, against which the quality and security aspects of software can be measured. As discussed later, some standards do exist, but they are not universally accepted.

Systemic Risks

Even if software or equipment is robust and carefully tested and scanned for vulnerabilities, the system chain is only as strong as its weakest link. Also, the more components and pathways that are linked together, the greater the chance that something will not quite match up or that components or links have weaknesses that can be exploited. There is greater potential for more and riskier vulnerabilities as more systems within a company are integrated, and as more organizations link their systems with those of business partners and customers. Adding to the exposure, new capabilities, such as Web services, are designed to combine the processing capability of many independently built and supported components.

Outsourcing invariably adds another dimension to what is already a complex set of interactions. Take Web services, for example. Still in their formative stage, Web services require the ability of programs within a unit or belonging to different units of an organization or among organizations to interact with one

5. Security continues to be a top priority with Bill Gates and with Microsoft's customers, as described in [3].

another through a standard set of interfaces. In concept, this is not unlike object-oriented programming, whereby a programmer will utilize a library of objects, enabling him or her to pull standard routines or objects that perform common functions into the program.

Web services, however, can be structured as an extreme form of outsourcing, since each unit of the service can be incorporated into a program through the program's accessing the unit to perform specific standard functions, such as credit checking. The dependence upon the security of the third-party provider of the particular service is extremely high, particularly as business-critical functions might be performed by the remote service. How such services are warranted and how both sides accommodate change will become major challenges. The need for security and reliability is great, as any unauthorized changes or lack of availability would have instant impact on all the systems using a particular service.[6]

Another trend having serious security implications is grid computing, wherein, for example, a computer program is broken down into components that can be processed on many computers within an organization, across known organizations, or across the Internet. In the last case, the program manager may not even know where the processing machines are or to whom they belong. As the form of grid computing migrates from processing to database handling, the issues of privacy and confidentiality become even more significant.

The ultimate security nightmare arises with the intersection of Web services and grid computing, where applications developed by a diverse group across possibly many organizations are run on machines that might reside in unknown places with data spread across a mysterious network of applications and systems.

Operational Risk

Operational risk results from deficiencies in an organization's management information, support, and control systems. These deficiencies represent one of the more significant areas of risk. Certainly up until the recent accounting and control debacles at major corporations, such as Enron, Tyco, and WorldCom, the focus for many high-flying companies was on functionality, usability, and appearance (i.e., reputation). The underlying control capabilities needed to ensure the lawful and correct running of systems and processes were given short

---

6. There is an equivalent in Business Process Outsourcing (BPO), as it relates to workflow components. Here, each step of a process can be separated into individual components, any one of which might be outsourced.

shrift. If adequate systems did exist, those responsible for running those systems and processes were delinquent.

With outsourcing, matters of management and control become even more crucial because functions are often divided among organizations in seemingly arbitrary ways. The combining of two or more operational systems introduces its own set of problems, inconsistencies, and vulnerabilities. Ironically, it was the ability to subjugate the control and auditing of a separate entity that exacerbated the Enron debacle, since such insourced entities were created in order to hide misdeeds.

From an outsourcing organization's perspective, the fact that specific operational processes may be given over to a third party raises many questions about the operational integrity and security of the other party. Consequently, customers exhibit an increasing interest in objective reviews and assessments, such as that provided by a SAS 70 report, which goes beyond the provision of IT services by adding operational functions.[7] There are other certifications, such as TruSecure Enterprise Certification, SysTrust, WebTrust, and Trust-e, that specifically address the IT and information security functions.

Operator and Administrator Risk

Many security-related problems can be attributed to the human factor. When strong system and operational controls are not in place, an organization depends heavily upon its system operators and administrative staff to ensure that computer systems operate according to their design and purpose. Operators and administrators tend to be fairly low in the organizational hierarchy both in terms of pay and education, yet they have enormous responsibility and authority. An operator error can cause a system to operate inappropriately or fail entirely. A simple slip by an administrator can expose highly confidential information to unauthorized persons. Consequently, significant effort should be expended on automating administrative and control systems to reduce operator intervention to a minimum and to remove the decision-making responsibility from low-level administrators.

When outsourcing, many of these administrative and operational functions are transferred to the service provider, resulting in another degree of separation. This real concern must be addressed through stringent due diligence and, where possible, retaining or overseeing control. Retention of control is

---

7. The Statement on Auditing Standards No. 70 (SAS 70) is an auditing standard developed by the American Institute of Certified Public Accountants (AICPA), which is used by a service provider to provide independent assurance that control objectives are met and control processes are adequate. Details of the SAS 70 are available at http://www.sas70.org.

possible but difficult to implement.[8] More usual is the situation in which the service provider manages the operation and submits management reports to the client, so that the latter can oversee the operation from afar.

Complexity Risk

As described earlier, any arrangement that adds a third party will increase complexity, because the interactions between the organizations must be added to the internal activities within each organization. The more complex an arrangement of interacting systems, operations, and human beings, the greater is the chance of error or damage, unintentional or otherwise. Therefore, one can assume that managing an outsourcing arrangement will be more difficult and require more effort than if the outsourced functions ran totally in-house.

That is not to say that an organization should not outsource. Clearly they often should and they do. However, when all the benefits of outsourcing are evaluated, they must be set against the additional risks and effort that increased complexity produces.

Life-Cycle Risk

There are many life cycles in the IT world, the best known being the system development life cycle (SDLC)—the process whereby a system is designed, developed, tested, and implemented.

Security aspects of system development are frequently neglected. For the highest-quality systems, security considerations need to be included and security features need to be built in from the outset. Each stage of development provides an opportunity to take a more secure approach, as well as to insert security assessments [4]. The risks in the SDLC are of particular importance when applications and systems development are outsourced. Applications development is among the more recent IT functions to be outsourced. However, with the recent availability of large offshore pools of highly educated, well-trained programmers at reasonable cost, and of low-cost, high-bandwidth communications, this form of outsourcing is expanding rapidly.

Other life cycles relate to the newness of technology. The reliability and efficacy of new hardware and software can be low since they frequently contain bugs, errors, and manufacturing defects that must be resolved over time. For

---

8. Early in my career, I implemented a production control system (called UCC-7 when supplied by University Computing Corporation (UCC), then becoming CA-7 after Computer Associates bought UCC), which enabled the client organization, for which I worked, to manage the running of applications at the hosting service provider (or facilities manager). I can attest to the fact that this type of arrangement is difficult to achieve and requires considerable effort.

equipment, most failures occur when units are new and later when they wear out, with the in-between period showing good reliability, as in the well-known "bathtub curve" (see Figure 2.1).

The pattern for software is somewhat different, as shown in Figure 2.2. Here there is an initial relatively rapid improvement as early, more obvious errors are detected and fixed. Over time, new errors are found and resolved, making for a continuing drop in failure rate. There is no wear-out period as such for software, although withdrawal by the vendor of maintenance support on obsolete software will mean that any failures in such software will not be resolved, or will be addressed at a lower priority compared to supported software. However, when software is replaced with newer versions, the failure rate will generally jump up again and the pattern in Figure 2.2 will repeat itself.

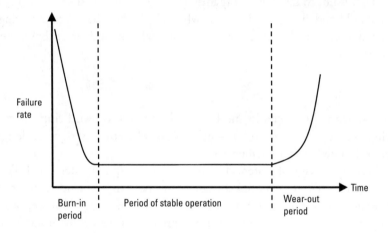

Figure 2.1 Hardware failure rate over time.

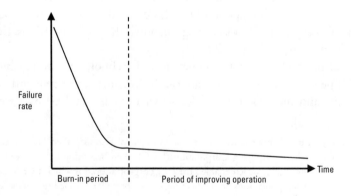

Figure 2.2 Software failure rate over time.

The combination of failure rates of new hardware and software can be complex. If the equipment and software are combined, as they are with so-called "appliances," then the failure rate pattern will likely be of the form shown in Figure 2.3, which is a combination of the curves in Figures 2.1 and 2.2. This is not often the case. Generally, equipment will break and have to be replaced, with existing software reloaded onto the new hardware. On the other hand, new software may well function on older, in-place equipment, which is passing through its period of stability. Whatever the situation, it is the combined failure rate that pertains.

Sometimes an organization will outsource to gain the benefits of new technologies through providers who have already moved beyond the initial failure period. To the extent that technology is new and unknown to the client but well known and familiar to the service provider, the use of the outsourcer yields considerable benefits. One should be concerned, however, if a technology is first being tested and used by the service provider for your environment, as it might be unreliable.

Risks of Obsolescence

While there are risks tied to introducing new technologies, as described above, there are also risks relating to obsolescence. Replacement parts and trained service engineers may no longer be available for older equipment. Often with computer equipment, in particular, we see the cost of maintaining older machines often exceeding the total cost of ownership of new equipment. Not only does the higher cost of maintenance reflect the reality that older technology is more expensive to fix, the manufacturer is likely using maintenance charges as an incentive for customers to buy new equipment, which is cheaper to maintain and service. Falling costs exacerbate the planned obsolescence phenomenon.

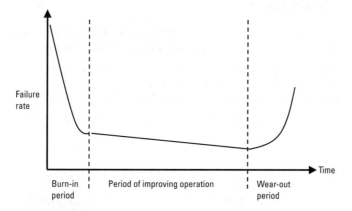

Figure 2.3 Combined hardware and software failure rate over time.

Software has not experienced the same downward plunge in cost per unit of capacity or capability. However, older software does become more costly to maintain than new software and lacks desirable features and capabilities.

While some service providers use leading-edge technologies, others may choose to prolong the life of older technologies. In the latter case, they may be locked into obsolete platforms by customers who are unwilling to change or upgrade to newer technologies. Whatever the reason, both customers and service providers need to evaluate periodically the efficacy of their current technologies to determine whether they should be upgraded.

In addition to the operational and support issues, security issues exist. Old versions of software may no longer be supported by the vendor, and unsupported software is a security risk. First, the software vendor will not fix newly discovered vulnerabilities in older unsupported products and, second, there is a greater chance that a hacker will have had more time to discover vulnerabilities in longer-running products.

Vendor Viability Risk

Vendors produce hardware and software that may be used by both or either the customer and the service provider. When a vendor goes out of business and can no longer support a product, the company using that product must deal with the possibility of the product breaking and being unrepairable. This issue applies to hardware and software, as well as services.

Careful due diligence before committing to a vendor can reduce this risk. Mitigation of vendor risk also includes reducing dependency on a single vendor and designing systems to be flexible so that they can be ported to other platforms with relative ease.

Risk of Poor Quality Support

Vendors and service providers not uncommonly assign their most able support personnel to their largest, most lucrative accounts. Those customers who do not fall within this privileged category often receive lesser support service. Any negotiation of service level should ensure that the best possible support is provided. Even entities that consider that they have little leverage can adopt techniques that will encourage suppliers of goods and services to provide top-quality support.

Conversion Risk

Conversion from an existing in-house operation to a service provider, as well as setting up a new function at a third-party site, can be rife with problems. If the members of a functional area see that it is to be disbanded once the conversion is done, they will not be likely to cooperate unless specific incentives have been agreed upon in advance. Even with an entirely new operation, insiders may be of the opinion that they should be in charge of the function. Any sense of dissention or disgruntlement must be followed up and protected against, since an employee or contractor who harbors resentment is more likely to try to damage systems or facilities.

Risk of Dependency on Key Individuals

Very commonly one or two experts are knowledgeable in specific critical applications, networks, systems, or processes. The loss of such subject-matter expertise can be extremely detrimental to the ongoing operation and support of these systems. When an existing operation is outsourced, it is quite likely that those expert individuals will decide not to remain with the operation, even if it is clear that they are needed. It is crucial to the future stability of an ongoing operation to identify rapidly those individuals who are critical for the smooth running of systems and to encourage them to stay on.

Both the customer and the service provider may have a number of such individuals. However, the customer may not be aware of who is important to the third-party operation and who is not. It is incumbent upon those arranging the service relationship to make sure that this concern is addressed by both customer and service provider.

Summary

Outsourcing presents organizations with security-related risks—as does deciding *not* to outsource. The underlying principle of this book is that knowing what the risks are and taking them into account make for better outsourcing decisions. In this chapter, we have laid out the risks. In what follows we shall discuss how to deal with them.

References

[1]   Schneier, B., *Secrets and Lies*, New York: John Wiley & Sons, 2000, pp. 154–155.

[2]   Axelrod, C. W., "Protecting the E-Commerce Infrastructure," *Electronic Commerce Advisor,* November/December 1999, Vol. 4, No. 3, pp. 13–20.

[3]   Taft, D. K., "Gates Has Mind on Future Tech: Security Tops Microsoft Chairman's 'Think Week,'" *eWeek*, March 29, 2004.

[4]   Graff, M. G., and K. R. van Wyk, *Secure Coding*, Sebastopol, CA: O'Reilly & Associates, 2003.

3

Justifying Outsourcing

So you think that you should outsource your major IT functions, such as network and computer management, applications development and testing, and customer support and, perhaps, even some of your information security functions? How about really diving in with both feet and seeking an offshore provider of services so as to reap the enormous cost and productivity benefits that these faraway places promise?

Professed Reasons to Outsource

Is your primary motivation to hand over responsibility to a third party so that you will not be on the hook when things go awry? Well, think again, because the function may move out the door, but the responsibility might very well stay behind, lurking in the shadows. On whose door will management knock if the service expectations are not met, or if the charges are higher than expected, or if the third party goes out of business—suddenly, and without warning? The inevitable question from management in such soul-destroying situations is "Whose idea was this in the first place?" as all eyes bear down on you, if you are unfortunate or unwise enough to have stayed around.

Perhaps you think that you are going to save piles of money for your organization. But are the savings real? How about sharpening your pencil and going over those numbers again? Did you include all those intangible costs? You have probably fully accounted for intangible benefits as if they were already in hand. But what about hidden costs? Are you still trying to keep them out of sight? And don't forget the possible delayed costs of extricating yourself from a relationship turned sour? Were they included in the initial analysis or not?

Probably they were not. Perhaps you should have put more effort into calculating the numbers ahead of time and remembered to put in a contingency cushion. Here management's question will be: "Why didn't you tell me we would be hit with such-and-such costs?"

Do you believe that you chose to outsource a peripheral function so that you could concentrate on your core businesses? Well, now you are more on track. This line of reasoning could make sense and may even be true. Your plan may not work out as expected, but at least outsourcing stands a chance of producing the desired benefits, that is, if you are positioned to take advantage of the situation. But don't expect the kudos for the additional business opportunities or revenues to come to you. The sales and marketing staff will be sure to take the largest share of the credit. And worse, even in the face of success, an ungrateful management might ask: "Well, why didn't you suggest this years ago?"

So it is for those who propose risky ventures such as outsourcing. You can be faulted whether or not the outsourcing venture is successful in terms of service, cost, and capability. So why do it at all? Clearly there must be more to this outsourcing business than meets the eye.

The Basis for Decision

The outsourcing decision is often highly subjective, even when the decision-maker has gone through an extensive quantitative analysis. Determining the costs of a particular outsourcing venture usually involves a fair amount of estimation and judgment. Cost estimates can be inflated or understated, or a cost category or two might be omitted entirely, either accidentally or intentionally. However inaccurate cost estimates might be, quantitative estimates of benefits usually have very broad ranges, particularly for those that are intangible. It can be extremely difficult, if not impossible, to place an accurate value on certain intangible benefits, and any valuation is likely to be highly subjective and engender significant error. Clearly, in such situations, personal bias can be the deciding factor, overriding any amount of precision in the cost analysis.

Reasons for Considering Outsourcing

Perhaps the best place to begin is to list and discuss the reasons one might give for considering outsourcing as an alternative to in-house functions. Some reasons are obvious and inarguable, while others are fuzzy and highly debatable. Sometimes a reason may appear obvious, but it might become the basis of heated arguments, politicization, and polarization.

I reviewed a variety of sources, some of which reported on surveys of those in a position to use information technology outsourcers, and others which presented reasons based on direct experience [1–4]. It was an interesting exercise, especially as the same item can be a driver to one person and a risk to another. For example, a reason to outsource is to benefit from a particular expertise offered by the service provider. Yet, at the same time, there is a feeling that the in-house staff is not being given access to the feeding trough of knowledge.

However, let us willingly suspend our disbelief and come up with a list of good reasons to outsource. Here we shall discuss the arguments in favor of outsourcing associated with costs, performance, security, expertise, support, and financial arrangements.

Cost Savings

Saving money is usually at or very near the top of the list of reasons to outsource. It is very difficult to justify a third-party service that is more expensive than performing the same service in-house, unless there is a significant material difference in the type or quality of service.

The challenge at hand is to calculate the full cost of performing the same tasks internally or externally over a particular time period, which would generally be the number of years over which a third-party agreement is expected to run. Different periods, such as three, four, or five years, might be considered, in order to determine the minimum time for which the arrangement must be in place to recoup initial costs through future savings and benefits.

Labor

Often the largest cost of service provision is for labor. For in-house full-time and part-time staff, there are a number of categories of cost. They include salaries, overtime, benefits, and payroll taxes for internal staff. For contractors and consultants, there is an hourly or daily basic rate, with a premium for overtime. The basic consultant rate covers salaries, benefits, and so on, as well as profit. For internal staff paid vacations and holidays as well as sick days must be added, whereas for consultants these are included in the basic rate applied to actual time spent on the job.

Various overhead costs, such as those related to facilities occupied by the staff (e.g., rent, utilities), administrative costs (e.g., secretarial staff, costs of printing, copying) and management, can be handled in a variety of ways. Within a company such costs as facilities and administrative costs are generally depicted as allocations from the corporate cost centers to the specific staff cost centers. The cost of management and corporate staff may be included in administrative costs or may be specifically assigned to individuals. This is also true of service providers and consulting firms, although here the senior managers are often billed directly, whereas administrative support staff is included as a percentage, such as a surcharge of 20% of total other charges.

It should be noted that, in calculating internal costs, contractors and consultants may be engaged in support of the in-house service in addition to in-house staff. For third-party services, internal employee costs will likely be minimal, and most staff costs will be for consultants, even in the case where internal employees are transferred to the service provider. In Table 3.1, we show how staffing varies for internal or external services and the general degree to which the staff is provided internally or externally. This illustrates that some mix of internal and external staff is necessary regardless of the nature of the service, although the ratios can change dramatically. This is important to remember when costing out a particular service since accounting for internal staff in a third-party relationship and, to a lesser extent, the external staff assisting on an in-house service can be easily forgotten.

Besides costs directly attributable to individuals, other costs can be ascribed more generally to the role that a particular person has and what activities the person does in relation to that role. Perhaps the most obvious of these are travel-related costs, which include transportation, accommodation, meals, and costs related to entertaining clients. Often a consulting firm will charge travel-related expenses attributable to a project or service at cost with an administrative fee, as mentioned earlier. However, it should be noted that travel costs to a primary place of business are generally borne by an employee, whereas a consultant might charge for travel to the same client premises regardless of distance. For offshore service providers, the travel component can be considerable, not only in terms of airfares and accommodations, but also in the time required for the travel, which will be charged to the client.[1]

Other employee-related costs include those for training and attendance at seminars and conferences. Costs include those directly attributable to travel, accommodations, and registration, but also the cost of lost opportunity by not

Table 3.1
Staff (Internal and External) by Type of Service

	In-House Service	**Third-Party Service Provider**
Internal Staff	Full- and part-time employees	Minimal (relationship managers)
External Staff	Some consultants, contractors	Almost all consultants

1. The factors that affect the decision to use offshore and near-shore outsourcers are examined in a separate section. However, as we go through the general factors, I will point out aspects of those factors that pertain specifically to the selection and use of out-of-country service providers.

working during the training period. However, the training activity will probably more than pay for itself through higher productivity and effectiveness and new opportunities to create revenues and reduce costs. Companies often have formal standards for training, such as requiring so many days of training per year, or a minimum number of continuing education units (CEUs), for certain business-related or technology-related certifications. For consulting services, such costs are built into the rate, which includes an allowance for a certain number of nonbillable days per employee per year, some of which may be earmarked for training.[2]

Then there are one-time, per-person costs, such as those for recruiting, hiring, and firing. It can be more difficult for an organization to hire specialists than for a service provider or consulting firm to do so, since the latter can generally offer more interesting work, greater responsibility, more variety of work and environment, and a better career growth path. Thus, service providers may be able to save on these one-time personnel costs if being able to offer more attractive work environments and opportunities results in lower staffing turnover.

Various labor-related costs, and how they are calculated and assigned or allocated, are shown in Table 3.2 for both in-house and externally provided services. The main observation is that for internal workers the individual cost categories have to be defined and quantified, whereas for outside service providers most categories are included in a base rate. Of course, the service provider must go through the same definition and quantification of its internal costs to arrive at a suitable base rate.[3]

---

2. In difficult times, companies often cut back on training and other discretionary expenditures. Not investing in maintaining staff at the forefront of their respective fields can result in lower future productivity and reduced savings. It becomes a real issue in the outsourcing environment, where the service provider is motivated to keep up-to-date, but skills of internal staff can atrophy. This leads to greater dependency on the outsourcer by customers, with the potential for substantial rate increases and inability of the customer organization to seek better providers or move in-house.

3. It should be noted that only certain types of consulting and professional services proposals lend themselves to base-rate charging. Often, a service provider will charge based on some other measure, such as number of items processed per unit of time, or propose a fixed rate. What is even more interesting is that the revenue per internal employee and employee productivity is sensitive to whether or not the number of staff embodied in the outside services charges is included in the head count for these calculations. It can make an enormous difference in productivity numbers (e.g., number of calls answered or lines of code programmed) in particular. For example, the recent growing trend for outsourcing such activities as software development to countries such as India and China means that a certain amount of work can be done more cheaply. But it could be less productive in units of work per person, if the additional relationship management and project management staff and the likely larger numbers of programmers required are included in the calculation. Perhaps some of the noted increase in productivity seen recently in the United States is due in part in the conversion of head count–related costs to lump-sum fixed-price contracts.

Table 3.2
Labor-Related Costs for In-House and External Workers

	In-House	External
Ongoing Costs		
Salary	Specific cost	Included in base rate
Overtime	Percentage, say, 150%, of salary	Charged as a percentage of base hourly rate
Benefits	Percentage, say, 30%, of salary	Included in base rate
Payroll taxes	As required by taxing agency	Included in base rate
Travel and entertainment	Specific cost	Billed at cost or cost plus
Training	Specific cost	Included in base rate
Company car	May be taxable benefit	May be included in base rate or charged to client per mile
One-time Costs		
Hiring	Specific cost	Included in base rate
Firing	Specific cost	Included in base rate
Setup	Specific cost	Included in base rate
Overhead Costs		
Facilities (rent, utilities)	Specific cost	Included in base rate
Administration	Specific cost	Charged as percentage, say, 15%, of price
Corporate staff	Specific cost	Included in base rate or as part of administrative cost
Management	Specific cost	Charged on hourly basis and/or included in base rate of billable staff

Computer and Network Equipment and Software

The comparison between costs for equipment and software used in-house and which are either provided directly, as in the case of an application service provider (ASP), or embodied within a service, as for a business service provider

(BSP), can be difficult because such products are acquired in a number of different ways.[4]

Whether equipment is leased or purchased accounts for the most obvious cost differential. Leasing is reflected as a recurring periodic cost, usually monthly, whereas for purchased equipment, the company will depreciate the asset over a given number of years. Either way, costs include ongoing maintenance charges and, possibly, charges per unit of output, as in the case of a printer. Installation and de-installation charges are likely also, as are sales taxes and the like.

Software usually cannot be purchased; instead, the buyer is confronted with a periodic license fee plus a maintenance charge. There may or may not be installation and de-installation charges for software products, but there are often significant charges for professional services. Software pricing varies considerably, ranging from costs for unlimited licenses to very specific licenses according to the size and number of central machines on which the software is running, the number of end-users, the amount of use, and other factors.

Networks incur additional expenses for ordering, installing, maintaining, and de-installing circuits. Such costs are generally charged as a set fee per month for dedicated circuits, and for shared networks often on the basis of units of use.

The ready access to the Internet and proliferation of portable wireless devices has changed forever the way in which communications technologies are used and charged for.

All of the above examples indicate that there are certainly opportunities for quantity discounts based on the volume of products acquired. The discount can apply to either the service provider or the customer, but often a service provider will get a better deal than the customer, especially for specialty products, and may or may not pass such savings though, depending on the competitiveness of the market for those particular services.

With third-party service providers, the costs of equipment, software, services, and networks are usually rolled into a stated price regardless of whether the cost will change over time or the equipment has been fully depreciated.

For offshore outsourcing, the telecommunications costs can be considerable due not only to the distances involved, but also because of the increased need to communicate due to different time zones. In addition, different countries have different equipment requirements, telecommunications tariffs, and rules and regulations.

---

4. There are many types of service providers. Prevalent are ASPs and BSPs or Business Process Outsourcers (BPOs). In general, ASPs offer customers use of proprietary applications or customized off-the-shelf computer applications, where the customers interact directly with the computer applications housed with the ASP from their organization's location. For BPOs, the customer usually deals with persons who offer an interactive services, such as help desk services, and the outsourcer's staff interacts with appropriate computer systems.

For internal use, the cost can vary widely based on not only how the products have been acquired but on whether or not they are shared with other applications.

Facilities

People and equipment require space, furniture, heating and cooling, electrical power, light, and air. In particular, they not only require a regulated physical environment, but also supplies, food, drink, bathroom facilities, and more.

Space, fixtures, equipment, and furniture can be rented or purchased, and, if purchased, depreciated for tax purposes over a number of years. Buildings are amortized over decades compared to depreciation over a few years for equipment and furnishings. If a building is purchased, the owner must pay for property taxes and utilities, such as electricity, gas, and water, and maintenance and support of the facilities, including the costs of janitorial and security staff. Sometimes the costs for utilities and maintenance are passed through to the renter, while in other situations they are included in the rent.

These various facilities costs can be determined explicitly for in-house operations but are factored into the basic rate or the full price presented by service providers, much as was described for the costs of internal versus external staff.

Other Infrastructure Costs

In order to be all-inclusive, costs must include such items as security, business continuity, and disaster recovery. Some portion of these costs should be allocated to the particular service under consideration for outsourcing. In some cases, a third party will automatically provide the redundancy and capacity to fulfill the security and recovery needs. Indeed, many third-party services are offered specifically to fill such needs, namely, those from managed security services and disaster recovery services providers.

One aspect that should be carefully considered is the degree to which a customer organization might wind down backup sites after taking on a service provider and vice versa. In some situations the service provider serves as a complete backup, in which case the current cost of the in-house backup facility can be removed. In other cases, the impact of outsourcing one part of the business may have negligible impact on a backup facility that must remain in place, with marginally small savings. Particular care must be taken to ensure the continuation of backup services if they are moved back in-house or converted to another provider, or if the environment changes substantially, as might occur in the case of a takeover of either the customer or provider.

It should also be noted that if a function shares costs that are fixed and cannot be reduced in the event of outsourcing, then those costs have to be redistributed across remaining in-house functions. Consequently, the latter might become uneconomical and candidates for outsourcing.

We now turn to a number of other reasons for outsourcing, many of which also have cost components that must be included in the analysis.

Performance

An important reason for considering outsourcing is to achieve an improvement in performance that the service provider might offer both due to economies of scale and because of its absolute and relative size. Size, or scale, might give an organization the opportunity to provide sufficient work to keep second-shift and third-shift staff busy. Also, large scale can provide a variety of functions and opportunities which will help to retain the best available talent, who might not want to work in a less stimulating customer environment.[5] Additionally, the level of operational expertise is expected to be higher with service providers, due to the staff's greater concentration on, and lower repetitiveness of, tasks as compared to internal operations.

The relationship between service provider and customer is of necessity formal and specific, with particular service-level requirements often accompanied by charges for nonperformance and, occasionally, bonuses for exceeding requirements. Internal relationships are less likely to be as formal; furthermore, it is usually more difficult to press for nonperformance within one's own organization. Consequently, even with an internal service-level agreement in place (an increasingly popular practice), it is unusual for the customer to enforce such payment clauses of the agreement against other members of "the family." An advantage of third-party arms-length relationships is the greater likelihood that service-level performance will be aggressively monitored and pursued in the event of a provider missing a deadline or other performance measure. Therefore, service providers are usually more motivated to meet or beat agreed-upon service levels than in-house providers.

On the other hand, in a number of instances deterioration has occurred in service levels (to the extreme of no service) from third parties when, for example, a service provider runs into financial difficulty [5] or overly commits its limited resources and capacity.[6]

---

5. There is a paradox here. Service providers argue that they offer a more attractive work environment for specialists who would otherwise be bored and leave. Yet I recently asked a representative of a managed security services provider how they keep employees interested while performing routine and boring tasks, such as monitoring firewall logs. The response was that they rotate the staff after six months. This answer contradicts the frequent claim that service providers' staffs are very experienced in any particular area.

6. There has always been an issue with disaster recovery services as to their ability to handle a regional problem, such as a power blackout or snow storm, which results in numerous requests for service. This became an issue on September 11, 2001, when a large number of companies in the New York area declared emergencies virtually simultaneously, and some notable firms were not able to avail themselves of the services for which they had contracted.

Reliability

Improved reliability is a high-priority characteristic reportedly sought by those looking to contract with a service provider. Reliability is a component of performance—that is, it is a factor that drives availability, and availability is a key aspect of performance.

The study of reliability is an engineering field unto itself. Components individually have reliability characteristics, expressed in such terms as mean-time-between-failure (MTBF) and mean-time-to-repair (MTTR) that are estimated from experience with the hardware and software. When components are combined in series, their failure is additive and overall reliability decreases, whereas when components are combined in parallel, the overall reliability is increased. Therefore, by selecting more reliable hardware and software components, which have been suitably "burned in," and combining them so as to assure a measure of redundancy, the overall system is made more reliable, and hence more available.

Other factors to consider regarding reliability are business continuity and disaster recovery. Business continuity planning (BCP) and disaster recovery services (DRS) represent major outsourcing opportunities, since sharing services and facilities with other customers can reduce the cost to each participant considerably. From an availability perspective, BCP and DRS provide a high level of assurance that an organization can survive and recover from a major disaster such as a fire, hurricane, earthquake, or bomb.

From a customer's perspective, the time at which these seemingly random failures take place can be very significant. In [6, 7], I distinguish reliability and availability as seen from the users' perspective from the view of reliability and availability by the vendor or service provider. Availability is only significant from a user's perspective for periods during which the person normally has access to systems and networks. Failures during off-hours essentially don't count. That is why companies often contract with vendor service departments for short response times during critical periods and are willing to pay a substantial premium, perhaps 20% to 50% of the base maintenance fee, for such services.

It is really availability, rather than reliability, that is of interest to customers and the customers' employees. But availability alone does not meet the service requirements. A system or service can be up and running, but it meets the performance standards for the customer only if all the contracted systems and services are available. That is to say, if systems are available but are operating erroneously (for example, they may be operating on a corrupted database, or a function within a program may not be running properly), they are not meeting the service requirements.

Integrity

The requirement that a system be running properly and accurately is one aspect of integrity or usability. In order to maintain such integrity, a service provider must develop, adopt, follow, and enforce policies and procedures to establish and implement protective controls. The provider must be able to monitor and review all activities by subjects (such as end users or programs) to determine and verify who has gained access to specific applications, functions, and data and to review the frequency and timing of successful and unsuccessful access attempts. The service provider must also have plans in place to respond to the observation of any unusual activities or intrusions in order to prevent further abuse, repair any damage done, and pursue and prosecute perpetrators, as appropriate.

Quality of Service

While service levels, availability, and, to some extent, integrity are measurable and can be managed against the numbers, quality of service is by definition less tangible. It is a combination of these quantitative measures along with the intangible aspects of performance. Particularly important here is the degree to which the service provider is proactive in anticipating and resolving issues before they become critical. Through such actions, a service provider can differentiate itself from internal providers and competitors.

Because quality of service is subjective yet very important in the selection of a service provider, a potential customer needs to do due diligence, primarily through talking with references very familiar with the subject outsourcer. Other more measurable factors can be included, such as the growth in the number of customers, the length of time the customers have stayed with the provider, attrition rates, and percentage of renewals. These factors are all-important and should be included in the justification analysis, but are not as valuable as the honest opinions of current and former customers.

Security

Another factor high on the list for those deciding on whether or not to outsource and how to choose the service provider is security. Much like reliability, security involves a broad range of characteristics. The mantra for security is confidentiality, integrity, and availability (CIA). We have already discussed integrity and availability under the rubric of performance and quality of service, so what is left to discuss is confidentiality.

Confidentiality

In the discussion of security, we see a fair degree of confusion among the terms confidentiality, privacy, intellectual property, and proprietary information. In general, we use these terms to discuss the handling of information that should be viewed and can be changed by a select population, not necessarily the same group in each case. The issue of confidentiality receives a huge amount of attention from legislators and regulators, particularly in the financial services and health services industries.

The rapid advances in technology, particularly those that allow virtually universal access from practically anywhere to information stored within the databases of government agencies and private organizations, have by far outstripped the ability of organizations to control access to such information and suitably secure it. However, the increasing number of widely publicized abuses, with millions of cases of theft of identity and other personal information occurring each year, has caught the eye of governments. The result is a large number of laws and, for certain industries, regulations designed to protect individuals' personal information. The significance of this trend to outsourcers is that regulators in some industries, such as financial services, are demanding that customers perform exhaustive due diligence on prospective service providers in terms of their security.[7] That is to say, banks in particular are performing extensive evaluations and security assessments in practically every area of security, including system access, awareness, business continuity, disaster recovery, and physical security. BITS has produced an *IT Service Provider Expectations Matrix* [8], which provides a very extensive set of due diligence questions and requests. Table 3.3 shows the covered categories and subcategories.

One highly motivating reason for this relatively sudden and very pressing need to achieve the level of due diligence shown in Table 3.3 is the laws in the United States. They have, in particular, made senior management and boards of directors of major corporations personally responsible for any unauthorized disclosure of customers' nonpublic personal information (NPPI). This information might include full name, Social Security number, date of birth, and account numbers.

Security and Trust

As indicated above, the examination of the status of service providers' security posture extends well beyond the usual technical and operational controls. The examination investigates hiring practices (using background checks, testing for evidence of drugs), security awareness programs, and access to buildings and facilities (especially data centers).

It is rapidly becoming a baseline requirement that service providers demonstrate that they can adequately protect and restrict access to the confidential information of their customers and, in some cases, the private information of their customers' customers. Because third parties are, by definition, not legally

---

7. See, for example, Office of the Comptroller of the Currency (OCC) Bulletins 2001–47 and 2002–16. The former looks at third-party IT service providers in general and the latter relates to offshore IT outsourcing in particular. Available at http://www.occ.treas.gov.

Table 3.3
Summary Categories and Subcategories as Outlined in BITS Expectations Matrix [8]

Categories	Subcategories
Security policy	
Organizational security	Information security infrastructure
	Security of access by third parties
	Outsourcing
Asset classification and control	Accountability for assets
	Information classification
Personnel security	Security specified in job definition
	User training
	Responding to security incidents and malfunctions
Physical and environmental security	Secure areas
	Equipment security
	General controls
Communications and operations management	Operational procedures and responsibilities
	System planning and acceptance
	Protection against malicious software
	Housekeeping
	Network management
	Media handling and security
	Exchanges of information and software
Access control	Business requirements for access control
	User access management
	User responsibilities
	Network access control
	Operating system access control
	Application access control
	Monitoring system access and use
	Mobile computing and teleworking
Systems development and maintenance	Security requirements of systems
	Security in application systems
	Cryptographic controls
	Security in system files
	Security in development and support
Business continuity management	Aspects of business continuity planning
Compliance with legal requirements	Compliance with legal requirements
	Review of security policy and technical compliance
	System audit considerations

or, usually, physically part of customers' organizations, their ability to conform to these stringent security requirements is more difficult to achieve and represents a major risk of outsourcing, particularly offshore outsourcing.

An oft-quoted reason for using third parties is that they must have high security standards because their business depends on their demonstration of secure facilities and services. However, trusting to this belief is a mistake. It is certainly not true in all, or perhaps even in many, cases. If a third party can demonstrate such high security standards, it can be a very good reason to choose a service provider, especially one that can help with security itself.

Expertise

Another major reason to outsource, alluded to in the section on performance, is having access to highly qualified personnel, who may not be otherwise available to the hiring organization. In a number of areas, particular in information security, demand for highly qualified and experienced practitioners far outpaces the supply, particularly in government agencies where compensation levels are relatively low. Also, a particular organization may not have adequate work to keep highly qualified personnel busy, whereas a specialty service provider will. For example, security specialists working for service providers can also benefit by being exposed often to many situations, such as hacker attacks, which an employee of the customer's company would not experience to such a degree. The analogy is that one would prefer to go to a surgeon who does several of a particular procedure each day compared to one who may do the procedure twice a month on average. Though both are qualified, the former benefits from more frequent exposure.

Customers should be forewarned that, while a service provider may have presented staff with exemplary credentials, it may not be planning to assign those particular individuals to your account. It is important that customers understand exactly who is to be assigned to their project and in what roles. Specific staff assignments should be included in the service agreement.

Also, as described earlier, highly competent specialists are not likely to be satisfied doing the same routine—even though they are extremely good at it—year in and year out. Service providers claim to offer their specialized staff better career growth and opportunities than customers do. That may be true in many cases. However, the flip side of this is that the best, most experienced practitioners may well be swapped out of the position agreed upon. If the specialist were forced to remain in the same position as a result of contractual stipulations, then he or she might pick up and leave the outsource altogether, causing a major loss for the customer.

There are several answers to this problem. One is to ensure that the service provider has redundancy in the form of several individuals on staff with the high level of expertise and extensive experience required for the particular role. Another solution is to have the service provider automate the role, thereby incorporating the knowledge into an expert system. Yet another is to fully document the role so that someone with lesser expertise can perform the function.

In any event, access to expertise that is in short supply can be a significant driver in the decision to outsource.[8] It is one of the major factors driving the movement of offshore outsourcing to countries such as India, Ireland, and China, where there are increasingly large pools of low-cost, highly educated engineers and other professionals.

Computer Applications

Whether the outsourcer is an applications service provider (ASP) or not, the majority of, if not all, services that are provided by third parties embody computer applications, either as explicit offerings or built into an overall service and not necessarily visible to the customer. The customer, the service provider, and/or a software vendor may have developed these applications, jointly or independently. Because of the tight integration of computer applications into service offerings, much of the outsourcing decision revolves around the design, development, implementation, and operation of applications and interfacing such applications with other systems and processes.

It requires time, money, and frequently the effort of many specialists, expert in computer systems, technology, and specific business areas, to develop and maintain these computer applications. Quite often, a company will decide that having a third party take care of the headaches that come with application development and operation is preferable for a number of reasons discussed next.

Insufficient In-House Expertise

As described earlier, an important reason for using third parties to develop and run computer systems is that the customer organization may not have sufficient work to justify or interest highly skilled in-house persons. Part and parcel of the lack of expertise is the retention issue.

---

8. The U.S. government established a program to train security professionals. The government has instituted a program whereby it pays for the education and training of professionals in exchange for a commitment that the graduates will spend a stated amount of time working for their government sponsors. The first crop of graduates had surprising difficulty getting positions with government agencies, which appeared reticent in accepting newly minted graduates of the programwho might supplant more experienced personnel.

Retention

The competitive market for particular specialty skills may make it difficult for a customer organization to hold on to capable, trained individuals. Often, the preferred solution is to avoid the issue by using an outsourcer.

Compensation Limitations

Customer organizations may have difficulty recruiting the desired caliber of person or may have an issue with the compensation that such individuals demand in the marketplace. Budget-constrained customers may not be able to offer competitive incentives, such as stock or stock options, to their professional staffs.

Shared Costs

An individual customer organization may not be able to justify the cost of building a particular application. On the other hand, it might be able to afford the cost of application development and modification if the costs are shared with other organizations through the conduit of a service provider intermediary.

For systems that provide competitive advantage, not being able to build or modify systems might lead to loss of market share, reduced profits, and a negative impact on the image of the organization. In cases where regulators require certain capabilities by a given deadline, the ability to build new systems or change existing systems means the difference between surviving or not. Such considerations arose as a Y2K issue, when many companies decided to outsource rather than analyze and change millions of lines of program code.

Prompt Software Version Updates

Although there is appeal in not having to upgrade versions of software and apply patches when errors or vulnerabilities are found, in today's world viruses and worms can spread globally in seconds. Therefore, keeping software and systems up to date is even more important. This not only maintains the service provider's image as progressive, but it also reduces vulnerability in the face of ever-growing threats. Outsourcers are often more apt to perform upgrades because they tend to be somewhat more sensitive to implications that their systems are insecure.

The incentives for updating software are the same for in-house and external situations, but often the in-house program is not given a sufficiently high priority and inadequate resources are assigned to this effort. Updates are more likely to be a priority for a healthy outsourcer.[9]

---

9. The updating of software is one of the first activities to be jettisoned at an ailing outsourcer. If this is observed, it is a red flag to the customer.

Speed to Market

By having a large, flexible team of specialists to deploy to a priority system, a service provider can help a customer organization bring a particular application or service to market more rapidly than would be possible using in-house resources.

New Revenue Opportunities

Customers can exploit the broader range of capabilities offered by service providers in order to generate higher revenues and profits. Sometimes a business opportunity starts out small and grows over time. In such a case, an organization may be unwilling to make the initial investment in developing systems and services in support of the opportunity, but may find that, if priced appropriately, a service provider might reasonably support the volume of business, particularly in its early stages.

Fluctuations in Volume of Projects

A particular issue that organizations have regarding their application development shops is the fluctuations in volumes of work due to available opportunities, business cycles, and other factors. Service providers offer two benefits here. First, they may be more able to deploy staff to other projects. Second, by using service providers, the customer organization avoids laying off and rehiring personnel in response to fluctuations in workload.

Lower Customization Costs

While not always the case, it is sometimes easier for a third party to customize its systems and services for a particular requirement than for a customer organization to do so. One reason for this is that service providers likely build their systems to be readily adapted to the individual requirements of their customers, compared to more directed and less flexible in-house systems.

Lower Integration Costs

Service providers must be able to integrate their systems efficiently with those of customers and business partners. The ability to rapidly convert a customer's systems and processes is usually a determining factor in a service provider's success and can be a significant differentiator among services. The service provider's systems and processes are designed to facilitate this requirement to adapt quickly to multifarious environments.

Support

Service providers need strong support capabilities to survive in a competitive marketplace. Support takes many forms, such as a help desk that assists those using the services and embedded systems, or sophisticated technical support to deal with problems arising from a failure of the systems or networks to operate properly.

Help Desk

The help desk function for a service provider is much like an internal help desk except that its support personnel are likely to be better qualified to respond to problems. The service provider's personnel see problems and issues across a number of customers, resulting in a higher likelihood that they have confronted a particular problem many times before. Their experience level will likely have improved more rapidly in a multicustomer setting.

That is not to assume that internal or external help desk staff are particularly well trained, or that a service provider's staff is inherently better than internal staff. There is stronger motivation, however, for the service provider to present the best support image that it can. This is because customers can easily leave a provider, whereas in-house "customers" are captive.

It is quite common for companies to locate their help desk facilities in remote areas, including offshore locations, where a large, cheap labor pool exists which is reasonably well educated and hungry for employment. However, in order to justify this approach, a certain critical mass is necessary to assure that the required infrastructure and management is cost-effective despite cheaper labor. Often, a service provider supporting many customers can justify the establishment of a remote, cost-effective help desk capability better than those at customer organizations. Despite providing much-needed employment and money to less economically buoyant parts of the world, the image of the help desk job is quite negative in the United States and other developed countries—it is often viewed as a menial, boring job that attracts poor quality candidates. This may be truer of the large urban marketplace where there are many vocational choices. It is less true in areas, such as those with high unemployment or suburban areas where employees do not wish to commute large distances or have other personal reasons to be near to home, that any employment is desirable, particularly part-time employment.

In an interesting anomaly that, in certain countries, such as India, a help desk job is well respected and much sought after. According to Stephanie Moore of Forrester Research, not only is a help desk position highly regarded in India, with many candidates seeking relatively few jobs, but those companies outsourcing help desk services go to great lengths to make the location of the help desk transparent to customers calling in. For example, for the U.S. market, the candidates must be extremely proficient in English, but receive additional training to speak with an American accent and to use vernacular and buzz words relating to the specific service supported. Furthermore, the help desk staff members are given American pseudonyms. Ideally, a customer calling in has no idea of the location of the help desk facility—it could be in Florida or India for all they know.

Technical Support

Advances in communications technology have facilitated the trend towards remote technical support and service, particularly of the 24/7 variety. While it is possible and not uncommon, to have three-shift technical support domestically, outsourcing to foreign countries in different time zones makes for a much larger pool of engineers available around-the-clock within their normal working hours. With the cost of broadband long-distance communications lines coming down, linkages within organizations and between customer organizations and outsourcers are more feasible both technically and economically.

Financial Arrangements

The use of a third-party service provider can significantly impact a company's profitability, depending upon the payment options available from the outsourcer.

Price and Sharing

The cost of service can be charged to the customer by the outsourcer in a number of ways. Perhaps the simplest, and often the most appealing, is a monthly cost, which is based on level of resource use and agreed-upon service levels. Because the service provider frequently allocates certain resources across a number of customers, it is possible to come up with a menu of service costs based upon the degree of sharing. A customer organization commonly buys some combination of shared and dedicated resources in its service package.

Perhaps the most illustrative example of shared resources is in disaster recovery services (DRS). The whole raison d'être for such services is the notion that, at any given point in time, only a small subset of customers might need to use particular services. Providers typically offer a number of levels of service based largely on the degree of sharing and the low probability of customers declaring near-simultaneous disasters.

For generic DRS, such as providing access to off-site central processing and data storage, or desktop facilities, resources are made available to customers, up to a predetermined quantity (e.g., number of workstations) on a first-come, first-served basis. At this lowest level of service, providers typically overbook facilities. Consequently, the agreed-upon resources may not be available in total or even in part, if there are many customers competing for those same resources. The DRS vendor will often take certain precautions, such as assigning specific shared resources among companies that are geographically dispersed, in different lines of business, or not dependent on one another. This type of distribution reduces the probability of simultaneous requests for particular designated resources.

Another option for overbooked resources is to apportion them in some ratio among customers, with the ratio based in some manner on the original request. For example, let us assume that Company A had contracted for 120 workstations and Company B for 60 workstations. The DRS vendor may build a total of 120 workstations so as to meet Company A's demand and to fully accommodate Company B if it were to declare a disaster and if Company A did not. If the two companies declared emergencies simultaneously, Company A would be assigned 80 workstations and Company B would get 40 workstations, based on an assignment proportional to the contracted numbers.

The next level of DRS service would be for a full dedication of resources to a particular customer. That is, in the above example, Company B decides that it needs to have 60 workstations under all circumstances. The DRS vendor builds 140 workstations, rather than 120, so that for a simultaneous emergency, Company B gets its 60 workstations, but Company A must make do with only 80 workstations, since Company A is on a lower-cost sharing plan. If only Company A declared a disaster, it receives its full allotment of 120 workstations. Company A's rate (cost per workstation) is lower than that of Company B since it is taking a greater risk, which allows the DRS vendor to build fewer workstations overall.

The highest cost per unit occurs when there is no sharing. This might be due to customers being unwilling to take the risk of not having their full complement of resources and facilities available, or it may be that the company's requirements are so specialized that sharing is not possible. In either case, the cost is high—possibly as high or higher than having an in-house facility. Why would a company choose a DRS facility if it costs more? The answer often lies in nonfinancial benefits of such a relationship, such as ability to hire capable, experienced staff, and not having to find a building and set up the facility. The ability to pay on a monthly basis, without having a large initial capital outlay, may also be a factor, particularly for a start-up company.

Many of the above issues apply to a variety of outsourcing arrangements, particularly those that involve setting up a specialized facility. Managed security service providers (MSSPs) are in a similar situation, except that they generally provide a primary service rather than a backup.

Impact on Costs

As alluded to earlier, depending on the size of the customer, the use of third parties provides a much greater and more flexible range of payment options, not all of which are available through an in-house facility.

The ability to pay per unit of use, often on a sliding scale with discounted rates for increased transaction volumes, is a way for organizations to introduce new services and products without high up-front costs. If the new business is successful and becomes self-sustaining, it might be worthwhile for the customer organization to convert from the outsourced service to an internal operation.

Tax-related financial benefits might apply to leasing through third parties versus buying equipment and software, based on depreciation calculations and estimates of the residual value of equipment were it to be sold. Also, a firm may not want to commit capital to equipment and facilities, preferring to lease or rent equipment and services and license software on a periodic basis.

Feasibility of Project or Activity

Sometimes it is necessary to finance the development and operation of a certain function or service by having a third party do the work at a predetermined rate. Many startups do not have the funding or the management resources to put everything together themselves, nor should they want to. More mature organizations can recognize significant cost reductions from outsourcing, which can turn an infeasible activity into a possibility.

For example, few organizations are large and globally dispersed enough to be able to justify 24/7 support for tasks such as monitoring firewalls, because this requires a high level of knowledge, training, and expense. A third party can spread such a function across a number of customers, which is cost-effective for each customer and profitable for the service provider.

This model provides the support necessary, beyond venture capital and other funding, to enable many companies to become profitable, which would have been impossible to achieve without outsourcing. For many mature organizations, the opportunity to outsource significant parts of their operations enabled them to return to profitable status or stay in business.

Summary

The justification of outsourcing centers on cost, responsibility, capabilities, and skills. Reduced cost or payments, shifting of responsibility, purchasing of scarce or expensive resources and facilities, and acquisition of hard-to-find or expensive-to-hire professionals—these are the major reasons to justify outsourcing. They may or may not be the real reasons in any particular case, but they are generally acceptable and politically correct. After all, an insider justifying using third parties does not want to present his or her own deficiencies or incompetence as the real reasons, although an outsider, such as a consulting firm brought in by senior management, might. We will address the potential disconnect between outsourcing proposals and reality later in what may be one of the more controversial parts of this book.

The Other Side of the Outsourcing Decision

When all the reasons that favor outsourcing have been brought out and substantiated to show significant benefits, we still don't have the full picture. Practically every one of the benefits carries with it one or more risks, which may, singly or in combination, destroy any hope of justifying outsourcing or availing the company of the service at all, even internally. Many of these risks relate to security and its related liabilities, as we will see in the following chapter.

However, one only needs to proceed with evaluating the offsetting risks if the benefits have been shown to be extensive and of high value. Otherwise, the decision-making process stops here. Let us assume that the anticipated benefits of outsourcing in a particular situation are substantial and that, if the negatives are not too great, the organization will be able to proceed. In that case we must see what risks abound.

References

[1]   "Network Computing E-Mail Poll," *Network Computing,* June 12, 2001.

[2]   Allen, J., et al., "Outsourcing Managed Security Services," *Network Systems Survivability Program,* Carnegie Mellon University, Pittsburgh, PA: Software Engineering Institute, January 2003, http://www.fedcirc.com.

[3]   Gareiss, R., "Analyzing the Outsourcers," *InformationWeek,* November 18, 2002.

[4]   "BITS Framework: Managing Technology Risk for Information Technology (IT) Service Providers," *Banking Industry Technology Secretariat, Financial Services Roundtable,* Washington, D.C., November 2003, http://www.bitsinfo.org.

[5]   Berinato, S., "Security Outsourcing: Exposed!" *CIO Magazine,* August 1, 2001, http://www.cio.com.

[6]   Axelrod, C. W.,"The User's View of Computer System Reliability," *Journal of Capacity Management,* Vol. 2, No. 1, 1983.

[7]   Axelrod, C. W., "The User's View of Computer System Availability," *Journal of Capacity Management,* Vol. 2, No. 4, 1985.

[8]   "BITS IT Service Provider Expectations Matrix: Review of Audit and Assessment Methodologies for Financial Institutions," *Banking Industry Technology Secretariat, Financial Services Roundtable,* Washington, D.C., January 2004, http://www.bitsinfo.org.

4

Risks of Outsourcing

In the previous chapter, we examined reasons for outsourcing certain functions to service providers. In this chapter, we discuss factors, such as hidden costs, phantom benefits, and broken promises, that might be used to argue against such a decision. We shall return to the references that were used for the justification of outsourcing as they also suggest what risks or negative experiences customers had with outsourcing.

Loss of Control

The other side of the coin to handing over responsibility and blame to service providers is loss of control over outsourced operations. It is debatable whether a customer does—or indeed can—avoid some or all responsibility through engaging service providers.

The most common view of outsourcing appears to be that the concerns generated by giving up control override any sense of relief at not having the day-to-day operational responsibilities. This trend may result from perceptions regarding the different goals and attitudes of internal and external staff towards service, profits, and survival. Clearly much of the concern stems from customers' suspicions, which may be justified, that the outsourcer does not have the same level of commitment to meeting service requirements as an internal group. After all, as the argument goes, internal staff is more closely aligned to other insiders and subscribes to the goals, mission, and culture of the customer organization. However, this may be somewhat offset by greater formality, as embodied in explicit service level agreements (SLAs), which almost always exist in arms-length relationships between customers and providers, and are seldom seen between internal departments or divisions.

There are fundamental differences in motivation, goals, and attitude between internal staff and employees of outsourcers. However, these differences are not the same for all organizations and all situations. They can vary with the relative size of the customer and outsourcer, both to one another and, for the customer, to other customers. They will depend on the nature of the relationship—for example, whether internal staff members were transferred to the outsourcer's payroll or not.

The differences might also relate to the type of service being provided and the relative skills required of internal and external staff. The differences will surely vary over time as the personnel in both customer and provider organizations change, as the nature of the services changes, as competitive pressures build in the customer's world and for the outsourcer, and as the economic environment changes, within the industry, regionally, nationally and, increasingly, globally.

In the following sections, we will examine many of the factors that can negatively affect the posture and effectiveness of customer/outsourcer relationships. We will consider what can be done to mitigate the impact of these factors. We will also attempt to anticipate how these factors are changing over time and which of them will be exacerbated or moderated by general trends in the outsourcing business.

The principal risk drivers are the viability of the service provider, relative size of the customer, conflicts in service level agreements, legal liabilities, knowledge transfer, and hidden costs. We will look at these in detail in the following sections.

We show in Table 4.1 the relative objectives of each of these factors for the customer and the outsourcer respectively. The similarities or differences in objectives between each party impact greatly how each approaches the service relationship. Where they are similar, each party should be willing to compromise in order to optimize the relationship. Where they differ, we have the opportunity for contention, misperception, and damaging behavior.

Viability of Service Providers

Perhaps the worst nightmare of the customer of third-party services is the prospect that the provider will fail and leave customers in the lurch without access to critical services and systems. There have been a number of immediate and dramatic instances of failure of managed security service providers (MSSPs), which threatened the ability of customers to stay in business [1]. A number of outsourcers have reconstituted themselves and are looking to grow in their new form [2].

Table 4.1

Opposing and Common Objectives of Outsourcers and Customers

Factor—Objective	Customer (In-House)	Outsourcer (External)
Cost per unit of service—Opposing	Customer wants to obtain the most service for the least cost by: Carefully defining and controlling the services and related costs; Requesting proposals from a wide range of providers; Negotiating the most effective price (not necessarily the lowest price).	Outsourcer's goal is to maximize long-term profitability through: High price-to-cost ratio; Proposing flexibility in pricing rules to allow for additional revenue generation; Large volume of standard services; High customer retention; Economies of scale.
Quality of service—Somewhat opposing	Customer wants guaranteed aggressive service levels, adhering to prespecified metrics, with high costs (e.g., nonperformance payments) if the outsourcer does not meet the service levels. Customer wants compensation for business loss.	Outsourcer prefers looser or nonexistent service-level requirements with minimal give-back in the event of not meeting any specified service levels. Provider wants to be responsible only for subscription fee.
Control—Opposing	There are two customer views: Customer retains control by having staff and capabilities in-house that can assert control. Customer hands over control and responsibility to the service provider and does not maintain in-house capability. Here, the reliance is on the service contract to ensure that third party performs and enforces requirements.	Outsourcer prefers having greater control since, among other benefits, it makes it harder for customer to terminate services and perform the services in-house or at a competitor's facility.
Viability of service provider—Similar	Customer wants to retain a service provider that is likely to be around for the duration of the contracted services, and extensions if needed or wanted. Customer does not want to have to react to a sudden change in ownership of the service provider (including none) that might lead to the discontinuation of critical services.	Outsourcer wants to be perceived as a long-term player and not an organization presenting the specter of failure. An ability to demonstrate long-term viability attracts more customers and is self-fulfilling since the additional business supports the outsourcer's remaining viable.

Table 4.1 (continued)

Factor—Objective	Customer (In-House)	Outsourcer (External)
Viability of service provider—Similar	Customer needs to be careful not to necessarily retain the lowest bidder since that firm could be in trouble and be desperately seeking additional business just to stay afloat and may not be successful.	
Viability of customer—Similar	A good cost-effective outsourcing deal can, in many cases, increase a customer's profitability and make it more competitive, therefore it is more likely to survive and compete effectively.	Outsourcer should concentrate on customers with a good record and realistic business plans and who appear to be outsourcing for the right reasons, rather than as a survival tactic. The rise and fall of the dot-coms represents an example of an industry whose demise threatened, and in some cases took out, otherwise healthy service providers and vendors. Bottom line: The customer needs to be able to pay its bills.
Setup—Similar	From the customer perspective, it should be relatively painless to establish the service relationship and its concomitant systems and services.	From the service provider perspective, it should be relatively efficient and fast in establishing the service relationship and its concomitant systems and services. This will accelerate the start of the income stream from the customer.
Discontinuance—Opposing	From the customer perspective, it should be relatively painless to sever the service relationship and its concomitant systems and services.	From the service provider perspective, it should be a relatively difficult and lengthy process, but inexpensive (to the provider) for the customer to extricate itself from the service relationship and its concomitant systems and services. This will extend the income stream from the customer as much as possible. The anticipation of the process being difficult also might discourage present customers from closing down their relationship. Another ploy is to engage the customer in as many of the outsourcer's services as possible, which will make extrication even more difficult.

Table 4.1 (continued)

Factor—Objective	Customer (In-House)	Outsourcer (External)
Operation— Somewhat similar	The services and systems provided by the outsourcer should integrate well and easily with other customer operations. This might require, in some cases, considerable customization of the services and systems.	The service provider also wants the systems and services to integrate well with existing customer systems and services, which the service provider is not able to replace or is not interested in doing so. However, the outsourcer's preference is for its customers to use the "plain vanilla" systems and services, with a minimum of customization. The more the systems and services are tailored to the meet the customer's requirements, the more difficult the support and the more resources required to maintain the specialized system and services.
Scalability—Similar	From the customer's perspective, the outsourcer's systems, networks, and services should be able to be easily scaled to meet increases in business volumes and changes in business mix. All this ties in with the cost model that customers seek, namely, elimination of fixed cost and pricing based on variability of activity volume (e.g., number of transactions).	For the outsourcer, it is advantageous for the systems, networks and services being offered to be scalable so that additional customers and business volumes can be accommodated easily and quickly. It is preferable for the incremental costs of the additional services and systems to be very low, but the market should be such that the outsourcer can charge substantially higher prices.
Complexity— Opposing	The systems and services might be complex "under the covers" but should be simple to use.	The systems and operations should be easy to maintain and change, but there should be a high cost of entry for customers and/or competitors trying to in-source and/or compete, respectively.
Ease of use— Similar	The systems and services should be intuitive and simple, requiring a minimum of training and fewer calls to the help desk.	The systems and services should be intuitive and simple, requiring a minimum of customer and technical support.

In order to reduce the risk of such failures, it is important that customers follow a clear, structured approach to minimize the chance of being subjected to such a failure or to reduce the impact if such a failure does occur. Before entering into a service-provider arrangement, the prospective purchaser of the services should perform a complete and detailed due diligence process [3, 4]. Additionally, the agreement between the customer and outsourcer should anticipate the potential failure of the service provider and include provisions for such an event. These provisions should include a set of contingency plans allowing the customer organization to avail itself of alternative facilities and resources or to take over those resources of the outsourcer that have been applied to the customer's particular service. The operational contingency plans need to be exercised and rehearsed on a regular basis to ensure that they will work.

At the time of failure, a predetermined response plan should be put into effect to protect the outsourcer's customers from the negative aspects of such a failure, which might include effecting negotiations with other vendors.

Reasons for Abandoning Service

There are many reasons why a company might go out of the service-provider business. Some are due to internal factors, such as poor management, inadequate funding, and employee misdeeds. Others relate to external factors, such as industry trends, downturns in the general economy, and mergers and acquisitions.

One of the most insidious causes for failure is damage to reputation. This can be real or perceived. But either way, the results can be the same—abandonment by existing customers, reticence of new customers to sign up, loss of key staff, and more.

A major factor can be broad awareness of customer dissatisfaction if it is made known through disparaging articles in the press, badmouthing among industry members, or other forms of communication. And it is not just the larger customers who can be harmful. Dissatisfaction expressed by smaller customers can be just as damaging to a service provider as complaints from larger customers, particularly if the smaller customers band together and give voice to their unhappiness through the press.

Mergers and Acquisitions

Mergers and acquisitions can affect customers in two ways. The most obvious is the acquisition of the service provider. The question then arises as to whether the acquiring company wishes to continue providing the specific service or prefers to close down or sell that particular operation.

In another scenario, a company might acquire an existing customer and then the latter or its owner may transfer to a competing service provider, perhaps the one that is already being used by the acquiring company. Another reason for leaving might be that the acquiring company already provides the service in-house and wants to internalize the outsourced services.

Such changes can threaten the existence of a service provider and represents some risk to the customer.

Relative Size of Customer

Generally, a particular customer is one of many serviced by the outsourcer and most likely accounts for only a small percentage of the total workload of the service provider.[1] Sometimes smaller customers feel that they are second-class citizens in the mind of the outsourcer, relative to larger customers from which most revenues are generated. Bigger customers may get special price breaks, customized services, and dedicated support staff—features that may not be available to the medium-sized and smaller customers at all, or may be unbundled and charged for at a high premium. In the event of general problems, larger customers may have their concerns addressed first, with small customers waiting until support staff is freed up from dealing with the larger customers.

Sometimes a large customer will successfully assert its dominance in order to obtain preferential treatment. However, if that customer is in contention for service with another even larger customer, it may itself have problems getting the desired attention. Also, in such a competitive battle for service, the customer may gain priority by making the most noise and escalating the issue to upper management at the provider. Smaller companies can avail themselves of this technique also and move up the priority ladder based on aggressive requests or special relationships with senior staff. Sometimes a customer might appeal to former employees who have transferred to the provider, thereby getting privileged access to decision-makers. Competition between customers for the provider's attention is a common situation. And it takes a top-flight service provider to be evenhanded in its treatment of customers.

In some situations, larger clients provide the economies of scale that make costs lower for everyone, including smaller customers. The latter should understand that the large clients might in fact be subsidizing them. On the other

---

1. If a service provider has many customers (for instance, more than 50), it is to be expected that the 80-20 rule, or similar, will apply, whereby 80% of business belongs to 20% of the customers. Sometimes the percentage is more skewed, with a handful of large customers and hundreds of relatively small organizations.

hand, the larger clients are often able to negotiate sweeter deals with the outsourcer just because of their size and volume of business. With their unequal risk profiles and different motivations, outsourcers and their customers approach the outsourcing relationship in different ways, as depicted in Table 4.1.

Quality of Service

One of the main reasons to outsource is the expectation of receiving better service from the outsourcer than from internal staff. This expectation is often based on the knowledge that there will be an explicit SLA in place, which can be enforced by the customer and which might bear remedies against the outsourcer for nonperformance. While companies are increasingly establishing SLAs for internal providers, they are often harder to enforce since everyone is a member of the family.

If an outsourcer loses a customer because of poor service, it is much less excusable. Of course, the perception of poor service could be misguided, or service expectations may not have been realistic in the first place. However, SLAs between customer and provider generally specify what constitutes acceptable service and what does not. Therefore, a base set of metrics exists against which to measure performance. The SLA is discussed in greater detail in Chapter 6.

There is a strong argument that the measures in an SLA may not adequately depict the perceived service. In an article by Jiang et al., quality measures are categorized into tangibles, reliability, responsiveness, assurance, and empathy items [5]. Some items are typical of those included in a SLA, whereas others are not. The quality measures include the following categories.

Tangibles

In *tangibles:*

- The service provider has up-to-date hardware and software.

- Physical facilities are visually appealing.

- Employees are well dressed and neat in appearance.

- Appearance of the physical facilities of the information systems unit is in keeping with the kind of services provided.

Reliability

In *reliability:*

- When outsourcer promises to do something by a certain time, it does so.
- The outsourcer provides services at the times promised.
- The customer insists on error-free records, and the outsourcer agrees.
- When users have a problem, the outsourcer's information systems units show sincere interest in solving it.
- The outsourcer's information systems units are dependable.

Responsiveness

In *responsiveness:*

- The outsourcer tells customers' users exactly when services will be performed.
- The outsourcer's employees give prompt service to users.
- The outsourcer's employees are always willing to help users.
- The outsourcer's employees are never too busy to respond to users' requests.

Assurance

In *assurance:*

- Behavior of the outsourcer's employees instills confidence in users.
- Users feel safe in their transactions with the outsourcer's information systems units' employees.
- The outsourcer's employees are consistently courteous with users.
- The outsourcer's employees have the knowledge to do their jobs well.

Empathy

In *empathy:*

- The outsourcer's operational hours are convenient for all their users.
- The outsourcer gives users individual attention.
- The outsourcer's technical units have employees who give users personal attention.
- The outsourcer has the users' best interests at heart.
- The outsourcer understands the specific needs of users.

The only item that can be related specifically to security or, more precisely, integrity of the service is the reference to error-free records in the reliability category. Many of the measures do not typically appear in SLAs, but are often key in evaluation and selection processes. Interestingly, security is only alluded to in one item in the assurance category in regard to feeling safe.

However, it is noticeable that there are no specific security metrics. The measurement of security characteristics is still in its infancy. There are no absolute standards and probably never will be, since the environment is continually changing and the needs of security are changing in response.

Since absolute security is not achievable, it follows that measures are likely to be relative. Some current standards are set and the actual operation can be measured against them. TruSecure Corporation, in defining their measures for certifying security posture uses the term "essential practices." This underscores the fact that the term "best practices" is not an accurate depiction due to the frequent occurrence of new threats and the discovery of previously unknown vulnerabilities. The latter could result from a detailed examination of the application or system code, a random event, or a directed attack by a computer worm or virus.

Nevertheless, the aspects of security that are characterized by system and network availability and system and data integrity are more measurable. Availability, in particular, can be expressed in specific percentage terms. However, even for availability, issues exist as to what are appropriate measures, since providers and users may have differing views, as described in my articles on the user's view of availability and reliability [6, 7].

Brandon and Siegelstein list occurrences, which make a system unavailable, in their book on contract negotiation [8]. These occurrences are:

- The system fails to operate.
- The system fails to operate in accordance with formal specifications.
- The system operates inconsistently or erratically.
- The system is in the process of being maintained or repaired.
- A hardware or software component of the system is inoperative, which renders the entire system useless for user purposes.
- The system is not operated because there is potential danger from operation of the system to operators, employees, or customers.
- There is a defect in software supplied by the manufacturer.

These factors all affect the availability of a system to a customer's users, even though some factors may be controllable by the service provider and others are not. An important goal of the service arrangement is to establish that the outages due to controllable factors will be minimized. This is usually more difficult to do when the resources reside at, and/or are managed by, a third party.

Definitions

In order to assist in your determining what availability and reliability mean in this context, here are some definitions of applicable terms:

The *reliability* of a system is the probability that, when operating under given stated environmental conditions, the system will perform its intended functions adequately for a specified interval of time.

The *availability* of a system is the probability that the system is operating satisfactorily at any point in time, excluding scheduled idle time.

Intrinsic availability is the probability that a system is operating in a satisfactory manner, when used under given conditions, at any point in time, excluding idle time and downtime other than active repair time.

Operational readiness is the probability that a system is either operating or can operate satisfactorily when it is used under stated conditions.

The probability that a system is operating is a function of the mean time between failures (MTBF) and the mean time to repair (MTTR).

More detail in this area is available in the cited references and in standard engineering texts on system reliability. It is well worth learning some of these details. The availability component of quality of service is often the most contentious aspect since there is generally room for a range of interpretations and misinterpretations as to whether a service level is being met.

The Issue of Trust

It has become very important to ensure that third parties who have access to personal and confidential information are protecting that information from inappropriate disclosure and from misuse. In particular, customer organizations are increasingly being held responsible for securing and protecting customers' information. As mentioned earlier, a burgeoning body of laws and regulations holds boards of directors and senior management directly responsible for any breaches that disclose nonpublic personal information (NPPI), in particular to those who might exploit it for fraudulent endeavors.

The issue of trust has recently taken center stage in the health and financial services industries in the United States, the United Kingdom, Europe, and other countries around the world. A slew of laws and regulations require the protection of end customers' NPPI from unauthorized access and from misuse by those with or without approved authorization. In these and other sectors, there is also concern in regard to unauthorized and unintended disclosure of corporate and government confidential or proprietary information, as well as intellectual property.

Even prior to the extensive privacy and security legislation and regulation of recent times, which have focused on the protection of customers' identifying information,[2] there were very valid and forceful reasons to limit access to information when transmitted and stored electronically.

Such protection is not only altruistic but is often related to preventing competitors from gaining access to customer lists for fear that they would steal customers. In financial services, requirements keep information known to investment bankers away from traders, brokers, and other individuals who might attempt to use such insider information improperly. Such requirements also extend to third-party service providers who have access to the same information.

It is one level of effort to protect confidential, personal, and otherwise sensitive information within the confines of a single institution. Imagine how much more difficult it is to protect such information when it is obtained and processed by service providers, which may not be bound by the same laws and regulations as their clients. Of all the aspects of outsourcing, information protection is often the most critical, especially, as we have noted, in financial and health services, as well as government sectors, such as law enforcement and defense, where secrecy is paramount.

As will be discussed later, it is difficult and often costly to satisfy executive management, boards of directors, and regulators that sufficient care has been taken to safeguard the privacy of individuals' data. Safeguards include ensuring protection of information against unauthorized access or false manipulation during creation, transmission, storage, and retrieval operations involving third parties.

Another complication arises when different laws and regulations govern both the customer organization and the third party, particularly when located in different jurisdictions such as different states in the United States or different countries Accordingly, heavily regulated financial firms make extraordinary efforts to ensure that their service providers comply on their behalf and on

---

2. The U.S. Congress, along with other legislative bodies around the world, continues to express serious concerns over the proliferation of identity theft and the use of personal information against the interests of the owner of that information, namely, the private citizen. As mentioned previously, members of Congress, at a Subcommittee Hearing on cyber security at which I testified, clearly indicated that they had concerns about identity theft. In fact, I got the distinct impression that the issue of identity theft superceded cyber security in their minds.

behalf of their retail customers with relevant laws and regulations *as they apply to the customer organization.*

A U.S. financial firm, for example, is required by their regulatory bodies to retain and have quick access to certain documents for periods of several years. Therefore, in order to be acceptable to the financial institution and its regulators, service providers must arrange to offer and maintain such storage and access capabilities in their handling of those documents, in paper, electronic, or other form, in a manner consistent with the financial institution's regulatiory requirements. In such cases, it is not enough to have a statement or response from the service provider to the effect that the documents are stored and available appropriately. It is necessary for the financial firm to review the policies, standards, procedures, and other documentation relating to such data creation, transmission, storage, and disposal by the service provider *and by any subcontractors of the service provider.*

It is also good practice to test whether the outsourcer's stated policy and procedures are enforced and implemented. Either the customer organization or the service provider may hire third-party auditors or security assessment consultants to perform security and control assessments. Such specialty assessment firms are likely to do a more orderly, structured, and complete evaluation than an in-house staff might achieve, because they perform so many more assessments over a period of time than would an in-house group.[3]

With respect to support functions, an internal support group, whether a user help desk or technical support group, is usually dedicated to assisting internal personnel or direct customers of the firm. On the other hand, service providers' support groups will likely have many more customers vying for their attention. This raises concerns that an outsourcer's support may not be of as high a quality or as responsive as that of the firm itself, when the support function is internal. However, there is a strong trend towards outsourcing customer and technical support to third parties domestically and offshore, with mixed success.[4] Since, in many cases, support does not need to be colocated with the

---

3. Nevertheless, these third-party security assessments are not guarantees of absolute security, and should not be taken as such. Security assessment is not an exact science and, to a considerable degree, depends upon the expertise and experience of the testers. I recently had the experience where a second evaluation of the same application unearthed a vulnerability that had been missed by a prior assessment by a highly reputable firm. Also, the assessment is good only at particular point in time and should be redone whenever a major change in architecture or functionality occurs. It is recommended that security tests for highly critical systems be done with regularity and by different consulting firms. It is also very useful to have an internal group able to perform such assessments as an additional check, if such a group can be cost-justified.

4. In one highly publicized example, Dell Computer actually pulled back a help desk operation from India to a domestic U.S. facility because corporate customers were complaining that the quality of service was inadequate.

main service facilities, such support is frequently put in remote places where there might be a shortage of jobs and wages are lower. This also applies in regions where the cost of labor is less, as in near-shore and offshore locations.

Much of the evaluation of support is subjective and qualitative. The support area is rife with measurement problems. Service metrics include the number of requests handled per unit of time and in total, time to respond, and time to resolve the issue. Such measures usually are more relevant to the operation of the support group than to the customers. However, customers are certainly affected by the service levels, in terms of how long it takes to get through on the telephone (numerous rings, busy signal, on hold, or diverted through a complex automated response system), how knowledgeable the support person is, and how quickly and accurately the problem is resolved.

Sometimes, what appears to be a high service level, in terms of increased number of calls handled per hour, is not necessarily a good thing. A large on-line brokerage firm found that following the introduction of a telephone response system the number of calls increased dramatically, in part because the system was easy to use and individuals took advantage of the faster system to ask more questions. From the firm's perspective, there was little added value to the incremental calls since they did not generate additional revenues.

Customers often have concerns that the service provider will not meet required service standards. These concerns can usually be mitigated through contractual language. More likely, the service given is often in direct response to the service demanded. Customer organizations need to be willing to assert their contractual rights in getting better service, possibly through escalation or the threat of escalation to outsourcers' senior management. If that is not effective, the terms in the agreement need to be enforced, which might involve payments to the customer organization or reduced charges. If the matter is still not resolved, it may become necessary to take legal action and prosecute the terms of the contract, although this is clearly the least desirable action, since it will lead to strained relationships between customer and service provider and additional costs for both parties.

Performance of Applications and Services

Support is only one aspect of service. Another is the performance of the actual services, be they IT applications, operational services, or something else.

Again, SLAs should be designed to account for levels of performance of the contracted services. Here, too, metrics can assist. Measures of capacity, throughput, response time, and availability—particularly availability—are frequently used in SLAs to monitor performance.

However, since the outsourcer has profitability in mind, its goal is to provide service within the agreed-upon limits at minimum cost. Sometimes, if the penalties for not meeting the performance criteria are not onerous, the outsour-cer might find that it is cheaper to fail on the performance criteria than to add capacity and redundancy to meet or beat the criteria. It is important, therefore, to ensure that any payments back to the customer are sufficient to motivate the service provider to meet the service requirements.

It is also important for the availability criteria to be applied to significant times of day, days of the week, and so forth. A failure during a period of peak volume will have much greater impact than one that occurs during off-hours.

To maintain a proper balance between capacity and cost, it is necessary to establish the criteria up front and allow for changing requirements. Otherwise, performance needs of customers may not be met over time as the customer's vol-ume and/or the volumes of other customers increase.

Lack of Expertise

It can often be difficult to find third parties with a proven team of experts who are experienced and knowledgeable in a particular industry being serv-iced or in specific computer applications, programming languages, or system platforms. Customers should beware of bait-and-switch tactics. Vendors should provide lists of their staff along with their résumés as part of the outsourcer's proposal, and customers must insist that specific individuals be assigned to the project or service. Additionally, the customer should retain the right to approve any substitutes. Another safety measure is to ensure that the applications or activities outsourced can, if necessary, be insourced or contracted out to a differ-ent provider.

Hidden and Uncertain Costs

There are two main reasons why certain costs may be overlooked or hidden from the due diligence evaluation of service providers.

First, some costs are very difficult or practically impossible to quantify. Intangible costs might relate to such aspects as perceived quality of service.

Other costs are easier to define, but the probability of their occurrence is very uncertain. Such is the case with outsourcer viability. Reasonably good esti-mates of the cost impact of failure of a service provider can be made, but the probability that the outsourcer will fail is uncertain, particularly at the time of the evaluation. In fact, if outsourcers were known to be having financial difficul-ties at the time of the evaluation, they should not have been included in the short list of finalists. However, even though an outsourcer is in financial distress, it might continue to provide services. Additional funding (from a venture capitalist, for instance) could save the outsourcer or the provider might be acquired by another company, perhaps a competitor.

In the case of acquisition, services to specific customer companies may or may not be continued, at the choice of either the provider or the customer. Outsourcers are sometimes acquired by a competitor of one or more of their customers, in which case the latter might decide to terminate the service at the earliest opportunity. Some astute customers include statements in their contract with the outsourcer to the effect that either party can end the relationship, without termination payments, upon acquisition by a third party of either customer or provider.

The range of possible outcomes adds to the uncertainty. I have often heard, in response to negative financial news about a service provider, that "someone will buy the company and keep the service going." History has shown that such a resolution is by no means certain. Some form of risk analysis is called for in these circumstances in order to estimate the probabilities of each outcome and to project the corresponding costs.

In risk analysis, however, some costs might be hidden or excluded altogether, either unintentionally or through the analyst's ignorance or inexperience. More insidiously, an analyst may intentionally exclude costs to favor one decision, such as selecting one provider versus another, choosing insourcing over outsourcing, or staying in a particular business or not. Whatever the predisposition of the analyst might be, these intentional oversights or unintentional errors have to be dealt with differently, but they all must be confronted. There are well-publicized instances of major business decisions having been made due to errors or omissions in the calculations, as mentioned earlier.

While many domestic and offshore outsourcing decisions are based on known, tangible costs and benefits (such as cost savings), others rely on less tangible costs and fuzzy benefits for their conclusions. Furthermore, actual events have a major influence on the analyst's expectations of the likelihood and magnitude of future events. For example, the successful terrorist attacks of September 11, 2001, revised everyone's expectations of the frequency, scope, and impact of devastating terrorist attacks. Legislators and regulators have responded with conservative backup and disaster recovery requirements, particularly in critical sectors such as financial services.

The greatly increased expectations of the probability and magnitude of terrorist attacks, the wars in Afghanistan and Iraq, the threats posed by North Korea and other nations, and the potential for the global spread of diseases (such as SARS) have raised management concerns about offshore outsourcing. As a result, management has focused on contingency planning, business continuity, and disaster recovery for offshore facilities.

In response to these concerns, management in many domestic organizations using offshore service providers launched investigations of outsourcers' contingency plans in the event of a war or other disruptions. Management wanted to know whether domestic facilities and capabilities could take over in the event that offshore facilities were no longer available. Of course, similar requirements apply to domestic outsourcing, where the chance of war may be less but the expectation of terrorism is high. Suddenly, the security and continuity risk equations for critical functions such as technical support and applications development changed and are now considered subject to the whims of terrorists. The huge increase in expected losses resulting from recent terrorism, wars, and health epidemics, in addition to the vagaries of the economy, has created a much greater willingness to expend funds to mitigate such risks with increased investments in security, business continuity, and disaster recovery.

Such potential losses were not anticipated when originally evaluating many outsourcing proposals—how could they have been? In hindsight, the analysis was in error. Had such terrible events been factored in, the decision to adopt a particular outsourcing arrangement might have actually been reversed in some cases to avoid the newly recognized risks or the costs of mitigating them. While some analysts favor a high reserve to allow for extremely uncertain events, such as acts of war or terrorism (often termed "force majeur"), it was far more common not to allow for such highly unlikely scenarios prior to September 11 than subsequently. Of course, one might argue that the telecommunications industry did not, as a whole, consider the potential bursting of the dot-com bubble, which in many ways was far more devastating financially to many organizations and individuals than the various terrorist acts.

Table 4.2, illustrates the differences between situations in which there is an understatement of costs and/or overstatement of benefits and situations in which the expectation of something happening was explicitly included or not.

In Table 4.2, if the analyst misses something that should have been anticipated, that is a sign of incompetence. If the analyst misses something that someone expert in the area would likely miss also, he or she is not to blame, because

Table 4.2
Predictable and Unpredictable Oversights

	Likely to Be Anticipated	**Unlikely to Be Predicted**
Oversight (Accidental)	Less usual—reason for concernabout the ability and/or intentions of the analyst	Usual situation
Hidden (Intentional)	Fraudulent	Unprofessional (given the benefit of the doubt)

events that could not have been guessed in advance occur frequently. If the analysis intentionally omits something that should be generally known by someone familiar with the area, it is a fraudulent act and, if provable, needs to be dealt with severely. If an analyst omits something that is difficult to know about or it is hard to estimate its impact, the analyst is being professionally dishonest if he or she chooses not to disclose that such an event could happen and would affect the analysis if it did indeed happen.

Limited Customization and Enhancements

Going into an outsourcing arrangement, it might appear that the systems and/or services meet most if not all of customer's requirements without the need for future enhancements. However, situations change over time, both for the outsourcer and the customer organization, and need to be renegotiated if they were not in the original contract. Most changes of this nature are readily accommodated.

On the other hand, a customer's business might change due to external market forces or new laws and regulations, and the demands on their outsourcers change accordingly. To the extent that the demands of a customer and the provisions in the outsourcing agreement diverge, there are implicit as well as explicit costs to the customer related to satisfying the discrepancies, even to the extent of having to transfer to a different service provider or to an in-house operation.

Knowledge Transfer

The more functions and roles that are outsourced, the less likely is it that the internal staff can support those functions should they be moved back in-house. In order for an organization to maintain its best bargaining position and to retain critical internal staff, the latter must be kept up-to-date by means of training programs and/or via the transfer of knowledge from the outsourcer to the customer. Rotation of customer staff through the service provider on a prespecified schedule might be feasible. Of course, the outsourcer will probably not be enthusiastic or supportive of such an exercise, since it is in their interest to keep customers dependent on them.[5]

---

5. I once was involved in an effort to move a computer system in-house from a "facilities manager," as host service providers were once called. We were able to achieve a great deal on the operational side—taking over the entire computer job production-control system. In this way, the internal expertise was built up.

The cost of not maintaining a knowledgeable cadre of internal staff can be considerable in the long run. The impact can include loss of negotiating power in terms of costs and services, difficulty in moving to another service provider or in-house, and the danger of being totally dependent on a third party whose strategic direction might not match that of the customer. For the most part, these costs are difficult to measure and are usually excluded from the evaluation of the outsourcing relationship, but they are real costs.

Shared Environments

A major concern, especially among firms in highly regulated industries such as financial and health services, is one customer gaining access to information about another customer. Beyond the risk of having a competitor get access to proprietary information, there would be the strong possibility that a firm is not in compliance with laws and regulations. Such a case is not purely a business or reputation risk, but puts senior management and boards of directors in jeopardy if found to be negligent about ensuring that customer information is protected.

With a function operating totally in-house, there is little likelihood that other companies can access information—unless, of course, industrial espionage or information warfare occurs. However, if these same systems and data are moved into a shared environment, such as an outsourcing arrangement, this new, very serious risk appears. How should this risk be mitigated? There are several possible approaches, such as vulnerability analysis and tests and enterprise security evaluations and certification. But, it is important to note that the outsourcer's status might change.[6] The customer needs to be notified in a timely fashion.

Legal and Regulatory Matters

Increasingly, legislators and regulators are looking at the issue of the security of customer data. The risks related to not protecting customer data adequately apply not only to the individuals tasked with managing those information assets but also to senior management and the board of directors. The real strength of these regulations lies in their application whether or not the information is in the hands of the organization to which it was originally entrusted. That is to say, a firm's management is just as culpable if the disclosure took place from inside a

---

6. I know of a situation where an ASP was considering moving its own computer facilities from in-house to a hosted service. It was only by chance that the customer got to know about it, much to their chagrin.

third party not under the former management's direct control. This has led to a frenzy of due diligence, particularly by the larger U.S. banks, which are subject to the Gramm-Leach-Bliley Act and the consequent regulations by the Federal Reserve Board, Securities and Exchange Commission, and other agencies.

Certainly, from a basic perspective, the cost of the newly required and intensive due diligence efforts and the risks associated with not meeting the regulatory requirements need to be included in the evaluation of all outsourcing arrangements, particularly where customer NPPI is transferred to and from the outsourcer.

The long-term effect of these requirements is likely to be a reduction in the number of service providers serving highly regulated markets and a consolidation into a relatively few major players. These stringent requirements also suggest that some form of globally recognized certification standards needs to be developed and the means of attaining them established. While certifications might increase initial costs, they tend to lower the longer-term aggregate costs because certification standards must be met periodically, perhaps annually, versus being continually subject to verification.

Summary and Conclusion

When all the risks of outsourcing are considered, one wonders how anyone ever makes the decision to use a third party. However, there is plenty of evidence that these deals are done frequently and are often satisfactory from both buyer's and seller's perspectives.

The purpose of this chapter is to make the reader aware of the risks and pitfalls involved in the analysis and evaluation of third-party service providers, particularly from the security aspect. Once aware, the evaluator should be able to develop a satisfactory analysis and service arrangement and, consequently, arrive at a decision that is justified through the consideration of all factors, and not the neglect of an unpleasant few. For the latter will surely raise their ugly heads and negatively affect the area of outsourcing. Better to be prepared in advance for the appearance of hidden costs and the possible occurrence of unlikely events than to be taken by surprise.

References

[1]   Berinato, S., "Security Outsourcing: Exposed!" *CIO Magazine*, August 1, 2001, http://www.cio.com.

[2]   Wright, R., "The Hosts with the Most: Three Hosting Companies Revamp Their Channel Strategies. What's in It for VARs?" *VAR Business*, June 2, 2003, http://www.varbusiness.com.

[3]   Allen, J., et al., *Outsourcing Managed Security Services*, Carnegie Mellon University, Pittsburgh, PA: Software Engineering Institute, January 2003, available at http://www.fedcirc.com.

[4]   "BITS Framework: Managing Technology Risk for Information Technology (IT) Service Providers," *Banking Industry Technology Secretariat*, Washington, D.C., November 2003, http://www.bitsinfo.org.

[5]   Jiang, J. J., et al., "Closing the User and Provider Service Quality Gap," *Communications of the ACM*, February 2003, Vol. 46, No. 2, pp. 72–76.

[6]   Axelrod, C. W., "The User's View of Computer System Availability," *Journal of Capacity Management*, Vol. 2, No. 4, 1985.

[7]   Axelrod, C. W., "The User's View of Computer System Reliability," *Journal of Capacity Management*, Vol. 2, No. 1, 1983.

[8]   Brandon, D. H., and S. Siegelstein, *Data Processing Contracts: Structure, Contents, and Negotiation*, New York: Van Nostrand Reinhold Company, 1976.

5

Categorizing Costs and Benefits

In Chapters 3 and 4, we discussed the positive and negative aspects of outsourcing in general terms. At some point, however, management will want to know what outsourcing will actually cost, what savings can be expected, and what the return on investment (ROI) will be.

In this chapter, we will analyze how to categorize the specific items that need to be included in the cost-benefit equation of an outsourcing proposition, so that you can make a case for such a proposal before the appropriate approving body within your organization.

Structured, Unbiased Analysis—The Ideal

Many organizations, particularly government agencies, already use detailed templates and work sheets for such evaluations—the techniques are by no means new. However, in the approach described below, we will expand upon those templates in order to take into account the peculiarities of outsourcing, since few business decisions involve so much emotion and subjectivity.

As previously stated, analysts' preferences and predispositions often bias the evaluation of outsourcing. It is well known that analysts, from time to time, make the numbers work in order to come up with the answer they want. This is not necessarily fraudulent since the analysts' bias might be subconscious and impact only the subjective components of the analysis. For example, an American individual of Irish descent might feel more comfortable with offshore service providers from Ireland because he or she is more familiar with the country and subconsciously consider the risk less there than in other countries.

However, an analyst who believes that he or she would be personally affected negatively by the decision to outsource might intentionally bias the results. Therefore, many organizations have objective third-party consulting firms perform the analysis. Objective is the questionable word here, because sometimes the third party has a business interest in the outcome. For example, the consulting firm may believe that it has an opportunity for a sizeable transitional engagement were the decision to be made in favor of outsourcing versus retaining the functions in-house, which would not generate additional consulting work. Any firm contracting for a third-party analysis should be aware of this issue and should avoid such conflicts of interest.

Next we will describe both objective and subjective measures, as well as those that demand a degree of reasonableness in order to minimize bias on the part of analysts, decision-makers, and other stakeholders.

Costs and Benefits

Some costs and benefits associated with outsourcing are known with a high degree of precision and certainty. These include labor costs for predefined tasks and rent and equipment leases for which contracts already exist or for which expenses can be predicted accurately. Comparable benefits might include labor, rent, and equipment lease cost savings, if they are made on the same basis and use the same assumptions.

The spectrum of the cost-benefit continuum runs from certain, known, and tangible costs and benefits to those that are uncertain, unknown, and intangible. First, we will identify a number of cost-benefit classifications [1].

Tangible Versus Intangible Costs and Benefits

Tangible costs can be observed and measured. They appear on the books of organizations and can be audited. Tangible benefits are realized or potential cost savings and revenue increases, which can also be measured and audited.

Intangible costs and benefits may be easy to identify, but they are always much more difficult, if not impossible, to measure with any degree of accuracy.

Objective Versus Subjective Costs and Benefits

Tangible costs are objective in nature, but tangible benefits are subjective because, while a cost saving or revenue increase may be real, attributing it appropriately to a specific effort can be difficult and very much a matter of opinion.

Intangible costs and benefits are subjective, sometimes highly so, even though estimates can be obtained from objective third parties.

An example is the use of industry-wide statistics of losses, due to computer worms, viruses, and hacker attacks, in order to justify spending on security tools. While the statistics, which are themselves questionable as to accuracy, provide general trending data, they are not valuable in estimating specific events. Furthermore, the stronger the security protection in place, the less the potential impact of a particular threat, so that the loss from any specific event is conditional upon the measures already implemented.

Direct Versus Indirect Costs and Benefits

Costs and benefits are handled differently depending on whether they are direct or indirect. Direct costs or benefits can be attributed to a specific activity or group. Indirect costs and benefits, on the other hand, are incurred or achieved in another area and are allocated or assigned back to other activities or groups.

Controllable Versus Noncontrollable Costs and Benefits

This differentiation is between costs and benefits that the analyst or decision-maker can change or influence versus those that he or she must accept as given. In general, tangible, direct, and objective costs and benefits are considered controllable, but those categorized as intangible, indirect, and subjective are not.

Certain Versus Probabilistic Costs and Benefits

Some costs and benefits can be expressed in precise absolute terms, that is, they are known with a high degree of certainty. For instance, contractual payments for equipment and software are certain. However, uncertainty needs to be factored into some costs and benefits, since either their magnitude or their very occurrence is questionable. Usually, for probabilistic costs and benefits, some expectation is established, and estimates of magnitude and probability are made. In some cases, a decision tree is created whereby the probabilities of various outcomes are stated and the magnitude of each outcome is estimated. By multiplying probability by magnitude and aggregating across all probabilities, an "expected value" is obtained for use in the analysis.

Fixed Versus Variable Costs and Benefits

To paraphrase a common saying, in the long run all costs and benefits are variable. However, the term of a typical outsourcing contract, which is usually in the two- to three-year range, but can extend to as long as 10 years, allows for some costs and benefits to be considered fixed. Such long-term fixed costs include building leases or mortgage payments.

Variability is a function of time, resource level, and/or activity level. If the latter is related in some form to the costs and benefits, then assumptions can be made regarding the so-called independent variables (e.g., activity level), and the dependent variables (i.e., costs or benefits) can be calculated. Sometimes the relationship is not "well behaved" and is "disjoint," meaning that it can jump from one level to another level at a certain value. Such disjoint or binary behavior can result from a number of situations. A frequent example in economics is power stations, which come in very large, expensive increments, namely, another power station. Each power station is characterized by enormous one-time fixed costs. Assuming that the power demand of homes and businesses in a region, which is served by a single station, reaches and exceeds the capacity of that station. The next incremental unit of demand will, at least theoretically, call for the building of a second power station. Is it fair to charge the incremental user the whole expense of the power station? No. Should existing users be asked to share the cost and see a doubling of costs? That would not be popular. Instead, the power authorities build on the expectation of using most of the capacity of the second power station so that costs will remain about the same as before. For a period, they will not recover the cost of the new power station—unless, perhaps, they can sell the power to some other region—but, over time, the initial fixed costs and the ongoing running costs will be recovered. Benefits, namely, the revenues from the power, are variable for the most part.

Fixed and variable costs often, but not always, consist of one-time and ongoing costs, respectively, as described next.

One-Time Versus Ongoing Costs and Benefits

It is important to distinguish between one-time costs, such as the purchase price of equipment or a software license, and the ongoing costs of maintenance and the like. Benefits, which may occur at a single point in time or can be spread over the life of the project, do not necessarily track costs. Usually benefits are realized only after much of the expenditure has been made. The cost and benefit flows are illustrated in Figure 5.1 for a typical internal application development project. This type of diagram also applies to customizing and/or installing off-the-shelf products, including security-related products. Benefits are net of ongoing costs

This phasing of costs and benefits means that they cannot be compared in an absolute sense—the time value of money must be considered, as will be discussed later in this chapter.

Table 5.1 provides descriptions of costs and benefits falling into each of the categories and subcategories defined above.

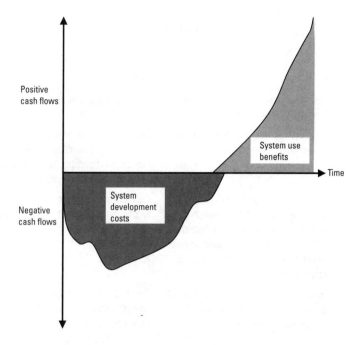

Figure 5.1 Costs and benefits related to the system development process.

Following are the major items of costs and benefits falling into the categories shown in Table 5.1.

Tangible-Objective-Direct Costs and Benefits

As mentioned above, this category includes most of the costs and benefits that would be recorded in the books of the organization and are almost always contained in an analysis, although some costs may be omitted or ignored, usually accidentally.

Labor Costs

The direct costs of employees, contractors, and part-time staff include wages, overtime, and the cost of benefits, such as a health plan (if applicable) and payroll taxes. Job-related travel and accommodation are also directly assigned to specific individuals and are therefore direct. Also, if a car is part of the employee's package, the cost of the car is a direct cost attributable to an individual.

Equipment and Software Costs

Computer and communications equipment, as well as other equipment such as manufacturing machines and computer software, are assets that are owned by an

Table 5.1
Costs and Benefits by Category and Subcategory

Categories	Costs	Benefits
Tangible	Costs that are measurable and can be recorded and reported	Benefits that are measurable and able to be recorded
Objective	Expenditures as reported in the books and records of the organization.	Cost savings or revenue enhancements that can be directly attributed to a specific management decision or internal or external event, and can be recorded and reported
Direct	Specific, measurable costs. Major categories include labor (full-time, part-time, contractors, consultants), computer hardware, computer software, communications lines, software, and equipment	Cost reductions due to specific cuts in headcount, equipment, software, and the like
Indirect	Costs of other departments allocated to specific resources, such as personnel, equipment, space, utilities	Cost reductions due to savings in overhead and allocated costs, such as reduction in head count in administrative areas, leased space (if it can be sublet or the lease terminated)
Subjective	Costs that are not clearly defined and are subject to the discretion of the analyst	Benefits that are not clearly defined and are subject to the discretion of the analyst
Direct	Opportunity cost increases attributable to not having engaged in a specific activity or resource	Opportunity cost savings such as the reductions in cost by not having to hire and retain staff for a particular purpose
Indirect	Opportunity costs not directly attributable to any particular activity or resource	Opportunity cost savings not directly attributable to any particular activity or resource
Intangible	Costs that cannot be measured with precision or at all	Benefits that cannot be expressed in terms of specific cost savings or revenue increases
Objective	Costs incurred from, say, inadequate experience based upon certain known measures	Benefits not realized, such as those due to wrong mix of staff
Direct	Increased cost of staff and other resources due to, for example, inadequate or lack of training program	Increased productivity due to, for example, conducive work environment that has been purposely introduced
Indirect	Increased costs due to external factors outside the control of the organization	Increased productivity due to external factors outside the control of the organization

Table 5.1 (continued)

Categories	Costs	Benefits
Subjective	Costs resulting from lack of motivation, loyalty, camaraderie, and so forth, and subject to the discretion of the analyst	Benefits not realized because of, perhaps, lack of loyalty and motivation, and subject to the discretion of the analyst
Direct	While these costs are fuzzy in nature, they can be attributed to specific activities or resources	While these benefits are fuzzy in nature, they can be attributed to specific activities or resources
Indirect	These costs are fuzzy in nature, and also cannot be attributed to specific activities or resources (e.g., country risk)	These benefits are fuzzy in nature, and also cannot be attributed to specific activities or resources (e.g., reputation, goodwill)

organization or leased or rented from a third party. Either way, they are a direct cost of the operation, although not necessarily attributable to employees. In fact, much equipment and software is acquired to perform a particular function, and therefore is related to specific activities.

Furniture and Fixtures

As with equipment, furniture that is either purchased or rented is a direct cost and is assignable to a resource. However, fixtures are usually considered part of the building and, as such, are more likely to be considered an indirect cost.

Third-Party Services

Pricing of services from third parties can be directly related to specific costs, particularly the hourly or daily rates of consultants and contractors. These rates are based on the direct cost of the contractors' salaries and benefits, as well as allocated overhead costs and a margin for profit.

For the buyer of these services, such costs are tangible and direct, since they are measurable and can be specifically assigned to particular activities. For the service provider, on the other hand, these charges are a combination of direct and indirect costs. They are considered to be fully variable by the customer, in contrast to internal staff, whose costs contain both fixed and variable components. Consequently, the cost impact of the addition or removal of consultants is easy to determine.

In other situations, a proposal from third parties may be fixed-price, if it involves a specific deliverable. Fixed-price contracts do not specify an hourly or daily rate (at least for the basic work, although add-on work may be quoted that way). Here the cost is binary—either the full amount is incurred or nothing is done or charged for. Again, from the buyer's point of view, such costs are direct in that they can be assigned to a specific activity and are highly measurable.

As was mentioned in an earlier chapter, it is advantageous to know with precision the direct costs of services, whether they be fixed or variable, since such external costs are generally more manageable and predictable than the internal costs of equivalent in-house services.

Tangible-Objective-Indirect Costs and Benefits

Indirect Costs

Indirect costs fall into virtually any resource category; however, the most important are labor, equipment, software, space, and utilities. Typically, these charges are accumulated in specific cost centers and then allocated to specific direct-cost resources based on some algorithm, such as in proportion to the number of personnel or square feet occupied.

Often costs, such as other cost center charges, that are considered indirect when they are incurred internally become direct costs (to the customer) when incurred by a service provider. For example, administrative costs are generally considered indirect, yet they will often be included in the hourly rate of consultants. Sometimes they will appear as a specific percentage of those other changes added on to the cost of the project and charged directly to the customer.

Backup, Continuity, and Recovery

A category of indirect costs that is growing rapidly in size and importance, due largely to concerns surrounding terrorism and increasing access to real-time systems through the Internet, is backup, business continuity, and disaster recovery. There is frequently confusion with terms such as business continuity and disaster recovery and with backup, recovery, and restart. Usage does vary, but for our purposes we will use the following definitions:

- *Business Continuity Planning (BCP)* is the establishment of plans and procedures for the recovery of business functions of an organization following some damaging event. BCP might include relocating staff to another site that has basic infrastructure in place or able to be rapidly deployed, so that critical business functions can continue to operate.

- *Disaster Recovery Planning (DRP)* involves backing up the primary infrastructure by establishing separate data processing and communications facilities that will operate to support the business units should the primary facility suffer a damaging or destructive event. This is often termed "offsite backup." The backup site might be "hot," meaning that it is kept in an active state of readiness should there be a need to switch from the primary site; "warm," meaning that certain initiating procedures are needed to bring up the backup systems, which are already fully loaded with the requisite software and for which the data can be quickly recovered; or "cold," meaning that software and data need to be loaded and initiated from scratch.

- *Onsite backup* refers to the location of redundant hardware and software within the same facility so that, should a system break (usually an equipment failure), processing can be switched to the backup system. For critical, high-availability systems, a separate unit will determine the health of a system at any instant in time and switch automatically to a hot backup.

- *Recovery* refers to the process whereby the compromised systems are brought back to normal operating condition. This will most likely involve restoration and restart processes.

The costs and resources described in this category are called into active service when an event occurs that disables or destroys the primary facility, although they should be exercised by periodic tests and rehearsals.

These capabilities include:

- Onsite backup and recovery of data, processors, and networks and the restarting of application programs;
- Offsite recovery of business functions (business continuity) where the primary infrastructure (i.e., computers, networks) remains intact;
- Offsite backup and recovery of the primary infrastructure functions (disaster recovery) with business units intact.

Onsite backup, recovery, and restart capabilities might well be included as part of the original system acquisition, although often they are not. If they are, then the costs are taken as direct. If not, they could be included in some broader based set of costs, which are then allocated across all systems within a particular configuration.

Business recovery, which involves setting up alternative office space and all necessary supporting facilities, and infrastructure recovery, which involves setting up secondary data centers and related computer equipment, software, and staffing, costs larger organizations in the tens of millions of dollars per year. This cost is often charged to some central corporate account and then allocated to other cost and profit centers rather than being directly assigned to specific systems.

Information and Physical Security

Some aspects of security are attributable to specific resources, programs, and data and are allocated directly to those resources. However, much of the costs of security and security functions are general organizational expenses, which are allocated to other costs centers, the costs of which may or may not be further allocated to direct cost items.

Indirect Benefits

The formal allocation process for indirect costs seldom applies to indirect benefits. Indirect benefits realized by one department, perhaps as a result of the activities of another department, are not generally allocated over several areas, but are frequently claimed by the areas that see the benefits directly. It is usually difficult in a corporate environment for a particular area to claim cost reductions in another area as its own benefit, even though the first area is responsible for the second area's savings. If both claim the benefit, we have double counting.

The major elements of indirect benefits follow.

Backup and Recovery

Not only are backup and recovery functions considered to be indirect costs, they also yield indirect benefits. One such benefit is a reduction in business interruption insurance premiums for the organization implementing such recovery capabilities.

Information and Physical Security

The benefits of security are very difficult to measure. Much has been written on security metrics, but the development of meaningful measures is as distant as ever, particularly as the threat and vulnerability environments are rapidly evolving and mutating. In many respects, the best event is a nonevent. The benefits of security relate to the prevention of potential attacks or misdeeds and the mitigation of and recovery from any events that do occur.

If we accept that security benefits are the avoidance of costs that would be incurred were security to be breached, it is certainly possible to measure the direct and indirect costs that are incurred as a result of inadequate security. Such costs—hopefully incurred by someone else—can be used to estimate what would have been lost had security not been effective. By applying some probability of occurrence in an unprotected environment, a measure of indirect security benefits can be estimated and used as a representation of the indirect benefits of the security program.

Losses due to security breaches can be felt in a number of ways and in different areas. Important examples include:

- Credit risk—somewhat tangible, objective;
- Liquidity risk—somewhat tangible, objective;
- Reputation risk—intangible, subjective;

- Legal and compliance risk—intangible, somewhat objective;
- Operations risk—intangible, subjective (includes security risk).

Tangible-Subjective-Direct Costs and Benefits

Tangible, subjective direct costs and benefits are specific to resources that are assigned to a task or activity. They can be measured, although choice of the particular measurement, or metric, is discretionary, or subjective, on the part of the analyst.

For example, such a cost is the direct cost of an offshore employee who is paid in local currency. Here there may be subjective discretion as to what exchange rate to use in a cost-benefit analysis. Usually an organization will have a specific policy as to what rate is appropriate—and it is almost certainly some published number—but even among published numbers, there are ranges and variations.

Another element of subjectivity in offshore outsourcing relates to person-equivalents. Is one offshore employee exactly the same as one on-site employee? Usually not, but it is difficult to measure the person-equivalent of an offshore employee. Undoubtedly additional effort is required to manage offshore operations. Additional effort is also expended on splitting tasks so that any jobs requiring specific local expertise are performed on-site, whereas generic tasks are done offshore.

The earlier example also applies to direct benefits. To the extent that the costs saved as a result of using offshore staff is calculated in a specific currency different from the local currency, and uses a subjectively selected exchange rate, the offshore cost of resources can be made to look more or less favorable. This situation is more complicated if costs and benefits are calculated using different exchange rates. While this might not happen internally, it might well occur for external consulting staff, where the third-party provider might gain an additional advantage by using an exchange rate more favorable to it. The agreement between the organization and the service provider, and even internal agreements, need to ensure that the source of, and criteria for selecting, the rates be standardized across entities, even though the choice may be arbitrary.

Tangible-Subjective-Indirect Costs and Benefits

This category includes those measurable costs and benefits, which are generally allocated and assigned to specific direct resource costs and benefits, respectively, subject to the discretion, or the subjective view, of the analyst. For example, the costs of heating and cooling, or the cost savings of finding an efficient way to heat and cool a location, are certainly tangible and measurable in themselves, but the way in which the respective costs or savings are allocated to human and equipment resources can be based on any of a number of factors, such as square feet, number of people, and amount of equipment installed and running. Of course, if each section of a location is individually metered, the discretionary component is eliminated and the cost is in the tangible-objective-indirect category.

Benefits are usually claimed by the specific department that implemented the cost-saving method, although the other departments will see a benefit in reduced charges allocated to them.

Intangible-Objective-Direct Costs and Benefits

In this category, the cost or benefit is specific and attributable to a particular direct resource, but not all aspects are fully measurable. An example of such a cost is the loss of productivity that results from lack of training, poor computer response time, or inadequate supervision of outsourcing. Even when productivity is measurable in specific units, such as number of calls to the help desk or number of calls lost, attributes such as customer service are measured subjectively. The loss is calculated by comparing the productivity against some standard or goal, which might be based on other similar operations. And the cost is clearly directly attributable to the labor resources, which are usually direct.

However, some aspects of the cost of reduced productivity are not so easily identified, even though their impact can be measured—it is just that the costs cannot be specifically attributed to a particular aspect. This situation is very common and is probably subject to the most misinterpretation. Whether a particular component is responsible for a shortfall of revenue or an increase in cost cannot be readily determined, because those responsible for the specific component will usually question the relationship. And since this component is intangible, it is difficult for management to point to the source, and, even if they can, the resulting estimate might be highly subjective.

The quality component of service provided, which may not be measurable, is certainly affected by training and supervision.

Intangible-Objective-Indirect Costs and Benefits

These costs and benefits result from known factors, often external to the organization, that affect an organization's indirect costs and savings in a specific way, but are not easily defined or measured. This often occurs when internal and external factors are known to impact less readily discernable internal costs and benefits; that is, there is not any judgment involved in stating that such a relationship exists, only in measuring the effect.

An example is a change in the exchange rate, which certainly affects any indirect costs and benefits associated with offshore resources. However, the new exchange rate might support the analyst's opinion that certain resources are becoming less competitive globally than others on a relative basis or that resources in other nations have become more competitive, even though quantifying the impact is virtually impossible. The analysis is further complicated by other factors affecting the decision, such as the leveling off of one country's appeal just as another is gaining market share.

Intangible-Subjective-Direct Costs and Benefits

Intangible, subjective costs and benefits are the fuzziest of all since they are neither readily discerned nor measured objectively. These types of costs and benefits—particularly benefits—are the most difficult to analyze and raise the most questions in an analysis, particularly given an attempt to quantify them. The most important examples are goodwill and reputation. Goodwill has value if it is preserved and loses value if an organization's reputation is besmirched.

It is similarly difficult to assign such costs and benefits to a specific resource so that it affects the cost of that resource. However, a situation is possible where the reputation of a company hangs on that of one individual or a select group. When that person is in good graces, he or she highly augments the value of specific products or services, but if that reputation is sullied, then the impact on costs and benefits can be immediate and dramatic. The billing rate of a service provider might be reduced if something bad happens, and the provider might have to reduce staff because of a loss of business due to the damaged reputation of the high-profile representative.

Intangible-Subjective-Indirect Costs and Benefits

This category is similarly difficult to analyze, although here the fuzzy aspect applies to indirect costs and benefits. Thus, an offshore facility for which the country risk is high, due to the high likelihood or war or terrorism, for example, can lead to increased costs of security. Security is an indirect cost as it is allocated across cost centers.

Next Chapter

In the next chapter, we will demonstrate how the cost-benefit classification should be part of the information gathering process, leading to an analysis of internal versus external providers of service. We will show where the weaknesses and strengths of such an analysis lie and demonstrate how the analysis leads to the selection decision.

Reference

[1]   Axelrod, C. W., *Computer Productivity: A Planning Guide for Cost-Effective Management*, New York: John Wiley & Sons, 1982, Chapter 4.

6

Costs and Benefits Throughout the Evaluation Process

In Chapter 5, we examined costs and benefits related to outsourcing as to whether they are tangible or intangible, subjective or objective, and direct or indirect. This breakdown gives the reader an idea as to which characteristics of costs and benefits should be considered when evaluating an outsourcing opportunity.

In this chapter, we look at specific costs and benefits that accrue at each phase of the evaluation process used in deciding whether or not outsource and how to choose an outsourcer. It is certainly worth remembering the categories delineated in the previous chapter when enumerating the costs and benefits at various stages of the evaluation process.

Triggering the Process

For organizations that have not done any material outsourcing in the past, there will likely be one or more events that will trigger looking into this option. For organizations that have previously outsourced projects and functions, their decision to outsource further, from less-critical to core functions, will likely be based on their prior experiences. That is to say, many companies will test the water by first dipping in a small function or task that is not critical to the business. If that experience turns out to be positive, then the company is likely to consider extending the range of services performed externally. If not, there will likely be retrenchment of existing contracts.

We will now look at some of the triggers that might cause someone, or some group, within an organization to look at the prospect of outsourcing for the first time or to consider expanding into previously untried areas. One or more of the following triggers is experienced by a decision-maker, usually initiating the evaluation process:

- An outsourcing vendor calls and offers to describe a brand-new, red-hot service.

- A peer in another company describes a great new service they have been using.

- An article in a magazine or newspaper describes an exciting new outsourcing trend.

- A television program or news item runs about outsourcing.

- A seminar or conference treats outsourcing as the main or subsidiary topic.

- In-house units do not provide satisfactory service.

- Finding, hiring, and retaining high-quality staff to support a function in-house is a hassle.

- The staffing problem is exacerbated by the need to use fast-moving, leading-edge technologies (such as many of the information security technologies), for which the supply of experts and practitioners is severely lacking.

- The in-house function causes continual and debilitating problems that create dissatisfaction throughout the company.

- The pressure to reduce costs and, at the same time, improve service is extreme.

Once obscure, the term outsourcing is now in everyday use, and the concept of using a third-party service provider for critical business and information technology functions is now commonplace. Additionally, more people than ever before are being asked to evaluate and decide upon the suitability of outsourced services to a particular situation. But these individuals often have insufficient knowledge, experience, and understanding to perform an exhaustive evaluation of outsourcing options. Furthermore, the area of security is often given short shrift or is analyzed inadequately, whether or not the primary function of the outsourcing is security.

When a company, nonprofit organization, academic institution, or government agency is a start-up, it may not want to take on the burden of establishing and operating a payroll department, for example. Other potential areas for outsourcing include building a computer systems capability or engaging in a wide variety of support activities. These are not generally considered to be core business functions. Or a business may be too small to achieve the critical mass needed in some of these areas even if they are considered to be core functions, forcing the use of third parties as sole supplier or in conjunction with internal staff as the only reasonable solution. In other cases, organizations may be already running specific functions in-house and might, at some point, determine that transferring those functions to a third-party service provider is more cost-effective. The internal staff in many organizations is unlikely to have had much direct experience of outsourcing and therefore falls into a similar category as for start-ups, namely, that they may be uninformed and/or inexperienced.

Perhaps a company has already tried outsourcing and then, based upon external changes, unmet expectations, increased internal capability, or other factors, decides to insource (i.e., move the function back in-house). Or conversely, the organization has had a positive experience with an outsourcer and is prepared to engage service providers for increasingly critical activities. In other situations, with circumstances having changed, the cost-effectiveness of an in-house operation may become superior to that of an outsourcer. One example of unmet expectations is that the cost savings and/or operational benefits initially expected were never fully realized or the quality of service never reached the desired, and contracted, level.

Often a willingness to outsource is expressed at a high executive level, but then it is more intuitive than analytical. The analyst's responsibility is to quantify this interest to the extent possible and to integrate the results into a cost-benefit or return-on-investment (ROI) analysis.

Different Strokes

We will first look at the different approaches associated with various types of organization and stages of development. This is illustrated in Table 6.1.

The nature of an organization on the broad spectrum of size, stage (e.g., start-up, mature), sophistication, and willingness to outsource, can go a long way in determining the approach that it might take and how it responds to the results of such an analysis.

Practically all companies, at any stage and of any size, outsource at least one function, such as payroll processing or tax accounting, not considering this instance to be true outsourcing since they have never performed the task as an internal function.

Analysis of Costs and Benefits

In this section, we travel chronologically through the outsourcing decision-making process and consider the costs and benefits at each stage.

Table 6.1
Decision Factors based on Nature of Organization and Approach to and Reasons for Outsourcing

Nature of Organization/ Outsourcing Approach	Reasons for Outsourcing or Insourcing	Examples of Outsourcing or Insourcing Options	Relevant Decision Factors
Start-up—open to outsourcing	Concentrate available resources on core business functions Too small for the cost-effective running of certain noncore functions in-house, therefore may be better to take advantage of economies of scale of outsourcer	Outsource noncore functions to third parties or cosource more critical functions with service providers, where cost is secondary to getting the required work done. Hire part-time staff into the function or cosource with a third party until the function is large enough to move in-house effectively Outsource a function if it does not grow to a critical mass for effective in-house operation	Comparison of costs of insourcing, outsourcing, and cosourcing Comparison of benefits of various alternatives Analysis of viability of service providers, particularly those supporting critical functions Ease of hiring internally versus outsourcer's attractiveness to potential employees Threat to intellectual property, and confidential and private information
Established self-contained operation—little or no outsourcing	Concentrate on and excel at core business functions Reduce cost per unit and total costs to remain competitive Make costs more predictable with respect to changes in volume and over time	Outsource only noncore functions to third parties Retain in-house those functions offering competitive advantage	Comparison of costs Comparison of benefits Availability of in-house versus external expertise Ease of hiring internally versus attractiveness of outsourcer to potential employees Ability to retain key staff Potential threat to intellectual property, and confidential and private information, if certain functions are outsourced

Table 6.1 (continued)

Nature of Organization/ Outsourcing Approach	Reasons for Outsourcing or Insourcing	Examples of Outsourcing or Insourcing Options	Relevant Decision Factors
Established organization amenable to outsourcing where it makes sense	Concentrate on core business functions Reduce cost per unit and in total Make costs more predictable with volume changes and over time	Outsource noncore and/or possibly critical functions to third parties in order to get them done, where cost is secondary to getting the required work accomplished timely and of good quality Outsource functions that do not achieve internal critical mass	Comparison of costs Comparison of benefits Viability of service providers Availability of in-house versus external expertise Ease of hiring internally Attractiveness of outsourcer to potential employees Ability to retain key internal staff Potential threat to intellectual property, confidential and private information
Currently outsourcing one or more functions— satisfied with results—looking to outsource further	Further concentrate on core businesses and outsource noncritical functions Reduce cost per unit and in total Make costs more predictable with volume changes and over time	Outsource noncore and/or possibly critical functions to third parties in order to get them done, where cost is secondary to the work needed Hire part-time staff into the function until it is large enough to move in-house or outsource the function if it does not grow internally to a critical mass	Comparison of costs Comparison of benefits Analysis of viability of service providers Availability of in-house versus external expertise Ease of hiring internally Attractiveness of outsourcer to potential employees Ability to retain key staff Potential threat to intellectual property, confidential and private information

Table 6.1 (continued)

Nature of Organization/ Outsourcing Approach	Reasons for Outsourcing or Insourcing	Examples of Outsourcing or Insourcing Options	Relevant Decision Factors
Currently outsourcing one or more functions—looking to bring some or all of the functions back in-house	Gain greater control over function(s) Improve morale and motivation of internal staff Meet new business and technical requirements that cannot be achieved by third party Reduce cost per unit and in total	Insource the more critical functions to ensure that they get done as desired	Comparison of costs Comparison of benefits Availability of in-house versus external expertise Ease of hiring internally versus attractiveness of outsourcer to potential employees Ability to retain key staff
Organization going out of business—has no outsourced functions	May need to outsource certain support services, which were previously performed in-house, during the winding-down process	Outsource specialty services that are specific to going out of business (e.g., firms that specialize in selling off products and fixtures) Hire specialists in the financial aspects of dismantling and selling off parts of a business	Comparison of costs Comparison of benefits Analysis of viability of service providers Availability of in-house versus external expertise and willingness to stay around—might need incentives to retain experts Threat to intellectual property, confidential and private information—these assets may have considerable liquidation value
Organization going out of business—has outsourced functions	Will need to decrease, then terminate, the outsourcing relationship consistent with the winding down of the enterprise as a whole—this will likely be highly dependent on the contractual relationship between customer and outsourcer	To the extent possible, arrange for smooth exit from outsourcer, considering applicable penalties and restrictions If going bankrupt, then bankruptcy process will determine actions	Threat to intellectual property, confidential and private information—these assets may have considerable liquidation value Retention of records consistent with legal and regulatory requirements Minimization of impact on customers and debtors

Table 6.1 (continued)

Nature of Organization/ Outsourcing Approach	Reasons for Outsourcing or Insourcing	Examples of Outsourcing or Insourcing Options	Relevant Decision Factors
Service provider may be going out of business—has buyer to continue services	Need to decrease, then terminate, the current outsourcing relationship consistent with transitioning to the buyer—this may involve minimal disruption if the current services are maintained, or could result in major disruption if buyer decide to move customers to another service	To the extent possible, arrange for smooth transition from one outsourcer to another	Transfer and retention of records consistent with operational, legal, and regulatory requirements Minimization of impact on customers
Service provider may be going out of business—has no buyer on the horizon to continue its services	Need to find alternative services, either in-house or with another provider, in order to avoid discontinuance of services	If it is determined to remain in outsourcing mode, arrange for smooth transition from one outsourcer to another If it is determined to bring services in-house, which may be more likely following the negative experience of the current outsourcer failing, arrange for smooth transition from the existing outsourcer to in-house facilities	Comparison of costs Comparison of benefits Analysis of viability of service providers Availability of in-house versus external expertise Ease of hiring internally Attractiveness of outsourcer to potential employees Ability to retain key staff Threat to intellectual property, confidential and private information

The Evaluation Process

As stated above, a particular event usually triggers the consideration of outsourcing specific corporate functions and capabilities. Sometimes, because of critical business needs or political factors, some assessment steps are bypassed.

However, for a complete and accurate assessment, well-defined steps should be addressed, the first of which is the evaluation process.

The cost of evaluation occurs only if a decision involving potential change has to be made—otherwise the effort of evaluation and subsequent phases are obviously not required. Consequently, the cost of evaluation is rightfully attributable to the outsourcing decision.

Internal staff, outside experts, or a combination of both perform the evaluation. The inclusion of outside expertise is generally recommended if the internal staff is not familiar with the third-party service providers for the particular service to be rendered or if adequate internal resources, even those knowledgeable in the area, are not available for the project. However, in any outsourcing decision, if the function currently exists internally, including those internal staff familiar with the operation in the decision-making process is highly recommended. Two reasons apply: first, the staff's specific knowledge is of value to the evaluation and implementation of any outsourcing option selected, and second, they are more likely to accept and subscribe to the decision if they are involved in the process.

Requirements Phase—Costs

While, in some cases, the choices may be obvious, for the most part it is necessary to determine and document the requirements formally, particularly the security requirements, for the function(s), whether performed internally or externally. This requirements phase will be addressed specifically in a later chapter. However, for our purposes here, we need to be aware that a requirements-gathering phase is usually needed. The costs that generally result from the requirements phase follow.

Internal staff costs:

- Direct:
  - Salaries;
  - Benefits;
  - Travel and accommodation (flights, meals, hotels).
- Indirect:
  - Allocated overhead (space, telephone, utilities, computer systems, network supplies, mailing costs, administrative and managerial staff).

Direct consultant costs:
  - Hourly or per diem rate per consultant by category (e.g., manager, technician);
  - Travel and accommodation (flights, meals, hotels);
  - Administrative support;

- Supplies, copy services, computer rental.

Other costs:

- Direct:
  - Software licensing and maintenance;
  - Computer and computer equipment rental and maintenance;
  - Subscription to information and advisory services.
- Indirect, Intangible:
  - Not meeting user expectations;
  - Reduction in customer satisfaction;
  - Loss of reputation and goodwill.

Requirements Phase—Benefits

While less tangible, there are also benefits in performing a complete and orderly requirements phase. In fact, it is reasonable to state that the requirements phase is highly critical to the success of the project and represents the highest benefit/cost ratio of any of the phases in the decision process. Benefits of a careful determination of requirements, which are realized at later stages of the process, include the following.

- *Greater precision in what is needed*—This can lead to realistic estimates of the effort, and hence the costs, of effectively designing and implementing the project.
- *Lower implementation and ongoing costs*—Lower costs are a direct result of detailed, agreed-upon requirements, as there is a greater probability that the end result will meet requirements and expectations and that rework is reduced or eliminated.
- *Faster time to market*—The avoidance of rework or "scope creep" will result in a shorter project time to complete, other things being equal.

I hesitate to give estimates as to what the impact of these benefits might be in real terms. However, it is likely, based on experience and reading the computer press, that improvements of the order of 25% to 50% are attainable from investing enough time and effort in this phase, versus short-shrift requirements definitions. There is no question that inserting appropriate expertise at this stage, particularly persons with extensive experience in the particular venture being contemplated, can greatly improve the end product and avoid many of the pitfalls encountered in outsourcing.

Requests for Information and Proposals—Costs

Costs incurred at this stage are those related to preparing the Requests for Information (RFIs) and Requests for Proposals (RFPs). They include the cost of researching the information, assembling the document, putting together a list of recipients, reproducing and distributing the document, receiving the responses, following up if necessary, and analyzing the results. Internal staff, consultants, or a combination of the two do this. Many of these costs are hidden within the organization's general infrastructure, but uncovering them is illuminating and should be required. Not doing so, which is more frequently the case, leads to an underestimate of the costs of the entire outsourcing decision process.

Large RFIs and RFPs can require months of effort and incur substantial consulting fees to prepare and manage. The magnitude and expense of the effort is usually dictated by the anticipated size of the project itself rather than, say, the risk of a failed project. However, a strong argument exits for the spending level on RFIs and RFPs to be on a risk basis. For highly risky situations, such as out-sourcing of core IT functions or business processes or considering offshore service providers, emphasizing the information-gathering and evaluation stages usually pays off.

The above considerations do not include the substantial costs that are invested by the service providers that choose to respond. In fact, it is these costs that might have the greatest impact on selection opportunities. Smaller, less well-funded organizations may not to respond to an RFI or RFP because the cost may be prohibitive and they expect that a larger, better-known provider will win.

Consequently, smaller, obscure service providers may be self-eliminating, even though they might be very well qualified candidates.

It can be argued that third-party firms that do not spend highly on this process often offer better value for the money, since they do not incur the high marketing overhead. The irony is that the larger customer may never know this. Perhaps not until the smaller providers have established a foothold in companies not willing or able to pay the premium prices of the larger, better-established firms can they play in the larger arena.

It therefore behooves the decision-maker to simplify and streamline this part of the process or, if the project is a large, risky one, then consideration should be given to a paid information gathering and estimation process. In other words, a precursory project should be initiated. This could level the playing field and enable a larger group of contenders to participate, allowing the customer to benefit from a wider choice.

I have seen a difference in quotes of a *factor of four* for a particular consulting assignment between a single practitioner and a larger well-known firm. The small firm's principal was more qualified than the combined expertise of the team from the larger firm. The large firm presented a thick, colorful proposal detailing the extent of its expertise and assuring me of a quality product, even though their particular capability of the area in question was clearly limited, whereas the single practitioner offered a one-page proposal. We selected the small firm and received a much better product at 75% lower cost.

While the above example does not apply across the board, if in-depth due diligence is done, firms frequently benefit significantly from trawling for the more efficient and hungrier smaller players. The small firm may go out of business, but this risk exists for larger firms also, as experience with outsourcers has demonstrated.

So, how does this affect costs and benefits? RFIs and RFPs cost both the questioner and the responder money, but they provide significant benefits in terms of being able to select among contenders based on substantial information, thereby reducing the risk of a poor choice.

Costs to the Customer

The specific costs relating to preparing and processing of an RFI or RFP include salary, benefits, and overhead for internal staff and/or fully loaded per diem charges for consultants. The required tasks are:

- Determining that an RFI/RFP is warranted and should be prepared;
- Obtaining necessary approvals to proceed with developing an RFI/RFP;
- Researching the area for which the RFI/RFP is to be prepared;
- Preparation of the RFI or RFP document itself;
- Assembling a list of service providers to whom to send the document;
- Distribution of the document in physical or electronic form;
- Responding to questions from recipients;
- Receipt of responses;
- Analysis of responses;
- Preparation and presentation of conclusions.

Other related costs include those for:

- Research and advisory services, published reports, books, subscriptions;
- Telephone, computer, and other office-related costs;
- Travel and accommodation;
- Expenses relating to the printing, binding, and mailing of documents.

Costs to the Service Providers

The specific costs relating to responding to an RFI or RFP, are similar to those of the preparers and include salary, benefits, and overhead that apply to service providers' staffs working on:

- Determining that a response is worth the effort and should be prepared;
- Obtaining necessary approvals to proceed with developing a response to an RFI or RFP;
- Analyzing the RFI/RFP and determining the form and content of a response;
- Preparation of the response document itself;
- Preparation of a presentation, if required;
- Sending back the response document in physical or electronic form;
- Responding to questions from the potential customer over the telephone, via e-mail, or in person;
- Revising the RFI or RFP to account for changes determined as a result of a presentation or questions.

Other related costs include:

- Telephone, computer, and other office-related costs;
- Travel and accommodation, if in-person presentations are needed;
- Expenses relating to the printing, binding, and mailing of documents.

Requests for Information/Proposal—Benefits

Benefits to the Customer

A number of benefits to the requestor result from a well-constructed RFI or RFP development and activation process.

RFI/RFP Exercise Reduces Risk

In the first place, thinking through the requirements and coming up with questions to determine how well service providers might meet those requirements reduces the risk of missing critical decision criteria.

Focus on Real Contenders

The responses to the questions can eliminate outlying bidders and quickly narrow the field to a short list of perhaps three or four serious candidates. This reduces the effort for both customers and providers.

It is important here to differentiate form and content in the proposals. Large, well-heeled vendors proffer impressively produced proposals, which are lengthy, detailed, and expensively bound, often in color on heavy glossy paper. The recipient must see through the veneer and superficial claims and determine if real substance lies in these pages. Many such fancy proposals are pure boilerplate, with extensive chapters on the history and background of the firm, the firm's approach, and the broad range of skills and experience of the principals. The actual section responding to questions in the RFI or RFP may be minimal, demonstrating little understanding of the issues at hand and meager capabilities. Of course, this is not always the case—such large firms often are well equipped to handle the tasks at hand. However, the appearance of a proposal should not be necessarily taken as an indicator of the ability to do the proposed work well.

Documentation of Process

Later in the negotiation or during the service time itself, disagreement often arises as to what the RFP requested and what the proposal in response offered. Having these items carefully and fully documented provides for quick and less contentious resolution of disagreements.

Clearly the above benefits are intangible and cannot be readily measured in specific money terms. They can, however, be included in a risk assessment with broad estimates of how much the risk of problems can be reduced as a result of a sound RFI/RFP process. Two other major areas of risk reduction are described next.

Selection of a Cost-Effective Provider

While difficult to estimate, it is clear that a thorough RFI/RFP process can reduce the price that might otherwise be paid for services. A proposal will give pricing information, so that the customer can look at the range of prices and choose a service that provides more for less.[1]

Ability to Negotiate Strongly

If the short list contains several viable contenders, where the main difference is price, it should be easier to negotiate down the price or up the services than if

---

1. The best choice is not necessarily the lowest bidder. I know of one institution that regularly eliminates the five lowest bidders from consideration. While I question the appropriateness of what appears to be such an arbitrary cutoff, the institution stated that the criterion does reflect concern that very low bids are suspect.

there were only a single candidate. What is the value of this? I would say that a vibrant contest among providers can easily result in a 10% to 20% lower cost on the resulting services.

Benefits to the Service Providers

While clearly a great amount of work is involved in reviewing and responding to RFIs and RFPs, the process would not exist at all if there were not also significant benefits to the service provider. Following are some examples of benefits to be derived.

A Chance to Win the Business

The New York Lottery's publicity uses the phrase "you have to be in it to win it." This also holds true of service providers. If a vendor is not on the list, it cannot be considered for the work.

Consideration for Future Business

Even if the service provider does not win a particular contract, it is more likely to be considered for future RFIs and RFPs if it makes an honest and thorough effort to respond to each and every request, even if that response is "no bid." It is better, from a credibility and reputation viewpoint, to decline to bid on engagements that it cannot handle or does not have appropriate expertise or capacity, than to bid, win, and fail to perform satisfactorily. Conversely, if a provider does not respond at all, even to acknowledge receipt of the request and unwillingness to bid (for whatever reasons), it is likely to be struck from the list of contenders for future opportunities.

Recommendations to Potential Customers

Even if a provider does not win a particular engagement, the goodwill created from responsiveness and willingness to negotiate can yield the benefit that customers will develop a positive view of the provider, which may well be relayed to others. I have often heard statements such as: "We didn't go with XYZ, but were very impressed with their professionalism and would certainly consider them for future work and would recommend that you consider them also."

What is this all worth to the service provider? This is particularly hard to guess, but a service provider might see a 10% increase in future business resulting from a favorable RFI/RFP process. Furthermore, the service provider has a chance to capture the business being proposed—depending on the type of assignment and the number of viable competitors. The a priori chance of success generally varies between 10% and 50%. The service provider should estimate the probabilities of positive results and the possible value of these results, using a decision tree for the RFI/RFP submissions, responses, and outcomes such as the one shown in Figure 6.1.

Refining the Statement of Work (SOW)

The main purpose of the RFI is to gather sufficient information to decide whether or not to proceed with an RFP and, if so, the information obtained will assist the customer in developing a meaningful RFP. The RFP should contain the objective of the endeavor, a list and description of requirements, and a SOW on which prospective service providers can base their proposals.

The more complete and accurate the RFP, which depends to a significant extent on whether an RFI exercise was undertaken or whether access to a similar RFP was available, the more complete the SOW will be. Nevertheless, responses to an RFP by a number of vendors throws light on weaknesses or omissions in the SOW and may prompt a revision to it.

Here again, there is a tradeoff between additional time and effort spent on enhancing the SOW and savings that will result in the implementation of the

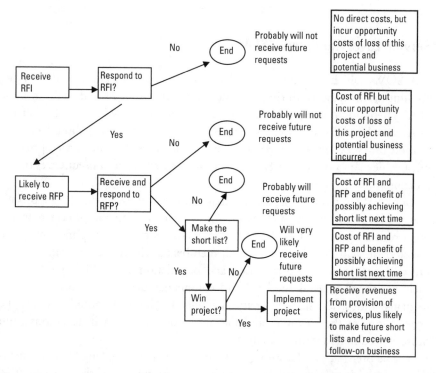

Figure 6.1 Outsourcers' decision processes for responding to RFIs and RFPs.

service itself. The costs here are simply the time and materials needed to make the revisions and redistribute the revised SOW. At this point in the process, the revised version of the SOW will likely be sent only to the short list of contenders, under the presumption that the changes were not material enough to warrant going through the entire RFP process again. Of course, that is not always the case, and it could be that the changes to the SOW are so significant that cycling back through the RFP process is warranted. From the customers' point of view, it is still better to spend the money at this stage than to go forward with a half-baked SOW. The costs down the line of a poorly structured SOW will certainly exceed by many times the costs of getting it right before embarking on the project.

While the benefits to the customer are clear, there are also benefits to the more ethical service providers, since they will be able to perform the assigned services to the customers' greater satisfaction and possibly less cost. Less scrupulous outsourcers may favor a less well-defined SOW as a means of upping their revenues after the fact; that is, they can turn any fuzziness in the SOW to their own fiscal advantage through costly revisions forced upon a then-dependent customer. Because of this prospect, it serves customers well to put in the additional effort to clarify the details of the SOW.

Service Level Agreement (SLA)

The SOW, which describes each phase of the implementation and how the account will be handled during the rendering of the services, feeds right into the SLA. Therefore, the more demanding and accurate the SOW, the likelier the SLA is to be tight and well structured. The SLA, however, should go well beyond the SOW in its specification of the measures that the service provider must achieve in order to satisfy the customer, as well as the consequences of not meeting those measures.

The SOW requires the attention and effort of those closest to the process that is being outsourced, such as the IT department and the project management office. Finalization of the SOW demands reviews and responses from the operational, as well as the managerial, members of the service providers' team. On the other hand, the preparation and negotiation of the SLA will bring in such additional areas as the legal and compliance departments (especially for regulated industries, such as financial services). The SLA should describe the expectations of the customer and the means of extrication if deviations from those expectations are not remedied.

The preparation of a strong SLA can be a demanding, lengthy, and expensive process, depending on the criticality and complexity of the services. It is, however, of great importance to the success of the outsourcing relationship and is, again, well worth the effort if done properly. The costs relating to the effort are much the same by category as those in preparing the requirements or RFI/RFP, except for the addition of legal and compliance talent, on both sides.

By this stage in the process, the expectation is that the service provider involved in the SLA negotiation will be the one to perform the services, barring some showstopper in the discussions. Consequently, with a high degree of certainty of the revenue, the outsourcer possesses a stronger willingness to invest in the SLA negotiation and to resolve open issues. Also in favor of resolution is the significant investment both parties will have already made in the process.

Implementation

The implementation process has several components, the costs of which must be recognized and included in the analysis as to whether or not outsourcing still makes sense. At the analysis stage, such costs are rough estimates. However, every effort must be made to obtain as accurate estimates as possible.

The components to consider are:

- The transition from in-house to third-party services;
- The implementation of management controls, and measurement, auditing, and reporting systems;
- The introduction of dispute resolution processes;
- The implementation and testing of emergency procedures;
- The development of a termination process due to expected or unexpected events.

Transition Phase

Perhaps the least understood and most underestimated phase of the outsourcing process is the transition from in-house to out-of-house. It is often accompanied by changes in information technology and business processes that alone are difficult to handle. Just listing the costs is a challenge, never mind quantifying them. And the benefits of a smooth transition are also difficult to quantify, although they become very obvious if one gets embroiled in a contentious or poorly planned transition.

Transferring from In-House to Out-of-House

While the outsourcer's salesperson uses phrases such as "transparent to the user" and "don't worry, we've done this a hundred times before," these assurances are cold comfort when one is in the midst of a crisis or experiencing cost overruns in the range of 200% or higher.

Most transfers involve a period of parallel operation, when the costs of two facilities are being incurred. Any underestimate as to the duration of this over-run period results in rapidly escalating costs, sometimes matching the cost of the entire transition. In a chapter on the "Financial Evaluation of Transition Technologies" [1], I suggested that cost overruns on client-server transition projects typically run 50% to 100%. Some outsourcing projects do involve the adaptation of old technologies to newer platforms, with comparable risks.

The obstacles to timely and on-budget completion of such projects are, in priority order:

- Underestimation of time and staff requirements;
- Change in corporate strategic direction;
- Shift in technology management;
- Unstable technology;
- Overrated project benefits;
- High cost of implementation [2].

These obstacles are not only relevant to the transition to client/server technology, but can be applied equally well to the transition to third-party services. Table 6.2 summarizes the issues and mitigation strategies as they relate to the above obstacles in the context of outsourcing services.

Specific costs and benefits related to transition are described next.

Costs of obsolescence (if in-house technology is obsolete and the outsourcer has more modern technology):

- Diminishing pool of required skills, leading to inflated costs;
- High and increasing maintenance costs for older equipment;
- High and increasing support costs for older software;
- Risk of discontinuation of vendor support;
- Lack of new features that may be taken for granted.

Transition costs include:

- Hiring of knowledgeable staff (high-salaried individuals);
- Training of existing and new staff;
- On-the-job learning (reduced productivity);

Table 6.2

Mitigation of Obstacles to Timely and On-Budget Completion

Obstacle	Related Issues	Mitigation Strategies
Underestimation of time and staff requirements	Reaching point at which adding staff causes drop-off in efficiency	Hire experienced managers who have led similar projects several to many times before
Change in corporate strategic direction	Changes in existing businesses and taking on new businesses call for flexibility	Ensure that there is sufficient scalability in outsourced arrangements to allow for business change, without penalties
Shift in technology management	Lack of continuity and support throughout the transition project	Break down project into component deliverables with fairly short-term deadlines
Unstable technology	Particularly true in outsourcing application development as complexity increases	Allow for possibility of technical difficulties and use seasoned internal and external staff
Overrated project benefits	Difficult to prove whether or not benefits have been realized	Discount intangible benefits and try to concentrate on direct savings
High cost of implementation	It is usually cheaper and easier in the short term to remain in-house with existing systems and services	Need to look at the longer term—some outsourcing arrangements run as long as 10 years

- Cost of redoing or reworking initial efforts;
- Loss of credibility from missed deadlines and inadequate systems;
- Lack of adequate project management.

Transition benefits, if outsourcing has installed more flexible and scalable technologies, are:

- Installation of an infrastructure and architecture for future work;
- Establishment of a knowledgeable team;
- More flexible, adaptable technologies that are easier to support and fix;
- Greater availability of more flexible and adaptable technologies;
- Availability of advanced design, development, and testing tools;

- Building of career-enhancing credentials for all those involved.

Again, quantification is difficult for many of the above categories, but some estimates are possible and should be made to get a good picture of the relevant costs and benefits. The key is to understand that there is clearly a need to go through such transition in order to reap the benefits of a new environment and, frequently, newer technologies. However, the existence and uncertainty of transition costs must temper these benefits. If these costs get out of hand, they can negate the advantages of the entire project.

Monitoring, Reporting, and Review

Enforcing SLA requirements requires measuring and reporting on specific metrics. These measures must have been part of the requirements, for both the RFI and RFP phases. Like security, auditing cannot easily be bolted on as an afterthought—it should be designed into the process from the start.

However, there are costs involved, both in the development and implementation of the measuring programs and the reviewing, reporting, and responding to exceptions when the service is in place. Generally the costs are minimal. However, there is a possibility of overdoing the collecting and reporting of metrics beyond what is truly informative and actionable. There are also different views of the measures, depending upon whether you are the customer or the service provider. I previously looked at application availability from the user's perspective [3]. The user is interested only in his application being available when and for how long he needs it, and is indifferent to its availability at other times.

Certain metrics are more difficult than others to measure and apply. This is particularly true of security-related metrics. Rather than using specific measures, generally the SLA requires that periodic security tests and assessments be conducted and that the service provider meet or beat standard industry practices.

Dispute Resolution

It is also important to have in place the means of resolving differences if, for example, a particular service level is not met in the view of the customer, but the service provider believes that it is met. The costs surrounding dispute resolution are among the more obscure, with losses on both sides. It becomes a matter of which side believes that it can benefit from pursuing a particular course of action, which very much depends on what they expect the outcome will be. It behooves both parties to agree up front how various contingencies will be handled—a kind of "prenuptial" agreement. It is clearly better to agree on what will be done if the terms of the agreement must be invoked.

Incident Response, Recovery, and Testing

There has been an increase in sensitivity to the possibility of major disasters—due in part to various terrorist events and natural disasters in recent years—and the ways in which they can be prevented or responded to. This has placed a significant emphasis on business continuity and disaster recovery by many critical business sectors and government. However, such backup capabilities can be extremely expensive to implement and test—and that cost has to be reflected in the cost of services.

The premium for a recoverable environment, versus one that is not, can easily add 25% to 50% to the cost of services, depending on whether the service provider is broadly dispersed or highly concentrated geographically. Whether or not a customer is willing to pay such a premium depends upon the criticality of the services being outsourced. Unless a company is in a regulated industry in which the provision of recovery capabilities is dictated in certain situations, the decision becomes one of risk analysis and the possible use of insurance to defray the risk.

Extrication

There can be a significant cost to both the customer and service provider if the arrangement is terminated either voluntarily or involuntarily. For one thing, another transition must be accounted for, with similar costs and risks of the transition, which must be incorporated into the original analysis. The transition may be orderly, if the separation is according to the contract's terms and conditions. Or it may be chaotic, as when the termination results from one or other party suddenly closing its doors or if it results from a dispute, rather than merely the lapsing of the term of the agreement.

What might the cost of ending the arrangement be? Since going into an arrangement, one may have certain expectations about how it may end, one should engage in an analysis based on the probability of each possible outcome and the costs or losses that might result.

Summary

The intent of this chapter is to show that the costs and benefits resulting from each stage of the outsourcing process must be all considered in a complete analysis. The costs and benifits of many of these phases, such as the requirements and RFI/RFP processes, SLA development, transition, and termination, are often omitted, primarily because accurate costs and benefits are very difficult to establish. However, such costs and benefits are important to consider. While their magnitude is much less than that of implementation, these costs and benefits could be determining factors in the outsourcing decision.

References

[1] Axelrod, C. W., "Financial Evaluation of Transition Technologies," Chap. 5 in *Handbook of Investment Technology,* K. Merz and J. Rosen, (eds.), Chicago, IL: Irwin Professional Publishing, 1996.

[2] "Why ITs Client/Server So Difficult?" *Client/Server Computing,* Vol. 3, No. 1, January 1996, pp. 48–49.

[3] Axelrod, C. W., "The User View of Computer System Availability," *Journal of Capacity Management,* Vol. 2, No. 4, 1985.

7

The Outsourcing Evaluation Process— Customer and Outsourcer Requirements

It is clearly a chicken-and-egg situation—having completed a cost-benefit analysis (CBA), the purpose of which is to demonstrate the feasibility of the project, we now return to the actual outsourcing decision process. However, before proceeding further, we will quickly review the financial evaluation methods in more common use today.

Investment Evaluation Methods

There are a number of ways in which an investment can be evaluated, such as cost-benefit analysis, net present value, return on investment, internal rate of return, and payback period. Each method has its supporters and detractors. Here are some brief definitions and descriptions of each method. More detail can be obtained from texts on financial analysis and capital budgeting.

- *Cost-benefit analysis (CBA):* This is the simplest method, although the determination of benefits is always difficult. CBA involves calculating the costs and benefits related to a specific project and then determining whether or not there is a positive net benefit. When there is, the project should be approved if money is available. The method does not account for absolute cost of a project, nor does it prioritize projects. It also does not account for the time it takes to complete the project and when benefits will start to be accrued.

- *Net present value (NPV):* This is similar to cost-benefit analysis except that the time value of money is incorporated into the analysis. It is based on the premise that a dollar held today will be worth more in the future because it accrues interest. For example, for a 10% interest rate, the dollar is worth $1.10 at the end of 1 year. Conversely, a dollar earned 1 year from now has a discounted value of about $0.91 today. The 0.91 is the discount factor. If costs incurred and benefits obtained are laid out across some future period of time (say, 5 years), then future negative cash flows (costs) and positive cash flows (benefits or revenues) can be discounted to the present to determine the NPV. In general, if the NPV is positive, the project should be considered. However, other factors, which might include intangible benefits, will determine whether the project's priority is high enough for it to be approved. In addition, for the NPV calculation, a single interest rate is assumed throughout the life of the project, which is generally not particularly realistic.

- *Return on investment (ROI):* This is merely the ratio of net benefits (or returns) to costs (investment), where net benefit (or profit) is total benefits less total costs. If the ROI is greater than zero, then the project should be considered. However, this method does not consider the time value of money, nor does it account for the absolute magnitude of the investment or relative magnitude as compared to other projects.

- *Payback period (PP):* The payback period is the length of time it takes for the flow of benefits to cover the costs. Benefits accruing beyond the payback period represent profits from the investment. Projects are compared on the basis of how quickly costs are recovered. However, the method does not account for the time value of money or the cash flows subsequent to the payback period.

- *Breakeven:* The breakeven is the point at which costs and benefits are equal. It corresponds to the payback period in that the latter designates the time at which the breakeven occurs. In addition, the breakeven is defined as an amount, namely, the project's breakeven point is $750,000 which occurs in the eighteenth month following initiation of the project.

- *Internal rate of return (IRR):* The IRR is to NPV as ROI is to CBA. The IRR is the interest rate, calculated from periodic cash flows, which would make the NPV equal to zero. Because of the nature of the mathematics, there will generally be two solutions to the IRR calculation, where one is clearly not valid for the purposes. The appropriate IRR is then compared to a minimum return or "hurdle rate" desired (usually some level above the cost of money to the organization) and projects with IRRs exceeding that rate are viable. Again, priorities are determined based not only on the IRR, but also on the size of the expenditures relative to available funding. Also, there is an implicit assumption that all cash flows are invested at the same IRR rate.

• *Economic value added (EVA):* This is a measure based on maximizing shareholder or stakeholder value. The method is associated with New York consulting firm Stern Stewart & Co. and is described on the Web site http://www.eva.com. This is mentioned in [1] along with four other methods, including ROI, NPV, IRR, and payback period.

Including All Costs

One should not go through the extensive and costly evaluation process, as described in this chapter, unless a preliminary cost-benefit analysis actually hints at the possibility of major benefits from outsourcing. Going into the process, the evaluator likely has some preconceived notion as to which way the analysis will go, although once the process is complete, the outcome can often be counterintuitive—which is the whole point of going through the ordeal in the first place.

There is a very high possibility that the costs of the evaluation process itself will not have been considered. If these costs were deducted from the cost savings, it might well transpire that the decision could hinge on the costs of the process. That is to say, with the addition of all the costs related to the evaluation process itself, the decision might be reversed. For example, if the net benefit of outsourcing is less than the cost of the evaluation, it would not be worth addressing in the first place. Of course, you will not know this until after the fact. Therefore, it should be expected that the value of outsourcing will exceed the cost, inclusive of evaluation costs, by a sufficient amount to make it worthwhile. That is, the analyst should have an a priori expectation that the savings net of process costs, however measured, will meet or exceed what is required by the organization. This is further complicated by the variations in evaluation methods described earlier, which themselves can produce very different conclusions, and each of which has its own anomalies.

To overcome these limitations, an organization might take a "portfolio" approach by recognizing in advance that not all analyses of potential outsourcing opportunities will yield savings. Here, there is an up-front recognition that any particular outcome may not yield a saving over the current approach—for example, the decision may be to preserve the status quo. Consequently, the cost is incurred without any measurable benefits, except that it enabled the organization to avoid an unprofitable move. The portfolio approach takes the view that, even though individual cases may not produce savings, across a multitude of analyses, there will be aggregate savings that exceed the total cost of all the analyses by enough to realize the required return or savings.

Here is a simplified example, in which an organization looks at two outsourcing opportunities. One is shown to yield savings over the life of the arrangement with a net present value of $500,000. In the other case, the outcome is to retain the operation in-house, so that there is no resultant saving. If the cost for each evaluation is $100,000 (although it is likely that this cost will vary with the type and magnitude of the service and other factors), then the net saving will be $300,000, even though there is a direct cost loss of $100,000 in one case. Whether the $300,000 net saving is acceptable depends on whether it yields a sufficient return on the investment needed to effect the outsourcing arrangement. It should be noted that for the individual analysis yielding a $500,000 gross saving, and a $400,000 saving net of the evaluation cost, the return may be acceptable, whereas the overall return from the portfolio of two investments might not meet return requirements. Clearly this becomes much more complex as the number and variety of prospective projects increases.

Few organizations will go through so explicit an analysis as this—more likely there will be informed guesses as to what is likely worth pursuing and what is not. When someone, with sufficient authority within the organization, decides that outsourcing a particular function might be a good idea, then the evaluation of the particular outsourcing venture is initiated. Ironically, when the origination of the desire to look at outsourcing comes from "on high" the "lowly" analysts may believe that the decision has already been made and that it is their task merely to provide documented justification that favor the boss's predisposition[1] (see http://www.eva.com).

A highly subjective aspect of the outsourcing decision is that of the inherent security of the service provider. Increasingly, companies are performing more detailed due diligence on service providers (as well as having their own security assessed by security consultants); but when it comes down to the final analysis, someone (most likely the chief information security officer or some other high-level executive) will usually make an intuitive determination as to whether the security is adequate to protect the assets at risk.

For the purposes of this book, we will make the overriding assumption that everyone involved in the analysis is seeking an objective, unbiased result,

---

1. To the extent that this conception, or misconception, is the overriding factor in the approach to the evaluation process, we might see the subjective weighting of the less-tangible costs and benefits in favor of the intended outcome. While this view may appear cynical, experience has shown this executive management influence to be prevalent. After all, the analyst is also looking to advance within the organization and may feel that this agenda is assisted by coming up with results that show the executives to be prescient and "on top of their game."

which is in the best interests of the organization and its stakeholders—otherwise we can stop right here (or should have done so much earlier!). Nevertheless, I will point out such areas in the evaluation process where someone's bias (or prejudice) could just possibly creep into the estimates of the less tangible costs and benefits. This is so that, at the very least, those responsible for the decision might know where to drill down for possible discrepancies.

Structure of the Chapter

In this chapter, we will address the following subjects:

- What issues need to be addressed along the way;
- Which items could and should be included at each step;
- The relative importance of the issues and items that we consider.

The goal of the exercise is to ensure to the greatest extent possible that everything relevant has been included, and that less important factors are not given excessive attention and weight, as an analyst might easily become enthralled with a minor details. We will also demonstrate how sensitive the decision can be to the less tangible, more intuitive estimates of costs and benefits. Distressingly, many such decisions are made based on incomplete and imprecise information. As we examine each step, emphasis will be placed on the information security aspects of the endeavor. Subsequently, we will look at the unique aspects of outsourcing actual security functions.

The Gathering of Requirements

In the beginning is a period of unstructured contemplation of whether or not a particular function or process should be outsourced. At this stage, the preliminary prediction as to the outcome of the analysis is made. Sometimes prediction is easy because the arguments, one way or the other, are overwhelming. Perhaps the function in question cannot be done in-house at the particular stage of an organization's development without incurring huge costs, perhaps many times the cost of having a third party perform that same function. However, even in such a situation, the best practice is to complete the entire evaluation process in order to determine *which* service provider to select. If little choice among service providers exists—that is, a dominant provider or couple of providers are being considered—the analysis may be perfunctory, but should still be done. Situations do change, such as new players entering into the fray or software products appearing on the scene, which might increase the feasibility of bringing the function in-house.

In addition, the decision to outsource varies greatly depending on how an organization compares with respect to business and technology. It matters greatly, for example, if an internal function already exists or whether it is necessary to create an entirely new process. Also, the stage of a company's business life cycle—start-up, rapid growth, mature, declining, in bankruptcy—has significant influence on the options that might be available and worth considering. These issues have been discussed in detail earlier, but bear repetition here since they refer to significant factors that are often omitted.

Business Requirements

In the BITS document [2], the decision as to whether or not to engage in IT outsourcing is considered a business decision, as indeed it mostly is. However, the technical component is also large, especially for the more esoteric areas of information security, where a critical success factor is the ability to implement and manage leading-edge technologies. One important reason for outsourcing, as described earlier, is to tap into frontier-technology products, skills, and abilities that are not readily available on the open market, but have been acquired and developed by leading providers months, if not years, ahead of the marketplace.

If the service being evaluated is already performed for the organization either internally or externally, a document should have been produced describing the need for such a service, as well as its scope, magnitude, and expected service levels. In the case of start-ups, such details may have been provided to venture capitalists in a business plan.

The motivation to examine other options—such as outsourcing a service that is being run in-house, changing an existing arrangement with a service provider, or transferring business from one service provider to another—will generally be the result of a number of triggers. These triggers, some of which were introduced in Chapter 6, may be generated by internal or external events that are related to time, performance, cost, or one or more particular incidents within or outside the control of the customer organization or the outsourcer.

Some examples of triggers, which might initiate a review of a current outsourcing or insourcing relationship, are as follows:

- *The end of the current term of the agreement* between the two parties, resulting in the need to decide whether or not to extend the term of the service, and at what cost, by renegotiating and/or renewing the agreement (time-related and event-related).

- *Downturn in business volumes* leading to reduced profits for the customer and/or the outsourcer. This might well result in the renegotiation by either party of the contract prior to the prearranged termination date (event-related).

- *Dissatisfaction with the service levels and quality of service* as a result of a drop-off in responsiveness by the outsourcer or its inability to scale up to handle greater volume at the same service level as before (performance-related).

- *Unexpected increases in costs,* possibly as a result of external factors such as inflation, or internal factors such as the need to build a new facility (cost-related).

- *Acquisition of the service provider* by another company that may or may not be interested in continuing the existing service arrangement (event-related).

- *Acquisition of the customer* by another company that may or may not use the particular service provider and may have strong views for or against using the service. Sometimes, if the acquiring firm has a different external auditor from the acquired firm, there may be a conflict between using a particular auditing firm's services (event-related).

- *Business dissolution of the service provider* (whether voluntarily or not) that forces a revision in the outsourcing relationship. Here the customer may be able to transfer its business to another provider or bring the service in-house (event-related).

- *Business dissolution of the customer* (whether voluntarily or not) that forces a change in the outsourcing relationship. Here the question relates to provisions in the contract for winding down the operation (event-related).

- *Exposure to information about successful outsourcing deals* through newspaper or magazine articles, newsletters, vendor or customer announcements, conversations with peers, attendance at conferences and seminars, and so on. The actions of peers, especially in the same industry, can greatly influence senior managers to view outsourcing positively and to consider outsourcing various functions themselves (event-related).

- *Exposure to information about failed outsourcing deals* through newspaper or magazine articles, newsletters, vendor or customer announcements, conversations with peers, attendance at conferences and seminars, and so on. The actions of peers, especially in the same industry, of similar size, can greatly influence senior managers to view outsourcing negatively and to consider bringing an outsourced function back in-house (event-related).

The object of the exercise at this stage is to determine the business justification for the service. Some services, whether performed internally or externally, are mandatory for every organization (e.g., payroll, accounting, legal). Others, such as training and strategic planning, are discretionary (at least in the short term), in which case a decision is necessary as to whether a service should be done at all at a particular point in time. The latter issue might hinge on whether viable opportunities to outsource the service exist at an acceptable cost and service level if, in fact, the service cannot be justified internally. Thus, one might not want to hire a training staff, but may well use a provider. Sometimes we see enormous growth in what appear to be marginal services if outsourcing is able to meet demand for lower costs and higher service levels, thereby opening up a new market. ADP's growth and dominance in payroll processing is a good example. Outsourcing decisions, by category of service, are illustrated in Figure 7.1.

In Figure 7.1, we differentiate between "discretionary" and "nice-to-have" services. Discretionary services refer to those services that in the long run may be

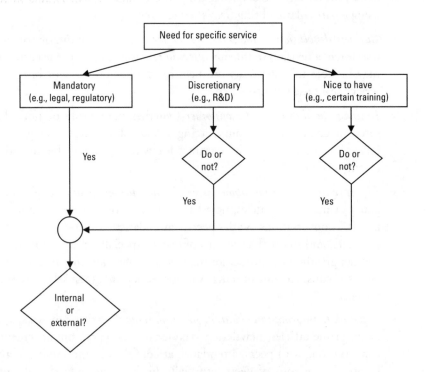

Figure 7.1 Outsourcing decisions by category of service.

needed for the future health and viability of the organization, but can be put off to a future date without significant negative impact. Arguably, such activities as research and development, training, advertising, and documentation of computer applications may be considered discretionary over some period of time. However, the consequences of reductions in spending on these types of activity may ultimately be far more costly in terms of lost future revenues from new products, drops in efficiency, lower morale of workers who are no longer well-trained, and increased maintenance costs associated with inadequately documented computer programs. A company may be wiser to borrow and spend money on these activities so that its future is not mortgaged. One might also argue that deterioration in these areas will likely lead to their being outsourced in the relatively near future.

On the other hand, nice-to-have services may affect the quality of the workplace but do not generally have a discernable impact on the company—although their advocates would argue otherwise. Nice-to-haves are often morale boosters. They might include attendance at marginally job-related conferences and lavish seasonal parties, which appear not to have a directly positive impact on the short-run profitability of the organization, but may contribute to higher staff retention and the concomitant benefits of a stable employee population. Experience has shown, however, that the strongest organizations in the long run are those that do not throw their money at frivolities in profitable times, but rather invest in programs that will serve them well in the difficult times that inevitably arise. Often, employees themselves would rather see profits return to them in compensation or invested in their future prosperity, and other stakeholders, such as shareholders, also want to see their companies build for the future.

In any event, the activities in discretionary areas may become viable if the services are outsourced rather than performed internally, or if they are in-sourced rather than performed by a third party, because perhaps one or the other is cheaper or more effective. Training is an area that should be considered for outsourcing. But, even a function that appears as innocuous as training involves issues, such as the protection of proprietary information and intellectual property, that must be taken into account during due diligence.[2]

For both discretionary and nice-to-have services, the decision whether or not to move forward with any provider—internal or external or a combination—may well come after the entire evaluation has been completed. Certainly one possible outcome is that the service cannot be justified in any form. Clearly,

---

2. I am aware of an embarrassing and potentially dangerous situation in which a firm hired an outside service to document a critical part of its computer applications, only to discover, quite by chance, that the owner of the provider had been convicted of computer fraud.

proceeding with the evaluation process only makes sense if the expectation of moving forward with change is 50% or more.

Assuming that proceeding is deemed reasonable, based upon prior analyses or experience, the next step is to specify the requirements. An excellent list of requirements is provided in the report issued by the Software Engineering Institute [3].

First, we will look at the business-related requirements.

Viability of Service Provider

In many ways, this is the most important component of the analysis because, if a provider does not pass muster here, it is hardly worth being included among the prospects. An added danger is that such a marginal vendor, if included, might come up with the most attractive proposal, driven by the vendor's attempt to survive at all costs, and the analyst may come under tremendous pressure to accept the lowest bid.[3]

Experience, particularly with some prominent MSSPs, has shown that even apparently well-funded outsourcers have gone out of business with little or no advance warning. It should also be noted that the person or persons analyzing the outsourcing opportunity might not have all necessary skills, such as being able to review, understand, and opine upon a company's financials. Certain issues should be left to the experts, particularly financial and legal matters.

Financial Analysis

Internal or external credit specialists should be asked to perform a credit check on the service provider. This type of review should include requesting or accessing a report from one of the companies that specializes in this area, such as Dun & Bradstreet. Additionally, if the service provider is a public company, the review should include going over its financial statements, including annual reports. If the service provider is privately owned, generally much less financial information is available and what is available is probably less comprehensive and useful compared to information about a public company.

The names of sources and managers of initial and subsequent funding should be obtained, if possible. Those companies heavily dependent on venture capital, for example, are likely to be much more volatile than companies able to fund their operations out of revenues. Consideration should be given to the

---

3. One analyst, who works for a major bank, said that he routinely eliminates the five lowest bidders from consideration. However, for many types of service, particularly in the information security area, there might not even be as many as five bona fide bidders.

number, size, quality, and length of commitment of current and potential client service contracts and product sales. Care should be taken when assessing the pipeline and backlog of work, as demonstrated by the number of high-profile cases of companies booking sales inappropriately.

Despite taking great care in reviewing financials, a customer organization cannot be absolutely sure of what is happening behind the scenes at a service provider or what matter might arise to overturn all the diligent analysis. As a recent example, the management of a well-reputed security consulting company was accused of using unlicensed software throughout their firm. Reports of defections of key staff and loss of customer trust can in a matter of weeks destroy a reputation that took years to build. Nevertheless, in the vast majority of cases, a thorough financial review provides a reasonably good picture of the financial health and prospective viability of potential business partners.

Marketplace and Business Prospects

Every organization operates in some form of marketplace. And no organization is immune from its vagaries. Therefore, the analyst should learn as much relevant information about the marketplace as possible to assess its impact on a particular outsourcing decision. However, evaluation of the marketplace is another area where the analyst might not have the capability, knowledge, or understanding to determine who the significant players are, how they stack up against one another, and, finally, how they might fit in with the requirements of the buying or selling entity.[4]

Subscribing to advisory services, such as those provided by the Gartner Group or Forrester Research (formerly Giga), can pay off since it is their business to be tuned into the vagaries of various IT-related markets, of which IT outsourcing is but one. Such advice should be supplemented with research on the Internet and in industry magazines and newspapers, as well as through discussions with peers in other, preferably similar, companies. The least reliable sources are competing outsourcing firms, which clearly have a different agenda to yours in that they will obviously downplay their own difficulties and perhaps exaggerate the troubles of others. However, from time to time, a vendor will disclose gossip containing information about a competitor that is worth trying to

---

4. For the most part, the analysis of outsourcing is done from the buyer's perspective. However, the providers of these services also have requirements of buyers in terms of financial capabilities (for example, the buyer's ability to pay its bills) or cultural acceptance to permit a productive working relationship. It is often indicative of solid service providers that they will perform their own due diligence on customers. This provides the added assurance that they have had other customers go through such an evaluation. This, in turn, means that the outsourcer has a better chance of getting paid and staying in business.

verify independently. That is, such heavily biased gossip can lead you down a path of investigation that will yield some beneficial information, which could save you from a costly mistake.

Health of the Economy

How are the sectors of the economy encompassing the buyer and seller of services doing? A poor economy may provide insufficient markets for outsourcers, resulting in paring of prices, lower profits, and increased likelihood of bankruptcy or takeover.

On the other hand, some outsourcers often do well in a down economy, because companies are looking to reduce costs and make costs more predictable—both potential advantages of outsourcing as described previously. In the early years of the twenty-first century, a poor economic climate in the United States has resulted in pressure on costs of doing business, which in turn has led to a surge in outsourcing, particularly in offshore locations such as India and China.[5] For the latter two countries, the cost per unit of service is a fraction of the equivalent U.S. domestic service, even accounting for the increased overhead due to managing the service remotely.

Probably the risk is higher from the outsourcers' perspective if customers are not able to sustain anticipated volumes or, worse, are not able to pay their bills. Of course, even in a recession some businesses do relatively well, so the outsourcers need to determine what portfolio of customers they should seek, by industry, company, size, and region. The general determination here is that it is difficult, if not impossible, to come to general conclusions, and each case needs to be evaluated separately.

Marketplace Matters

Is the market for the particular outsourcing services that an organization seeks growing and profitable? It is important here to segment the marketplace properly. For example, information security services can be divided into many submarkets, such as consulting services, advisory services, assessment services, and managed services. Some firms specialize in one or two of these, while others participate in several or most. Some firms sell security software products. Others remarket software products and/or bundle them into services. Some specialize in

---

5. An article [4] describes how revenues from software and computer services will grow more rapidly in China than in India, although the growth in India is expected to be substantial. This is because of the substantially lower wages in China, even compared to India. A chart from Gartner Dataquest shows 2002 revenues to be about $8 billion for India and $2 billion for China rising to about $27 billion each for China and India in 2006. With the growth rate so much greater for China, one might expect China to far surpass India following 2006.

information security; others provide general security services; and yet others, such as major accounting and consulting firms, provide security as one of many practices. The information security marketplace, which is relatively new, has seen many recent entrants, quite a few failures, and a significant number of mergers and acquisitions.

In recent years, the growth in the information security marketplace has been disappointing, despite major attacks on the Internet and organizations attached to the Internet. Heightened awareness and concerns about security following the September 11, 2001, terrorist plane hijacking and consequent destruction of the World Trade Center and part of the Pentagon did not result in major expenditures by businesses. However, when more funds flow from the Department of Homeland Security, the overall market probably will see growth, although it may be concentrated with a few large government contractors.

Furthermore, general spending on information technology in the United States has not shown growth comparable to that of the previous decade, with the exception of IT outsourcing services, particularly offshore outsourcing of application development and certain support services.

In 2004, we are seeing some measure of recovery both in IT and information security spending. It is too early to tell whether this is a brief upturn or if it is the start of a period of sustained growth.

Competitive Environment

Proceeding to the next level of analysis, we need to determine if a particular service provider is stable and can be relied upon to stay around to conduct its business. How is a service provider placed in its segment? Is it a leader or follower? Is it the only game in town, or does it face aggressive competition from like companies? Is the segment characterized by a few large publicly owned, or even employee-owned, companies or does a large number of privately held outfits exist? Have companies maintained their independence or is the segment rife with mergers, acquisitions, takeovers, bankruptcies, and defections? When a market is relatively new and still subject to all manner of upheavals, as is the case with information security, selecting a service provider is difficult and risky. To help make decisions in such an environment, one must gain as much market intelligence as possible.

An outsourcer looking at potential customers should go through similar assessments of customers' environments. It particularly needs to know whether the customer is a leader in its business segment, whether it is relatively large or small, whether it is growing or shrinking, and if it is financially viable. These considerations affect the reputation of the outsourcer as provider of advanced services to leading customers, the potential level of business, and the customer's ability to pay its bills in full and on time. If customers run into financial trouble, a domino effect adversely affects first other organizations that are customers of the outsourcer, and then the viability of the outsourcer. A failure by the outsourcer then impacts other financially healthy customers by endangering their services, which could severely damage and possibly eliminate even the strongest of customers if the service provided is critical.

Structure of the Business

As mentioned above, outsourcers and their customers may offer a single product or service, may be fully diversified across a wide range of business types and industries (i.e., be a conglomerate), or be somewhere in between. From a business perspective, the single product, single industry provider, or single customer is very risky—they can offer the highest returns, but they are also the most exposed to fluctuations in the economy and changes in technology and demand.

The dot-coms of the latter half of the 1990s and the turn of the twenty-first century were a prime example of a single dependency, namely, the on-line marketplace. The failure of dot-coms took out of business many companies that were not diversified into other markets, with relatively few exceptions. Those established companies, which saw the Internet as just another distribution channel, were not as affected by the crash, and most survived if their other businesses and channels were viable. A few dot-com companies, which dominate a particular segment, such as Amazon.com, eBay, and Google, have done very well in the post-bubble Internet economy.

Sometimes, a customer may be looking for a specialist—a service provider that concentrates on one thing and works to be the best there is in that particular area. In the information security arena, such a specialty could be "penetration testing," or the scanning of a customer's Internet-facing perimeter and the assessment of vulnerabilities discovered.

Frequently, a customer will seek a provider who offers a range of services, some of which might support and enhance others, as synergies are recognized and exploited. So, for example, an information security provider offering vulnerability assessments might also offer an alert and notification service of emerging threats, vulnerabilities, and patches relating to the customer's particular profile. First, the provider tracks threats, vulnerabilities, and software patch levels as part of its assessment services and, second, it understands the customer's environment. Further, if that same provider has a laboratory to test and assess security products, it may offer commercial off-the-shelf product security certification as an added service. While this example focuses on information security service providers, the same synergistic relationships apply to other outsourcers.

Major customers gravitate to well-established, stable, and diversified suppliers in order to reduce risk. Smaller, newer, and more cost-conscious customers might take on additional risk to get a cheaper price from a less established, more specialized outsourcer, particularly if the service is not core to the customer's business. Under this model, it is hard to see how start-ups grow to substantial size. Indeed, many small service providers fail, especially if a major customer decides to terminate its relationship. Other small outsourcers get bought by larger firms and then, in their new incarnation, take on the mantle of the owner. Others grow through gradually upgrading the quality and size of their customers and corresponding work engagements.

Nature of the Business

Customer organizations must not only consider what lines of business an outsourcer is in, they need to look at the specific characteristics of that business. They should consider the types of customer that the outsourcer serves (e.g., government, commercial, nonprofit) and the locations of those customers (e.g., concentrated in one or two metropolises, spread across the country, international). Of particular interest is whether the outsourcer has served one or more customers in the industry being researched, whether they are located nearby, and whether they are of similar size in both total business and size of service engagement anticipated. Discussions with such references should be part of the due diligence process.

Often a customer will look for a geographic match between itself and the service provider, particularly if the customer has a number of affiliates and subsidiaries distributed across many countries and it wishes to have some or all of these locations served. Today, with vast improvements in communications, including teleconferencing, electronic mail, instant messaging, videoconferencing, and voice over Internet protocol (VoIP), the location issue is less important than previously. Still, there are certain occasions and situations where face-to-face meetings are particularly valuable, and not readily being able to meet in person can be a hindrance.

Relative Sizes of Organizations

Their relative sizes as well as the absolute sizes of organizations can significantly affect the viability of the outsourcer and the customer and their relationship, as described in the following variations.

Large Customer, Small Outsourcer

If the customer is much larger than the outsourcer and the customer is the outsourcer's major source of revenue, there are a number of effects. The customer is likely able to negotiate price and deliverables aggressively, with the outsourcer acquiescing because of the importance of the account. On the other hand, the high dependency on a single customer makes the service provider highly vulnerable to changes in the level of business of that particular customer and, at the extreme, the termination of that business at the customer's option. This scenario is particularly dangerous for other smaller customers, which might have small but important services tied up with the outsourcer. Potential customers should be very wary of this situation if they will only account for a small part of the overall business of the outsourcer.

When the customer is much larger than the outsourcer, the customer has concerns that the smaller provider may not be able to stay in business. This does not generally discourage the customer from aggressively negotiating low prices and high service levels, to which the outsourcer is usually only too willing to agree in order to boast of the customer in its marketing and sales efforts. The customer must balance its desire for lower-cost services against the need to ensure that the outsourcer remains in business. Also, financial pressure might mean that the outsourcer will try to make up its shortfall by charging for additional services and not meeting the level of service expected by the customer, just to stay in business. For the customer, the resulting costs if the outsourcer fails will likely far outweigh the benefits of the initial cost reduction, in terms of risk to the business and need to transfer to another provider or to an operation in-house.

Large Outsourcer, Small Customer

The small customer derives a number of benefits from contracting with a large service provider—aside from the economies of scale that such a relationship brings, the customer is likely to gain better security, higher availability, and greater redundancy of systems and networks. The customer also gains access to the outsourcer's technologies, which might be more advanced than their own. Large outsourcers can usually afford to put advanced capabilities in place, whereas smaller-scale customers may not. Such outsourcers can also use these capabilities to enhance their competitive advantage in selling to prospects and in retaining existing customers.

From the customer viewpoint, choosing a large outsourcer is reassuring to the smaller customer, because of the greater chance of the provider's long-term viability. On the other hand, the outsourcer may have concerns about the customer's viability, although losing such a small customer might not result in much of a loss relative to the outsourcer's overall business.

Large Outsourcer, Large Customer

When both the customer and outsourcer are large, stable, viable organizations, the question of either one going out of business represents a lower risk than in other cases, but the risk is not zero. Large companies do get bought, suffer major declines, or are subject to losses of confidence that can cripple their effectiveness and result in slowdowns and failures.

For the most part, however, both types of organization can negotiate from a position of strength and come up with a win-win agreement whereby the customer gets good value and the outsourcer earns a fair profit. Many large organizations prefer to do business with other large organizations because so much of the risk is ameliorated.

Small Outsourcer, Small Customer

In some ways, this scenario is equivalent to the large outsourcer/large customer situation, in that both parties are evenly matched when it comes to negotiating strength and viability. Either party is subject to getting bought, suffering significant fluctuations in business level, and going out of business altogether. This is the riskiest situation but often the most common among smaller organizations. Small outsourcers have problems acquiring large customers, and small customers may not engage the interest of larger outsourcers, for whom the expensive setup required for small customers may not pay.

Service Requirements

Meeting Expectations

It is one thing to ensure that the business relationships are well founded, it is quite another to make sure that the level of service, as required by the customer, will be met satisfactorily on a continuing basis. What represents satisfactory service is expressed in a SLA, but it is clear from the many reports of failure of customer-outsourcer relationships that merely "putting it in writing" does not guarantee that the relationship will work. Fundamentally, quality of service is in the eyes of the beholder and accordingly the customer's perception of service quality and satisfaction count, no matter what the numbers indicate.

Two service providers can have identical commitments in terms of tangible and measurable service levels, such as throughput rate, capacity, response time, job completion times, availability, accuracy, data integrity, maintenance of confidentiality, communications and reporting, and responsiveness of technical support. Typical metrics include the percentage of messages handled per second within a specific time interval (e.g., 95% of response times less than 2 seconds), percentage of telephone calls to a support area that are answered within a specific period of time (or number of rings), and the percentage of the time an application is available.

Yet, even if these criteria are met consistently, the customer may still be unhappy. Customer satisfaction can vary enormously from one provider to another. Clearly, some features of service are beyond metrics—such as the knowledge and helpfulness of support staff and willingness to follow up and get the answer. An article in the August 2003 issue of the *Communications of the*

ACM discusses how CIOs should manage expectations, in this case the expectations of their superiors. It states that "...measures that address quantifiable efficiency like speed of processing are typically well understood and commonly used, but their usefulness is often limited. Other important measures...that address organizational/strategic effectiveness, value and popularity may not be well understood, widely used, or not used appropriately or consistently by organizations" [5].

It is reasonable to ask what items comprise service quality and how they can be evaluated if some aspects of service are intangible and not readily measurable. Jiang et al. assess both expectations and perceptions of service quality from the customer and provider viewpoints [6]. Ironically, typical performance measures may not jibe with user perceptions of good service, particularly in the IT arena. Jiang et al. look into the expectations, perceptions, and satisfaction gaps.

The management of customer satisfaction requires the convergence of expectations and perceptions of both customer and service provider. The goal is to reduce, or preferably eliminate, the gap in understanding between what the customer expects in terms of service level and what the provider thinks the customer needs. When that has been resolved and the service is implemented, a performance gap will arise if the customer's perception of what is being delivered differs from what the provider thinks is being delivered. Such a difference results in dissatisfaction. This gap needs to be put in specific terms and then fed back to both customer and provider in order to change perceptions regarding what level of performance is acceptable and to close the satisfaction gap. Without the feedback and the willingness to change, service levels will not generally improve.

The above-mentioned article shows that the crux of the service dilemma is indeed the management of expectations and the relationship. The authors state that the establishment of trust, based on prior track record, is indispensable and that "a relationship of trust with sufficient communication is the first line of defense against unrealistic and unmet expectations." CIOs are quoted as saying that "...perceptions are often not accurate. Evaluation at the executive level is often vague and impressionistic ...." Another CIO stated that "Surprises lead to failures—unanticipated outcomes, scope creep, cost overruns ...." [6].

Concentration and Dispersion of Business Operations and Functions

My article on the user, or customer, view of reliability considers how customers perceive the performance of the systems [7]. Trends that affect reliability result from the *concentration of power,* while other trends result from *concentration of functions.* These concepts can easily be translated to the outsourcing arena.

Outsourcing effectively distributes computational power and operational activities between customers and third parties, since even under the most drastic outsourcing scenarios some functionality is retained within customer organizations. For example, when the entire information technology function is outsourced or spun off, certain related business processes frequently remain with the customer. If some business processes are outsourced, others are retained. Otherwise, there would be no customer organization! Consequently, if something adverse should happen to customers' systems or facilities, customers might be affected less severely than they would be had certain operations remained in-house. The outsourcer will probably be operational and able to carry some additional load and perform additional services in support of damaged customers.[6] Conversely, if the outsourcer fails to provide contracted-for services for some reason—be it a failure in software or equipment or the business itself going bankrupt—then, depending on the size of the outsourcer, large segments of an industry or sector could be adversely affected. If the outsourcer provides core services, the impact could be enormous. For this reason, backup and recovery are a key issue in choosing an outsourcer. Also, outsourcers prefer customers that have business continuity plans in place so that a disaster at one location does not put them out of action.

Functionality may be less concentrated if business processes are included in the outsourcing arrangement. Increasingly, functions such as applications programming and customer support are being moved to external providers both at home and abroad. Again, advantages exist in terms of redundancy and resiliency if functional capabilities are dispersed. As discussed in a recent article, three U.S. financial regulatory agencies require key institutions to have redundant computer systems and networks and also to have operational staff distributed so that critical functions can continue, even if staff are not able to get to the designated backup site within an acceptable period of time [8]. Such requirements are being demanded more and more frequently as fears of terrorist acts and dependency on a few concentrated critical operations have increased enormously over the past few years.

The reliability of computer equipment has vastly improved over the last three decades. At one time, having to fix equipment failures was an everyday routine, with service engineers living on-site at major customer facilities. Back in the 1970s, most systems ran batch programs rather than real-time applications. While a breakdown in equipment was inconvenient, the delays were often tolerable because the expected turnaround times were relatively long with high

6. The tragic events that occurred in New York City on September 11, 2001, caused many organizations in and around the World Trade Center to seek alternative facilities and systems in order to try to remain in business. Although there were no contractual terms to force it, a large financial services outsourcer rapidly set up capabilities within its existing facilities to accommodate a subset of the staff, systems, and networks of several customer firms that were directly affected. While not a contractual obligation in this case, it was done to foster good customer relations and to keep the affected customers in business.

variances, and so the cost of outages of several hours or more were expected and tolerated by users, although not welcomed. As terminals and workstations were connected through networks to real-time or online applications, instant response and continuous availability became the users' goals. Discussions focused on *subsecond response times* for simple interactions with computer applications, and how a longer response would lead to marked declines in user productivity. Today, while tolerance exists for some delays for computationally intense operations, the push for speed continues, with even home users turning to high-speed telecommunications to accelerate the responsiveness of their Internet access.

As a side point, slower response is more tolerable if a system indicates that something is happening either by the appearance of comments regarding how much time remains for the process (such as a file transfer) or graphical meters showing percentage complete. Providing information on what to expect goes a long way towards satisfying service needs.

The usual engineering attributes do not adequately express the sentiments of most users, who view the computer applications as a means of getting work done in a timely and accurate fashion. Users are not generally patient with the lack of availability or responsiveness even when told how complex and difficult to manage such systems are and how remarkable their accomplishments. "Always on and available" is a minimum expectation, if not requirement, that users of systems believe is their due.

Customer View of Satisfactory Service

My article on availability examines the components of availability and its converse, downtime, from the user or customer viewpoint specifically [9]. The customer is generally not interested in the cause of an outage—only that the application is not available and how long it will be until it is back up again. Customers also have questions as to what information was lost and whether and when it can be recovered.

As the article describes, the system may be unavailable for a whole variety of reasons—some intentional, others accidental. For example, a system may be unavailable or available but not usable; in other words, the user can bring up an application on his or her workstation but the application is not operating properly—it might not accept data, perform calculations accurately, or generate results of requests. In negotiating an agreement with a service provider, these issues need to be investigated and addressed.

The makeup of downtime includes the time to realize that the system is down, subject to the definition in the SLA, the time the service engineers require to arrive on-site (if necessary) or to log in remotely, the time to determine the cause of the problem, repair it, and restore it to its condition before failure. The mean time between failure (MTBF) is a measure of the average time between failures. The mean time to repair (MTTR) is the average time a technician requires to get access, either physically or electronically, and then to fix, test, and bring back online the offending system. While these times give a decision-maker means of measuring, in relative and absolute terms, the performance of the provider, they give little guidance as to the impact of any outages in regard to the seriousness of an event, both in absolute and comparative terms. It is useful here to compare MTBF and MTTR performance across providers to investigate material differences. Such differences might arise as a result of the technological prowess of one vendor over another.

Technology Requirements

As described earlier, one of the key reasons why organizations seek to outsource certain functions is that they need a way to buy into new technology and capabilities and either cannot or will not do it in-house. With technology advancing so rapidly, firms commonly are overtaken and find themselves at a competitive disadvantage by being shackled with obsolete and expensive technologies that do not meet their needs. In some industries, the legal and regulatory demands may be so great that it is no longer feasible for a smaller firm to keep their applications and systems up-to-date, so they naturally seek help elsewhere. We also see that some service providers have an edge in respect to the technology they use.

The "Bleeding" Edge

A fine balance exists between engaging the latest technologies or waiting until others have tested them out before adopting them. The temptation is to get a lead over competitors by reaping the purported benefits of newer technology. However, because many innovative systems are beset by problems in the initial stages, one must question whether the risk is worth it. Even a proven track record is no guarantee of success. For example, the team that brought the world-beating SABRE system to American Airlines ran into major problems when they attempted to carry over many of their ideas and develop a system, named Confirm, for the hotel and car rental businesses. Confirm ran into major technological difficulties trying to implement a newer technology that could not be made to work. The effort disintegrated in a flurry of lawsuits.

When choosing a service provider, technology plays a major role, particularly for IT outsourcing and even more so for information security outsourcing. It is generally safer to select a provider with a proven track record and solid technology than to experiment with a glitzy new approach, particularly if you are a "beta" site, where the systems are being developed.

I have experienced situations where trying out the latest and greatest systems, using the most modern of architectures, has led to significant operational and financial problems. In one case, a third party was developing the first real-time on-line system and operations to handle a complex financial instrument. When a multimillion dollar shortfall appeared, I suggested using a service that had been in the business about a decade and had gained a reputation for solid, reliable, accurate work. Once transferred to the "old-line" provider, the problems were quickly rectified, and the provider was able to deliver quality service, albeit using an older technology.

I certainly do not eschew new technologies—I very much favor pushing ahead with more efficient, less-costly, easier-to-use systems. I merely recommend that innovative systems be approached with caution and that extra care be taken to test them thoroughly from start to finish. However, for rapidly changing technologies, especially those that pertain to information security, often the only choice is to push against the frontier. The risk of not having adequate protection and response capabilities is too high. In the next chapter, we will look at the information security space in particular because it is needed for pure-play information security outsourcing as well as a crucial part of every IT outsourcing arrangement.

References

[1] King, J., "Five Metrics for the Books," *Computerworld*, Vol. 36, No. 20, May 13, 2000, p. 40.

[2] "BITS Framework: Managing Technology Risk for Information Technology (IT) Service Providers," *Banking Industry Technology Secretariat, Financial Services Roundtable,* Washington, D.C., November 2003, http://www.bitsinfo.org.

[3] Allen, J., et al., "Outsourcing Managed Security Services," *Network Systems Survivability Program,* Carnegie Mellon University, Pittsburgh, PA: Software Engineering Institute, January 2003, http://www.fedcirc.com.

[4] Einhorm, B., and M. Kripalani, "Move Over, India," *BusinessWeek*, August 11, 2003, pp..42–43.

[5] Potter, R. E., "How CIO's Manage Their Superiors' Expectations," *Communications of the ACM*, Vol. 46, No. 8, 2003, pp. 75–79.

[6] Jiang, J. J., et al., "Closing the User and Provider Service Quality Gap," *Communications of the ACM*, Vol. 46, No. 2, 2003.

[7] Axelrod, C. W., "The User's View of Computer System Reliability," *Journal of Capacity Management*, Vol. 2, No. 1, 1983, pp. 24–41.

[8] "Interagency Paper on Sound Practices to Strengthen the Resilience of the U.S. Financial System," Federal Reserve System, Department of the Treasury: Office of the Comptroller

of the Currency, and Securities and Exchange Commission, April 7, 2003, http://www.sec.gov/news/studies/34-47638.htm.

[9]   Axelrod, C. W., "The User's View of Computer System Availability," *Journal of Capacity Management*, Vol. 2, No. 4, 1985, pp. 340–362.

8

Outsourcing Security Functions and Security Considerations When Outsourcing

In this chapter, we examine the outsourcing of security functions and security issues that arise from the outsourcing process itself. Not only is security an important subject on its own, but it is also a crucial component whenever an outsourcing arrangement is made. In many ways, the outsourcing of security as related to information assets, physical assets, and human assets is much the same as any other kind of outsourcing, but in other ways it is unique. While we have previously argued that a security component exists in every outsourcing arrangement, we still need to address the outsourcing of security itself when it is the primary function being outsourced.

Let us first try to put boundaries on the scope of this review in order to ensure that the list of categories is reasonably complete and comprehensive. We will do this by reviewing some of the standard classifications of areas that relate to security. One source is the 10 security categories of the CISSP Body of Knowledge[1], listed here.

---

1. As mentioned in the preface, CISSP stands for certified information systems security professional, a credential bestowed upon individuals who meet a number of work experience and knowledge criteria determined and examined by the International Information Systems Security Certification Consortium, Inc., in other words, the IISSCC or (ISC)[2]. In order to achieve the CISSP certification, a candidate must demonstrate proficiency in all ten components of the Body of Knowledge.

1. Security Management Practices;

2. Access Control;

3. Security Models and Architecture;

4. Physical Security;

5. Telecommunications and Network Security;

6. Cryptography;

7. Disaster Recovery and Business Continuity;

8. Law, Investigation and Ethics;

9. Application and System Development;

10. Operations Security.

Another source for categorizing areas of security is the ISO 17799[2], which was derived from British Standard (BS) 7799. The ISO 17799 categories are:

1. Business Continuity Planning;

2. System Access Control;

3. System Development and Maintenance;

4. Physical and Environmental Security;

5. Compliance;

6. Personnel Security;

7. Security Organization;

8. Computer and Operations Management;

9. Asset Classification and Control;

10. Security Policy.

Table 8.1 matches the CISSP Body of Knowledge categories to those of ISO 17799. As can be seen, they correspond quite closely to one another. Also, in the third column of Table 8.1, we show whether or not the specific security category readily lends itself to consulting or outsourcing services.

We will now go through each category and expand on the factors affecting security as they relate to third-party services, whether they are consulting services or outsourcing services, specific security services or not.

---

2. ISO/IEC 17799:2000, The Code of Practice for Information Security Management, is a security standard that provides high-level guidelines and voluntary directions for information security management covering 10 topics. More information on the standard is available at http://www.securityauditor.net/iso17799/.

Table 8.1

Relationship Between CISSP Body of Knowledge and ISO 17799 Security Classifications
and Appropriateness for Outsourcing

CISSP Body of Knowledge	ISO 17799	Appropriateness for Consulting/Outsourcing
Security Management Practices	Security Organization	Consulting firms will suggest various types of security and information security organization, with different reporting and responsibilities.
	Personnel Security	Part or all of personnel security is often assigned to an outside firm to handle since it requires specific subject-matter expertise. Here personnel security refers to safety of human beings (staff, visitors).
	Asset Classification and Control	Predominantly developed and implemented internally, but may be defined by laws and regulations and may be imposed on both customer organizations and outsourcers.
	Security Policy	Policy can be readily created through references to books, Web sites (such as http://www.sans.org), and the like, but also it is advisable to consult internal or outside counsel and/or consulting firms, since policy does have many legal implications.
Access Control	System Access Control	Usually handled internally, even when systems operations have been outsourced. However, it can be fairly easily outsourced if required security controls are put in place.
Security Models and Architecture		May be developed and implemented through the use of vendor-provided software and/or consulting services, since necessary subject-matter expertise is hard to come by. Qualified internal expertise usually gets assigned to other tasks.
Physical Security	Physical and Environmental Security	It is common to hire outside guard agencies and third-party employee-screening organizations. Here physical security refers to the protection of plant, equipment, and other assets from theft, damage, and/or destruction.
Telecommunications and Network Security		Establishing secure network, system and application architectures often requires the help of external subject-matter experts.
Cryptography		Generally not offered as a separate service—more often incorporated into another capability, which may itself be outsourced.

Table 8.1 (continued)

CISSP Body of Knowledge	ISO 17799	Appropriateness for Consulting/Outsourcing
Disaster Recovery and Business Continuity	Business Continuity Planning	Common to use third parties for off-site disaster recovery sites.
		Consultants are often used for developing and maintaining business continuity plans.
Law, Investigations, Ethics	Compliance	Externally supplied forensics experts are often brought in as needed, since such subject-matter expertise is generally hard to come by.
Application and System Development	System Development and Maintenance	Applications development and support are quite frequently outsourced—increasingly to offshore service providers.
		Training in secure coding practices is often performed by outside subject-matter experts.
		Assessment of the security level of systems throughout the application development life cycle is commonly outsourced, if done at all, to specialized security consulting firms or security practices of larger consulting firms.
Operations Security	Computer, Communications and Operations Management	Security aspects of operations and management of communications and computer systems can often be part of large multimillion, and even multibillion, dollar outsourcing agreements.
		Alternatively, just the security components can be outsourced, with actual operations management being retained internally.

Security Management Practices

The way in which security is managed varies significantly across organizations, and the degree to which those functions are handled internally or externally also differs from one organization to the next. We will now look at how these functions are dealt with by category.

Security Organization

Information security, or the securing of confidential information assets belonging to organizations and personal information belonging to individuals (customers, employees), has always been important, in order to protect such information from misuse. Increasingly, however, there are legal and regulatory requirements for the protecting of information, particularly information about individuals that is not of a public nature.

The roles, responsibilities, goals, functions, and structure of the security organization are realized in many ways. For example, the scope of information security can be limited to a high-level staff function, which determines policies and standards and sponsors security-related initiatives, or it may include line functions such as management of security devices, including firewalls and intrusion detection systems, and the management of access control. In some organizations, physical security, human (or personnel) security, business continuity planning, and disaster recovery fall under the responsibility of the security officer.

The reporting hierarchy also varies significantly, with the chief information security officer (CISO) or chief security officer (CSO) sometimes reporting to the chief information officer (CIO). In other companies and agencies, the CISO might report to the chief operating officer (COO) or general counsel or chief administrative officer (CAO). A recent article in *CIO Magazine* discusses how physical and information security are converging and how corporate responsibility for security is moving out of the IT area to report to the COO or chief financial officer (CFO) [1].

Accounting and auditing firms, general consulting firms with large security practices, and specialty security consulting firms regularly offer to analyze the general structure and culture of an organization and recommend how the information security function fits in most effectively. As with many consulting assignments, someone in the customer's organization often hopes that their particular agenda will be satisfied through the findings and recommendations of the consulting firm. And consultants sense pressure to support their clients' perceptions. Another determinant of how the information security function is structured is what others in the industry are doing. Here published survey results, magazine articles, discussions with peers, presentations at conferences, and consulting and research firms' pronouncements have the greatest influence.

The internal security structure also includes, and to some degree will determine, what functions might be outsourced to third parties. If the consulting firm also provides security outsourcing, or has alliances with companies that do, then one must consider any such recommendations by the firm as possibly being biased and having a potential for conflict of interest. It is therefore a better practice to hire a consulting firm with no such capabilities or relationships to help in evaluating one's organizational structure and functions.

Often the particular structure of the information security area is very much affected by the overall structure of the parent organization and its culture. A third party may not be familiar with these factors and may not be willing to take the time to learn. Furthermore, the customer might not want to pay for such a learning effort. It normally is well worth the cost, though, for the third party to factor in the culture, in particular, as otherwise the recommendations might be very much off the mark.

In summary, a third party's advice as to how to organize and structure the information security function can be helpful and reassuring if the consultants are sensitive to how a specific organization functions or is perceived to function. However, the advice can be damaging if the internal organization is misconstrued. Bringing a significant amount of good judgment to the table is necessary when making these types of decisions, since creating an ineffective security organization could well cause severe damage. Of particular importance is how the security organization aligns with the business functions. This critical factor will determine how the function is perceived, which affects how effective it can be.

Personnel Security

Personnel security can be interpreted in two ways. First, its goal is to protect individuals working for a company from physical, financial, and other forms of harm—this is physical well-being. Second, personnel security relates to dealing with personal concerns, which, if left unattended, might pose a security risk to the organization.

Physical Well-Being

Dealing with the physical aspect of a person's well-being can be considered simpler than handling other personnel-related issues. It involves such devices as:

- Performing thorough screening and background checks of new hires, contractors, and consultants;
- Having guards posted at entrances and roaming the floors;
- Requiring employees, contractors, and part-time staff show their identity badges;
- Having visitors sign in and be picked up and signed in by those they are visiting;
- Placing video cameras at strategic points, with security staff viewing monitors and storing videotapes.

Quite commonly, companies hire third parties to perform many of these functions. For example, few companies maintain a staff qualified to do the necessary background checks and perform comprehensive screening interviews. This field is a well-defined specialty, and many commercial agencies are available. On-site guards are often outsiders, although internal management staff is often mixed with guards supplied by third parties. In some cases, even the management level is made up of external staff, who often have law enforcement backgrounds.

At the executive and management levels, additional security may be implemented due to fears that executives are subject to kidnapping. Such a risk is considered especially high in certain foreign countries. In some situations, it is necessary to provide all employees with guarded, gated housing, protected travel (e.g., armored cars) and bodyguards in some cases, and a highly secured working environment. Such protection is an even more specialized field that is practically always staffed by third-party specialists.

Of course, this raises the important question as to who is checking on the checkers. There have been many documented cases of firms in the guard business unknowingly hiring ex-convicts because their own screening mechanisms are inadequate. Following the September 11, 2001, terrorist attack on the World Trade Center and Pentagon, it was discovered how unqualified, ill-trained, and suspect some staff performing passenger screening at airports had been.

Because human beings are the most important asset for many companies, the staff who select physical security agencies must perform comprehensive due diligence to ensure that those agencies do not increase employee risk. Danger to personnel is greatly increased if security agencies hire individuals who are in cahoots with terrorists or other criminals.

Law enforcement and emergency services organizations, as members of a particular community, draw upon the services provided at all levels by and for that community, whether it is part of a town, city, state, county, nation, or group of nations. In most situations, the costs of services for these organizations are paid from taxes collected from the community directly benefiting from those services. Smaller groups of businesses or citizens, rather than a particular organization, may hire security services and in some cases use local volunteers to supplement local public fire and police services. While one might loosely say that these services are outsourced, they are not generally subject to the type of outsourcing decision being handled in this book.

Other Human-Related Concerns of the Company

Job Security

The term job security has, of course, a different meaning—it does not mean securing the components of a job; it refers to tenure. Neither does tenure, per se, appear to affect the security of an organization. However, appearances are wrong here.

If employees feel insecure about the long-term prospects of their position or profession, they might become unhappy and, consequently, a threat to the organization to do the screening. A major risk is the insider threat that occurs when a disgruntled employee, who has both knowledge and access, decides to undermine an organization or to enrich himself or herself at the organization's expense. Thus a significant source of potential damage can be directly attributed to employees' feelings about job security.

Furthermore, the outsourcing of various job functions can affect the remaining employees' sense of job security, particularly if the jobs of those still employed are thought to be at risk. This situation is exacerbated if the outsourced jobs have been moved to an offshore service provider. In the latter case, the foreign country providing the resources is probably a less-developed, low-income country with a high-quality education system and a culture that encourages education, such as in India and China. In this case, a contributing factor to employee concerns is that the displaced workers have virtually no opportunity to be employed by the offshore outsourcer. Indeed a number of countries actively discourage the employment of foreign nationals.[3]

On the other hand, such employment is a possibility with domestic outsourcing, as outsourcers regularly hire staff from the customer organization as a means of importing expertise. In some cases, internal staff is transferred to the outsourcing company as part of the deal. In such a situation, job security in fact increases for certain individuals. When outsourcing is seen as largely a transfer of work and staff from one organizational entity to another, it can be thought of as a zero sum game. In fact, employees who are transferred may find that their future is more assured with the new outsourcing entity, which may be experiencing significant growth in staffing and profitability. The new environment might compare favorably to a more stagnant customer environment.

From a security point of view, such a transfer may be the preferred approach since it can reduce the number of disgruntled employees who could, as stated above, represent a threat to the organization's operation. These individuals are insiders with the knowledge to do real harm to their original parent organization if they so wished. In situations where jobs are lost, particularly when lost to offshore entities, employee resentment can be high and the risk of angry employees and ex-employees taking damaging action is correspondingly high.

The disgruntled employee is a danger in many situations, of which outsourcing is only one. Such resentment is often expressed by current employees who see their jobs disappear and respond by getting back at management and the company through subversive and destructive actions or by trying to capitalize on their inside knowledge. For example, such employees are more

---

3. Transferring existing staff often occurs when situations where the outsourcer, or facility manager, takes over an existing plant, such as a data center. However, it rarely occurs with offshore outsourcing. In fact, countries such as India have refused to allow U.S. workers to take employment, as in the sidebar "No Americans Need Apply" in [2].

likely to engage in fraud or embezzlement or to try to sell valuable proprietary confidential information.

Knowing that such dangers exist, how can the risks be mitigated? One way is to be honest with employees. That does not mean being entirely open and disclosing everything to them—that could undermine the organization as a whole and actually hurt the employees more. No, being honest means either to tell the truth or not say anything. If asked a direct question, management might say that they don't know (if that is the case) or that they are unable to answer the question at this particular time (if the answer must be kept confidential). Also, if possible, having employees involved in the decision-making process might alleviate ill will, if it is seen, for example, that tough decisions involve a survival issue for the organization and are not to be taken personally. Seeing the decision in broader economic terms might reduce hostility towards the organization and its management, and might deflect it towards political leaders, which may be more appropriate in some cases. Of course, the best rationale in the world is not much consolation to someone out of work and thrust into a difficult job market. If the organization can be flexible, it might assign some staff to other functions at the same facility or other locations. All this applies whether the job losses are due to outsourcing, offshore competition, weak economic times, new technologies, or other factors.

One related situation that particularly rankles employees is requiring them to train their replacements at the outsourcer or to stay around in dual mode until the transition to the service provider is complete. Often the magnitude of severance pay is linked to successful training of the replacement. Such an extension of employment, particularly under such hostile circumstances, might lead to damaging action by the employee who is to be let go, or to training in which the trainer omits crucial components, putting the environment at risk.

Transition Issues

Job security is also affected during the outsourcing transition itself, when employees become aware of the transfer of duties and that their employment with the outsourcing company may be for a limited time. During this period, if employees know that their positions are being eliminated internally, they may become difficult, especially if they are asked to train their replacements at the outsourcer. If employees are uncertain as to their future, they represent a danger to the organization in that they may be distracted, become careless, or purposely subvert the company. In any of these situations, threats to security exist that can be protected against even if they are unavoidable.

As mentioned previously, a generous severance, assistance in finding new work, or transfer to another position in the firm often alleviates employees' concerns and thereby reduces the chances that they will consider doing damage. Often, the receipt of at least part of the severance package should be contingent upon the employee agreeing not to take legal action against the employer. This further ensures that the employee will cooperate with the employer and not subvert its reputation or financial health.[4]

While job security, as described earlier, can indirectly affect the security of an organization's information assets, physical and emotional security while working on the job has quite a different impact.

Ameliorating the Concerns of Workers

Companies increasingly have taken on some measure of responsibility not only to protect the physical well-being of staff, but also, to some extent, their emotional, social, and financial states. In some ways, these latter aspects are as important as physical security to the employee. Accepting this responsibility is not purely altruistic on the part of the employer, because it yields considerable payback. For example, if the organization arranges for financial planning seminars or consultations and offers various forms of savings plans, employees may feel more secure financially and therefore be less likely to defraud the company.

Other benefits and services, such as the provision of day care for employees' children, may not have as direct an impact on the employees' financial health, but they can promote a positive and loyal view towards the organization. Employees with access to these benefits are less likely to jeopardize their comfortable status through destructive activities. In particular, assistance for employees who are having a particularly stressful time can result in major attitudinal changes, not only making the employees more productive contributors but also less of a security risk. Such positive support by an organization will deter employees from destructive activities because they have more to lose.

Asset Classification and Control

The categorization of specific information assets is generally the responsibility of the organization that owns the information. However, we are increasingly seeing definitions imposed by regulators, particularly in regard to information about individuals, such as customers or patients. Previously mentioned legislation, such as GLBA and HIPAA in the United States, impose strict requirements for protecting customer and patient data, respectively.

Along with classification of data come requirements for handling it protectively. Legislators and regulators are placing responsibility for protecting nonpublic personal information (NPPI) in the hands of organizations that

---

4. While this type of arrangement is presumably legal, as it is frequently used by conservative organizations, it smacks of bribery and has questionable ethical undertones.

gather such information from individuals, regardless of whether or not that information travels to third parties. Regulators in Europe, the United Kingdom, the United States, and other countries are increasingly demanding that financial and health services institutions, in particular, extend the oversight and protection of such data to when it is received, processed, stored, and distributed by third parties. Such third parties include offshore entities. Regulators also require that institutions be able to provide immediate access at any time to certain data and evidence of controls wherever it resides—internally or externally, domestically or offshore.

Data classes can be defined in various ways. One method is to assess what damage might be inflicted upon the institution, its customers, business partners, and service providers were the information to be accessed and possibly mishandled or misused by those who are not supposed to have access to it. Such unauthorized access might have been gained intentionally or by accident—either way, it is bad news. However, the judgments as to what damage might be incurred and what the chances are that damaging events will take place are highly subjective. In addition, the estimate as to the extent of the damage is extremely difficult to calculate because the harm will likely be to reputation and goodwill, which are particularly hard to quantify. Consequently, organizations usually provide examples of each category of information. In Table 8.2, we define various classifications and offer examples in each category.

The spectrum of asset classification is illustrated in Figure 8.1. As you can see, there are areas of overlap, as certain definitions can cut across several categories.

Once information has been categorized, it is necessary to specify the disposition of such data over its creation, processing, storage, transmission, and disposal, since each category is dealt with differently. We show how such handling applies across various categories of information in Table 8.3.

The data owner or, more likely, the owner of the application that generates and maintains the data establishes classifications for particular information. The importance of the classification is that its handling and disposal policy and procedures must apply whether the information remains within the organization or is passed on to an outsourcer.

Legislators and regulators are increasingly concerning themselves with the protection of data, particularly NPPI, that is in the custody of an organization, whether within itself or in the hands of an outsourcer. Thus, responsibility for the safekeeping of such data and ensuring that it is not allowed to be seen, copied, or misused by unauthorized individuals or organizations, and that confidential data is suitably disposed of, extends beyond an organization's own perimeter into outsourcers, both at home and abroad.

In order for outsourcers to satisfy these demands, they must accommodate the classification definitions and handling policy and procedures of the

Table 8.2
Asset Classification and Examples

Asset Category	Definition	Examples
Public	Information that is generally available in the public domain, the divulgence of which does not impact the organization, its customers, or its business partners.	End-of-day stock prices, newspaper or Web news articles, public Web site content, television and radio announcements.
Internal	Information that is readily accessible by those within the organization, such as employees, contractors, and (probably) service providers, but which is not generally available to the general public, the disclosure of this category is unlikely to damage the organization, its customers, or its business partners.	This category might include high-level descriptions of business systems and processes, from which nothing damaging to reputation and financial health can be developed, such as might otherwise result from disclosure of trade secrets and other intellectual property.
Confidential	Information which, if inappropriately disclosed or misused, could cause substantial harm to the organization, its customers, or its business partners. If such confidential data has to be shared with a third party, a nondisclosure agreement will need to be drawn up and executed, prior to sharing the information.	Confidential information might include such items as internal and external business communications, financial information about the company, its customers, business partners and/or service providers.
Nonpublic Personal	Information relating to individuals that may not be generally available to others and which, if compromised, could be used for bad purposes, including identity theft. If inadvertently disclosed, or otherwise compromised, the disclosure could lead to problems and inconvenience for the individual and loss of reputation for the organization. The organization might also incur costs to notify customers and provide assistance for restoring damaged credit ratings.	Generally includes a combination of information, such as name, address, and Social Security number.

Table 8.2 (continued)

Asset Category	Definition	Examples
Sensitive Personal	Highly personal information that generally should not be collected without a specific, valid reason, and for which the individual has given consent. If inadvertently disclosed, or otherwise compromised, the disclosure could lead to significant unwarranted problems for the individual and major remediation costs for the organization.	Such information might include religion, sexual preferences, and the like.
Secret	Very restricted information which, if disclosed to unauthorized persons, could result in major damage to the organization, its customers, employees, business partners and service providers.	This category might include information about upcoming mergers or acquisitions, detailed business process, intellectual property, employees' salaries.
Top Secret	Highly restricted information that is made available to a very select group and which, if used inappropriately, could result in a major disaster for the organization or others with an interest in the information.	Such information might relate to such areas as national defense (e.g., defense contracts). It could also include crucial intellectual property, such as the formula for Coca-Cola.

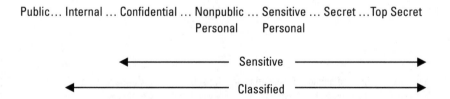

Public... Internal ... Confidential ... Nonpublic ... Sensitive ... Secret ...Top Secret
Personal   Personal

Figure 8.1 Spectrum of asset categories.

customer organization. Therefore, the handling of confidential and nonpublic personal data is the subject of much of the due diligence performed on third parties.

Table 8.3
Creation, Handling, and Disposal of Information by Category

Category	Creation	Handling-Processing-Access	Transmission	Storage	Disposal
Public	General—may be question of information's authenticity.	No special protection—questions of information's integrity and accuracy.	No special protection—question of information's integrity.	No special protection—question of information's integrity.	No special procedures.
Internal	Created by or via internal staff with supervisory review and approval as appropriate.	Designation as to being "for internal use" is desirable.	No special protection—question of integrity.	No special protection—question of integrity.	No special procedures.
Confidential	Created during the course of normal business operations.	Designation of "confidential" is required. Two-factor authentication required for remote access.	Should be encrypted if transmitted over public networks.	May have to be encrypted depending on location and protections in place.	Requires special precautions so as not to divulge content inadvertently, such as shredding paper copies, deleting and overwriting magnetic media such as disks and tapes, and so on.
Nonpublic Personal	Created during the course of normal business operations	Designation of "confidential" is required in all instances. Two-factor authentication required for access.	Must be encrypted if transmitted over public networks.	May have to be encrypted depending on location and protections in place.	Requires special precautions so as not to divulge content inadvertently.

Table 8.3 (continued)

Category	Creation	Handling-Processing-Access	Transmission	Storage	Disposal
Sensitive Personal	Question as to whether it should be collected in the first place. Created during the course of special operations.	Designation of "confidential" or "highly sensitive" is required in all instances. Two-factor authentication required for all access. Access is very limited.	Must be encrypted if transmitted over public networks.	Must be encrypted depending on location and protections in place.	Requires extremely stringent precautions so as not to divulge content inadvertently.
Secret	Created during the course of normal business operations.	Designation of "secret" is required in all instances. Two-factor authentication required for access. Access is restricted.	Must be strongly encrypted if transmitted over public networks.	Must be strongly encrypted depending on location and protections in place.	Requires special precautions so as not to divulge content inadvertently.
Top Secret	Created during the course of normal business operations.	Designation of "top secret" is required in all instances. Two-factor authentication required for access. Access is extremely limited.	Must not be transmitted over a public network.	Must be strongly encrypted at all times.	Requires particularly strict precautions so as not to divulge content inadvertently.

A number of high-profile cases involving third-party organizations, such as the data repository and analysis company Acxiom, have hit the headlines recently. In the Acxiom case, a former employee of a contracting company (i.e., an outsourcer) downloaded an encrypted password file, cracked it, and used this and other privileged information to download data about hundreds of thousands of individuals with accounts at major banks and credit card companies. In another case, several third parties analyzed data about passengers of an airline, Jet Blue, whose data the airline had agreed to share with a government agency in contravention of its own privacy policy. Subsequently, other airlines were found guilty of doing the same. These examples bring us to the issue of security policy and outsourcing.

Information Security Policy

Similarly as for asset classification, an organization can hire a third party to develop its information security policy along with accompanying standards, baselines, guidelines, and procedures. Third parties can also be used to implement a portal through which employees can gain ready access to the organization's policies and standards. External consultants are a recognized medium for introducing industry best practices quickly and efficiently.

First, it is important to differentiate among the various directives and advisories that make up the governance of an organization's information security. Coming up with reasonable definitions is important, since confusion among such directives or advisories makes it difficult to communicate internally and with outside parties. In general, policy is a high-level directive that expresses management's view of appropriate and required behavior under certain circumstances. Policy does not typically change much over time. For example, a information security policy statement is "employees must use company-provided electronic mail for business purposes." Probably, such a policy would not change over time, except when newer technologies, such as instant messaging, arise and cause the policy to be expanded to accommodate them. However, if the policy is stated in open-ended terms, such as "all forms of company-provided electronic communications, including e-mail, instant messaging," the policy will usually remain in its original form longer. But even so, new technologies and new uses of existing technologies might result in its revision.

Policy is more resilient to change than standards, which represent means of implementing policy. For example, a policy may state that "individuals must access data on a need-to-know basis." This will have a myriad of implications in terms of access control—which includes identity management or authentication and provisioning or authorization, as well as the mechanisms that facilitate these controls. When the need-to-know policy is applied at the application and operating system levels, it must be expressed within the standards, baselines, guidelines, and procedures that cover the specific architecture and hardware and software configurations.

When dealing with an outsourcer, an organization must ensure that the service provider complies with the customers' security policies where appropriate. Compliance can be achieved in a number of ways, which are described below.

Adopt Customer Policy

The service might agree to adhere to relevant customer policy in its entirety. This is the simplest approach from the point of view of the customer, but might entail considerable effort by the outsourcer, depending on the number and size of the gaps between the two sets of policy. There may also be national, regional, and local regulations that restrict whether the service provider can follow certain policy items.

Adopt Service Provider's Policy

The customer might agree to adopt the service provider's policy if the latter meets industry standards and is considered superior to the policy of the customer. It is quite likely that the service provider will have better policy, standards, and procedures, because they must satisfy many customers.

Evaluate Responses to Due-Diligence Questionnaire

If neither customer nor service provider is willing to share policy, standards, and procedures, the customer needs to determine the degree to which the service provider's policy, standards, and procedures meet its requirements by asking a series of questions as to the handling of various situations. Table 8.4 gives examples of security policy and standards and includes comments regarding their application and audience.

Enforcement and Compliance

The prospective customer, when evaluating policy, standards, and procedures of service providers, must carefully discern between the documented rules and how well they have been enforced and how well they are followed. Developing the rules is easy—making them happen is quite another matter. One of the better means of determining the quality of adherence to policy, standards, and baselines is to have a third party—an auditor or other assessor—review them to determine whether procedures are in place to ensure compliance and that such procedures are continually reviewed.

Table 8.4
Examples of Directives by Type

Type of Directive	Examples	Comments
Policy	Electronic mail, Internet use, remote access.	Generally applies to end-users, be they employed by the organization or doing work for it on a contractual basis (i.e., contractor, consultant, service provider).
		Minimal changes to policy over an extended period of time.
Standard	Operating systems—such as Unix, Windows, Linux—on servers, desktop personal computers, and laptops.	More technical, though still somewhat generic.
	Firewalls, routers, wireless.	Aimed at more technical staff.
	Following a standard somewhat ensures that control is maintained over how software and hardware are configured. This facilitates changes and emergency updates, if needed.	Likely to change only if there is a major new release of software or equipment.
Baseline	A specific implementation, which is expected to be followed closely, of a standard to, say, a particular version of an operating system (e.g., Windows, Unix, Linux).	Even more technical than standards and specific to a particular environment and version of software.
		Will likely have to be updated quite frequently, perhaps every few months as vendors modify their software and come out with new versions, often containing corrections to prior versions.
Guideline	A suggested means of following a standard that is proposed as a good approach but is not enforced to the same degree as a standard or baseline.	This type of suggested standard is meant for environments that require some measure of flexibility and variability.
Process	A relatively high-level series of tasks that is designed to enable those within the organization to comply with policy.	A process is to a procedure much as a policy is to a standard. The process is a management view of activities, whereas a procedure is specific to the person or persons performing the tasks.
Procedure	A lower-level process which generally captures a particular aspect or component of a process.	Procedures are usually required to be followed in detail and may involve many serial, and some parallel, steps, often requiring that forms are completed and/or checks are made to ensure that the procedure has taken place satisfactorily, or if not, the procedure delineates subsequent steps to recover from and repair error conditions.

Access Control and Identity Protection

Perhaps the most important aspect of security is control of access to an organization's information assets, as required in HIPAA and GLBA in the United States, as well as comparable non-U.S. laws such as the EU Directive and U.K. Data Protection law. This area is the cause for the greatest concern by individuals as well as legislators and regulators. Identity theft, which is the capture and use of other people's identifying information, usually to commit fraud, is epidemic. Not only does identity theft result in significant monetary losses, but the inconvenience, anguish, time, and effort that accompany it and remedies in response to it exact a huge toll on the general population and business. Furthermore, there is the recent recognition that individuals' or customers' nonpublic personal information is passed from one party to another, so that ensuring adequate protection by third parties is equally important.

The factors that protect persons' identities and the information that relates to them include authentication, authorization, and access management and control.

Methods of authentication, or means of knowing that someone is who he or she claims to be, take many forms, such as:

- Identifying codes along with passwords, magnetic cards, and security tokens (such as cards that change password displays every minute);
- Electronic certificates;
- Biometric features (e.g., fingerprints, retina scans);
- Other personal information (e.g., mother's maiden name, month of birth);
- Information readily familiar to the person but not to others (e.g., favorite color, favorite breed of dog);
- Out-of-wallet information (e.g., mortgage lender, car loan payments);
- Two-factor authentication (such as password and ID card).

These methods of authentication are summarized in relation to security level, technology, and cost in Table 8.5.

When someone or some system has been satisfactorily identified, they can then be given access to information and functionality (such as trading stocks, transferring money, or making purchases). Controlling who is entitled to access is without question the most demanding and difficult aspect of electronic commerce and system management faced by organizations today. It becomes additionally complex and difficult when a number of parties are involved, particularly outsourcers. Not only do the customers have access to information

Table 8.5
Relationship Between Access Control Security Level and Other Factors

Security Level	Representative Technology	Relative Cost	Examples of Areas of Application
Low	Identifier (ID) and password	Low cost of implementation. High cost of support.	Internet Web sites. General internal organization accesses.
Medium	Magnetic card and PIN (personal identification number)	Somewhat costly to implement (cost of card and its distribution and replacement). Relatively low support costs.	Automated bank teller machines.
High	Physical or software tokens Biometrics	High cost of implementation. Moderate-to-low support costs.	Access to sensitive or highly protected physical areas (e.g., data centers and sensitive applications).

and functionality, but so do many employees within the various processing organizations both within and external to an organization. It is important to ensure that the screening and background checks of all these employees are current, accurate, and complete. This is difficult enough to do with on-site employees, but is even more difficult for contractors, consultants, and employees of service providers, particularly those located in a distant country.

As mentioned earlier, U.S. regulators, particularly those with oversight responsibility for U.S. financial institutions (such as the Federal Reserve, the Office of the Comptroller of the Currency (OCC), and the Securities and Exchange Commission), as well as regulators in Europe, the United Kingdom, and other countries, are increasingly requiring executive management and boards of directors to bear direct responsibility for ensuring the protection of customer information and to answer for any deficiencies. The OCC, for example, has issued specific guidance for banks' transactions with service providers both domestically and abroad [3, 4].

The State of California pioneered stringent requirements in its recent law, SB 1386, which requires companies to notify customers living in California if they believe that customers' information has been compromised. Other states have considered passing similar laws, and, at the national level, several Federal banking agencies have issued proposed interagency guidance relating to the protection of sensitive customer information and the consequent notification of customers if their data is compromised. The latter is based on GLBA.

As legislators and regulators raise the bar on unauthorized access to and misuse of customer-sensitive nonpublic personal information, the need to ensure that service providers are taking the necessary protective steps becomes much more important as the price to be paid for failure, in monetary terms and loss of reputation, is continually increasing.

Application and System Development

Organizations frequently have third parties develop applications for them, and more and more they look to send that development, testing, and implementation offshore, especially to India, which has developed a large base of professionals with strong technical knowledge. This base is increasing rapidly as technical colleges and universities churn out record numbers of graduates. The combination of highly trained individuals, greatly improved infrastructure, and less-costly communications (particularly over the Internet) has served to promote cost-effective offshore development, despite increased overhead and logistics issues.

Application and system development has always been outsourced in order to gain expertise that may not be available at all or not available in sufficient quantities in-house. The big push into offshore programming came prior to 2000, when a huge demand for modifying programs to be Y2K-compliant forced organizations in North America and Europe, in particular, to seek help abroad. However, the initial motivation of a skills shortage has changed into one of cost reduction, as countries such as India, Singapore, and others are able to provide quality work at a small fraction of the cost of domestic U.S. and European IT workers.

A number of security concerns arise when outsourcing programming work both domestically and offshore. During the Y2K remediation effort, the fear arose that source code had been sent out to third parties and also that "back doors" had been written into software programs.[5] Back doors allow those familiar with them to gain unauthorized access to operating computer programs for purposes of doing harm, stealing information, or using the access to gain further access to other critical applications and data. Another risk is that theft of intellectual property will be used for competitive economic advantage.

As application development outsourcers increase their skill levels, they "move up the food chain" and work with and develop increasing critical

---

5. On page 37 of his book, Dan Verton suggests that it is highly likely that such malicious program code was inserted into remediated programs to enable a foreign agent to activate the code and gain access to, and control of, the computer applications at some future date [5].

applications, and they go beyond pure coding into system integration, testing, quality assurance, and the transition of applications from development and testing to production. I call this "function creep," and it can result in the outsourcer gaining increasingly detailed knowledge of systems supporting critical businesses. Suddenly the risk profile changes dramatically with the potential of large-scale compromise and destruction of critical parts of the infrastructure. Such increases in dependency can alter the "balance of power," making it extremely difficult for companies to extricate themselves should the political climate change for the worse.

Operations Security and Operational Risk

Every outsourced service contains some operational and administrative components, whether they consist of monitoring security devices, running computer applications, entering data, producing reports, or billing for services rendered. These comprise the typical human and human-machine activities and procedures that actually produce and manage the services. Whenever there is human involvement in a process, there is risk. Human participation means more significant risk of error, greater variations in quality, and differences in time to produce the service. It also entails the full range of security-related risks, including fraud, theft, damage, destruction, misuse, misrepresentation, unauthorized access, and inappropriate disclosure.

While electronic, electrical, and mechanical machines are far from perfect, they provide levels of reproducibility and consistency beyond which human beings are generally capable. Furthermore, machines are not intrinsically malevolent, although they can be programmed to be so.

Human-originated lapses, whether direct or indirect, may result in risk exposures and security breaches. Such human influences are exacerbated when third parties are involved. The client has relatively little control over who is employed by the service provider and comparatively little oversight as to what they are doing. This issue can be even greater when the facilities and workers providing the services are offshore, often thousands of miles distant, in a different culture with different values and laws and different ways of dealing with employees and others who commit crimes.

The methods of mitigating such operational risk, whether the service is domestic or offshore, include imposing control, improving training and awareness, and monitoring activities. Organizations, particularly financial institutions, increasingly delve deeply into the policies and procedures of their service providers to ensure the institutions' standards are met. I have used automated tools that were very effective in controlling the operation of remote third-party computer systems. Today it seems that U.S. banks in particular are being told by regulators that they are fully responsible for how third parties handle their customers' information. The best way of managing such processes is to have close oversight and, to the extent possible, a measure of direct control over third-party processes.

Security Models and Architecture

There is increasing recognition that an organization should build a specific security architecture in terms of *security services* being made available (such as authentication, authorization, monitoring and auditing, and administrative services), as well as the *structure of information security components* (such as the configuration of firewalls, routers, and intrusion detection systems) and *security management tools and services* (such as network scanning and vulnerability assessment).

Security Services—Framework

The basic objective of developing a security framework, into which to plug security-related modules that perform security services, is to increase control of security functions and reduce the cost and time-to-market of applications. A framework is different from an infrastructure in that a *security framework* is the substructure to which the various security services modules, such as purchased authentication and authorization software products or homegrown software, are attached. These modules should be replaceable without disturbing the overall structure or having to modify application programs to any significant degree. This means that, from a *security architecture* viewpoint, security services are not to be built into the applications themselves, but the applications should call upon the services as needed. This provides much more flexibility as to which services to implement, as well as much more control over a standardized security environment.

Security Infrastructure

On the other hand, a *security infrastructure* is the combination of security policies, standards, procedures, and devices (hardware, software or both) that make up deterrence, avoidance, prevention, protection, monitoring, reporting, and responding capabilities within the information technology functions of an organization. For example, the combination of intrusion detection and protection systems, personal and enterprise firewalls, desktop and gateway antivirus software, e-mail screening and blocking software or services, and Web-site blocking facilities represent physical renditions of security infrastructures.

Conversely, the establishment, awareness, and enforcement of policies, standards, and procedures characterize human and logical security.

Security Management and Control

Overlaid on the above are the *security management* functions, which comprise the management, control, and response aspects of operating the physical components of the security infrastructure. Additionally, the *security policy enforcement* functions consist of awareness, training, formal acceptance of policy, standards, and procedures by subjects (i.e., employees, contractors, and service providers) and the monitoring, auditing, and reporting of compliance. We briefly look at the various items in this regard.

Framework

The situations in which third parties might get involved with the framework are as consultants establishing the framework, helping to build it, and working to incorporate the various security services into the framework, as described in [6].

Such a framework comprises both a set of design standards and a physical realization of those standards, either in a commercial off-the-shelf (COTS) product or in custom-built software, developed internally or externally or through a combination of internal and external efforts.

The framework is a method of incorporating security services into the overall application system and network architectures of the organization, if they exist. The services might be in the form of software or product, such as a fingerprint reader and accompanying user registration and authentication software. Or actual services might exist, such as a third party performing the technical and management functions, as is the case in the models for public key infrastructure (PKI).[6]

Application to Service Providers

How do these models apply to third parties providing services to an organization? Ideally, any service provider will be in compliance with the policy and standards of the customer, and its architecture will be compatible with that of the customer organization. To the extent that this is not feasible—due to, for example, technology or cost restrictions or legal and regulatory requirements—

---

6. Public key infrastructure (PKI) has had a somewhat jaded history due to its complexity, cost, and lack of acceptance. Vendors have provided both the software to perform the functional and administrative tasks in-house, as well as offering PKI as a turnkey service.

accommodations that are acceptable to both parties, but particularly the customer, must be made.

The underlying approach here is to consider how any security-related services and products that have architectural and framework implications might be plugged into the framework or how they might fit within the overall security architecture and management and control systems. For example, an organization might be confronted with selecting a security access administration package, which comprises authentication and authorization components. Or an organization could be assessing whether outsourcing the help desk function makes both economic and operational sense. In both these cases, consideration must be given as to whether the functions fit into the existing infrastructure and can interface effectively with installed end-user and systems applications and computer operating systems.

Verification that this is the case in each situation may require a number of actions to be taken in the due diligence and proof-of-concept stages. Compatibility of products with the existing standards and infrastructure is determined by a review of the product's technical specifications followed by a well-crafted pilot test, if practicable, for products that meet specifications, such as compatibility with installed platforms (e.g., Microsoft Windows and Unix). Whether a product fits within the framework is determined by examining the types of interfaces available between the product and the framework and other components.

The same criteria apply when considering acquisition of management and control products to be run at either the customer's or service provider's sites, or both—the last being cosourcing. For example, an MSSP might monitor intrusion detection systems and firewalls installed on the customer's facilities or arrange for monitoring consoles to be installed both at the customer site and in the MSSP's facility. Which structure is selected will depend on the availability of expertise and resources at the customer. Also, the actual security devices may be located off-site, with the third-party provider hosting network and system assets and their corresponding protective products.

In all of these situations, compliance with customer policy and standards and compatibility with the customer's infrastructure are all important. If there are reasons why compliance cannot happen, the exceptions must be noted and risk-mitigating processes and systems must be put in place.

Physical and Environmental Security

As previously stated, it is common to outsource physical security for the protection of an organization's physical assets, whether or not specific assets have an information component. In fact, many security arrangements are decidedly low tech. However, the trend in physical access and environmental monitoring is toward remote centralized management and control, and the direction of such technology and related economics leads to unmanned guard stations being remotely managed from third-party facilities, including those at offshore locations.

Furthermore, as the control of physical access converges with access control for information assets, the nature of such functions is changing to pave the way for integrated physical and logical security. As the security system evolves to be all-encompassing, it will require a different kind of broadly based security firm to handle the nuances of a multidisciplined access management system. In some regards, this requirement pushes the consideration of outsourcers, since they are likely to have the requisite skills.[7] On the other hand, organizations may be reluctant to entrust so much of their security access to third parties, particularly a single third party as suggested by integrated systems.

Another aspect to consider, which might favor using a third party, is handling emergency situations in which disaster recovery plans are invoked. Here, an outsourcer might be able to cover a number of customer locations from its own control center, and thus easily switch the customer's security from a primary to backup location. This is very much preferable to trying to deal with the transfer of security functions within the organization, which exposes the company to a series of risks as described in my paper on the subject [7].

Telecommunications and Network Security

Telecommunications is among the earliest technology-based areas outsourced on a large scale. For example, the brokerage house Merrill Lynch gave up the deployment and management of its global voice and data networks to a major telecommunications company, as did Bankers Trust (which was later acquired by Deutsche Bank). These companies recognized the cost and difficulty of establishing and maintaining a global support and management function to handle communications with internal staff. They also realized that global telecommunications companies were better situated to handle the job, having already provisioned advanced centers throughout the world to handle their own requirements. So the match between customer and outsourcer appeared to be ideal.

Back then, prior to the Internet, high-speed, high-volume networks were made up of dedicated leased lines. Security of those lines was not a major issue as

---

7. An example of such a company is Kroll Associates, which started out in the physical protection field and diversified into information security. It seems less likely that an information security firm will migrate over to the physical side. However, as physical security becomes more computerized, this latter trend might develop.

access was restricted at either end. Important factors at that time (and today where dedicated lines are installed) were high availability and the rapid deployment and repair of lines. Recently, with increasing use of public lines as a means of significantly reducing communications costs, particularly over long distances, use of the Internet has greatly increased. This phenomenon raises the issue of securing the capacity used within the public networks and monitoring them to ensure secure traffic.

In response to this need, some companies set up security operating centers (SOCs), each staffed by persons with particular specialty knowledge. SOCs are more specialized than network operating centers (NOCs). Some security-consulting firms established their own SOCs and operated then as MSSPs, with the primary purpose of managing security devices such as firewalls, routers, and intrusion detection/prevention systems, for customer organizations.[8]

The nature of network security services provided now covers a broad range of device locations, device management, and event detection and response. System configurations vary from having devices at the customer's site, the outsourcer's facility, or both. The service provider will usually handle monitoring and reporting, but some customers favor a cosourcing arrangement whereby both the customer and outsourcer have control consoles and share management of the devices. I have always thought that sharing based on time of day and day of week makes sense, with internal staff providing the bulk of support during prime business hours and handing over control to the outsourcer for nights, weekends, and holidays. In this way, a certain level of expertise is retained in-house, so that the customer does not depend completely on the third party, which situation represents a risk, as described earlier. Some service providers report an event and leave it up to the client to follow up with notification of business units and the client's customers, along with remediation and restoration. In other cases, the outsourcer will provide full incident response support.

There is an increasing trend towards linking SOCs to NOCs, as well as merging their physical entities. Increasingly, security-only tools "talk to" network management software, and network engineers are becoming more familiar with the management and use of security monitoring, analysis, and reporting tools. Indeed, many security devices are implemented and controlled by the telecommunications staff. As discussed later, frequently network administrators first detect a security incident, raise the alert, and bring in the security team to assist, based on their specialized knowledge. The security team, on the other hand, is attuned to monitoring events in the outside world and

---

8. Among the early providers of security management services were Counterpane and ISS (Internet Security Systems), for which the services are based on specific security expertise.

determining any possible effects on the organization resulting from attacks on known vulnerabilities.

To date, most outsourcing has followed organizational lines, with security and networks being handled by different groups. Increasingly, with the merger of the operational aspects of security into the network and system environments, the line between security and networks is becoming fuzzy. We are likely to see a trend towards network carriers and Internet service providers (ISPs) providing more specialized security services. From technical and organizational perspectives, this makes a lot of sense, but it does increase the number of eggs in a single basket, and therefore increases the risk to the client organization if the service provider experiences viability or operational difficulties.

The main drivers towards outsourcing are a dearth of experts and lower cost for 24/7 coverage than for in-house operation. The major concerns are putting such critical functions into outsiders' hands.

Cryptography

When computer cryptography was developed, it was considered a product to be bought and applied to a particular situation. That seemed to work when the methods were quite distinct and highly technical in nature and where the actual transfer of encrypted data was sparse and the methods could be handled without setting up an expensive and complex administrative function. The situation changed markedly with the introduction of public key infrastructure (PKI), which immediately involved establishing a number of administrative functions and entities to authenticate users, and manage keys (e.g., issuance, registration, tracking, and revoking). The scaling up of the use of PKI made for huge implementation and management efforts, with complex rules and difficult handling of the various required functions. Therefore, a number of companies began offering turnkey management of PKI for large, medium-sized, and small organizations. Some of these same service providers offered to sell the product and have customers manage their own environments.

One of the major issues surrounding PKI and similar implementations is the high-level of trust that must be bestowed upon certificate authorities (CAs), whose function is to issue, protect, and revoke encryption keys. If the databases held by a CA are compromised, the intrusion leads to significant loss of credibility and a major problem for the customer organization, which must have keys revoked and reissued. Such a breach did in fact take place and was broadly publicized when several keys belonging to Microsoft were compromised through a VeriSign facility that inadvertently gave keys to unauthorized individuals [8].

Disaster Recovery and Business Continuity

Despite organizations' best efforts, disasters do take place, usually with security implications. To account for such events, firms maintain business continuity and disaster recovery plans, which are collectively referred to as contingency plans.

Disaster recovery and business continuity comprise several phases. The first is an analysis of the business impact of losing certain facilities and capabilities, followed by the development of a proposed plan for developing, implementing, and maintaining disaster recovery and business continuity plans. For our purposes, disaster recovery is the reaction to a loss of major computer and operational support capabilities, by relying on backup facilities when the primary site is out of action. On the other hand, business continuity relates to maintaining business capabilities if primary locations or capabilities of primary locations are disrupted and rendered inoperable.

Business Impact Analysis

Business continuity and disaster recovery plans should be based on sound risk analyses which compare the potential losses resulting from an incident, such as a fire or flood, compared to the cost of providing backup facilities. Such a business impact analysis (BIA) can be performed internally, using one of the many tools available in the marketplace, but this responsibility is often given to outside experts who specialize in such evaluations, often using proprietary tools.

Planning

Creating a business continuity and disaster recovery plan can be done in-house, but it is usually much easier and cost-effective to engage a third party to develop and maintain the plans. Maintenance is the most important factor, because such plans are often ignored after being enthusiastically put together. A third party can inject the discipline needed to keep the plans current.

Implementation and Testing

While putting together a plan and keeping it current are important, even more so is testing the plan periodically to ensure that it will work when needed. The testing and resulting revisions to the plan keep it viable. And the periodic retesting of the plan is required to ensure that it accounts for any changes in the business and systems environments.

Again, a third party might assist in the testing process, especially if the testing goes beyond the boundaries of the organization and involves business partners, suppliers, and others. Increasingly, organizations, particular large financial services companies, recognize the importance of testing business continuity and disaster recovery plans with their business partners.

Because provision of backup facilities that reasonably mimic the primary facilities can be extremely costly, it is common to engage a third party to provide backup facilities, which are generally shared among a number of customers. In this way, the high cost of building and maintaining the disaster recovery and business continuity facilities, systems, and networks is spread over a number of customers, while still providing reasonable assurance that the facilities will be available to all customers in the event of a regional disaster.

When third parties are retained for disaster backup and business continuity purposes, it is very important to protect the confidentiality of the organization's customer data and other sensitive and proprietary information, in particular throughout the recovery and restoration processes. It is highly likely that such data will, in the course of a recovery process, reside on shared computer resources. Establishing such trustworthiness at the service provider is not easy, but it is important. This can be achieved largely by means of a thorough due-diligence evaluation of the outsourcer, including understanding its security policy, standards, and procedures and reviewing physical security, application, system, and network security, and operational integrity and resiliency. In addition, secure procedures need to be set up and reviewed periodically.

Legal Action

Of all the areas covered here, perhaps the one most needing specific expertise is taking legal action when something has gone badly wrong, especially with respect to one's service provider. But legal advice should be sought well before there are indications of problems; it should be sought when the relationship is being created and contracts are being negotiated. Internal counsel, if available, can handle these issues; otherwise outside counsel must be retained.

If something bad does happen, despite precautions taken, a clear-cut investigation is needed, allowing for adequate information to be gathered and reported. Again, outside experts will often be called in because of their understanding of the due process of law. It is also important to gather uncontaminated evidence for the eventuality of a prosecution. It is so much more difficult to achieve this if the offending entity is a third-party service provider, especially when it is under another country's jurisdiction.

Summary

In this chapter, we have looked in depth at a broad array of security issues surrounding outsourcing decisions and operations. In the past, the level of trust of third parties seemed higher, but that may have been because the latitude available for misusing and damaging information and information systems was much less. Today our systems and processes are more tightly coupled and spread across the world, and much more of our critical information is at risk. It behooves us to recognize the security risks inherent in these new business models and to take the precautions necessary to mitigate those risks, since if they cannot be completely eliminated.

References

[1]   Koch, C., "Hand Over Security," *CIO Magazine,* Vol. 17, No. 13, April 15, 2004, pp. 48–54.

[2]   Worthen, B., "The Radicalization of Mike Emmons," *CIO Magazine,* Vol. 16, No. 22, September 1, 2003.

[3]   "Third-Party Relationships: Risk Management Principles," *OCC Bulletin 2001-47,* Office of the Comptroller of the Currency, U.S. Department of the Treasury, November 1, 2001, http://www.occ.treas.gov/ftp/bulletin/2001-47.txt.

[4]   "Bank Use of Foreign-Based Third-Party Service Providers: Risk Management Guidance," *OCC Bulletin 2002-16,* Office of the Comptroller of the Currency, U.S. Department of the Treasury, May 15, 2002, http://www.occ.treas.gov/ftp/bulletin/2002-16.txt.

[5]   Verton, D., *Black Ice: The Invisible Threat of Cyber-Terrorism,* Emeryville, CA: McGraw-Hill/Osborne, 2003.

[6]   Hartman, B., et al., *Mastering Web Services Security,* New York: John Wiley & Sons, Inc., 2003.

[7]   Axelrod, C. W., "Systems and Communications Security During Recovery and Repair," in *Business Continuity Planning: Protecting Your Organization's Life,* K. Doughty, (ed.), Boca Raton, CRC Press, FL: Auerbach Best Practices Series, 2000.

[8]   Lemos, R., "Microsoft Warns of Hijacked Certificates," *C-Net News.Com,* March 22, 2001, http://news.com.com/2100-1001-254586.html.

9

Summary of the Outsourcing Process—Soup to Nuts

Throughout the book, we have looked into various security aspects and components of the outsourcing decision. In this chapter, we will go through the steps in the process and describe how they relate to one another. This will enable the reader to put the various concepts, evaluations, and decisions into the context of an overall process. The events, tasks, and steps (or phases) that make up the typical outsourcing process are:

1. *Observe and respond to a trigger event.* Such an event causes someone in the organization (usually a member of the senior management team) to focus on a business or operational need for a particular enhanced or modified function or activity or to enter a new line of business. Similarly, in a start-up situation, the initiation of a new business or other form of organization might result in the need to consider outsourcing at the outset rather than establishing certain functions internally. Over time, a growing company determines that, at a certain level of activity, it might make more sense to consider internalizing certain outsourced functions. Typical events might include market forces or regulatory requirements. For example, for financial institutions, the burden of new regulations might make firms consider outsourcing some of their operational and IT functions rather than attempt to comply on their own. Here economies of scale will likely predominate. In other cases, the news that a large firm has outsourced a major function, to an MSSP, for instance, might get other firms' management teams to think along the same lines.

2. *Determine the actual business or operational need for the existing or suggested service or function.* This first step is important. Before making an outsourcing decision, the function or business must be justified in its own right, usually in the form of a business plan. There has to be a "leap of faith" in the business plan, since it might assume the use of service providers for various functions prior to actually determining the feasibility and cost-effectiveness of such decisions.

3. *Determine the scope, service requirements, and possible means of providing service.* This is the next level down from the business plan. If the plan is accepted in principle, the effort necessary to backfill the details is worthwhile. The full range of options for the service needs to be determined, whether internal, external or joint (cosourced), and whether the provider is domestic, near-shore or offshore, small or large, or relatively new or established.

4. *Perform research to determine the degree to which specific services are outsourced.* Find out about experiences others may have had with specific outsourcers and outsourcing in general. Today, the Internet is a rich source of free information through news and magazine articles, discussion forums, and associations. In addition, many conferences, proprietary research papers, books, and other commercially available items can be accessed. Through these resources, an organization gains access to the analysis and opinions of experts and, at conferences, seminars, and vendor-supported presentations, one can discuss experiences with peers as well as the speakers and panelists. Today, there are specialty conferences about outsourcing across all lines of business and government as well as industry-specific meetings. Each has its benefits. I have listed relevant books, articles, papers, conferences, Web sites, and other sources in the Selected Bibliography.

5. *Determine whether outsourcing is a feasible alternative as a result of the research.* In general, there will be favorable and negative views and experiences. However, changes of opinion are relatively inexpensive in the discovery and analysis phases. Once an organization embarks on the subsequent phases, a measure of commitment results from the investment in time and energy made to date. This alone can greatly influence the decision. After all, if someone or a team has spent months investigating the outsourcing alternative, it would be disappointing to realize that it is not feasible or is ineffective, and the effort would appear to have been a waste of time. Therefore, there is a self-fulfilling aspect of the process that should be recognized and removed. In any event, let us assume that the research has pointed to the

feasibility and potential benefit of outsourcing, so that we can proceed to the next step.

6. *Prepare and send out a Request for Information (RFI) to outsourcing service providers.* While good research can provide substantial information, particularly as to who the major players might be, there is no real substitute for the more detailed information that can only be obtained from the service providers themselves. Nevertheless, the cost of issuing and analyzing an RFI is not always justified. Depending upon the size of the potential service contract as well as the riskiness of the arrangement, or if the activity to be outsourced is highly critical, more detailed information may be warranted. Assuming that an RFI is worthwhile, it should be carefully crafted to provide all necessary information.

7. *Collect information from providers and perform preliminary analysis.* The results from analyzing the data obtained from the RFI will likely support or refute the original idea to consider outsourcing. If necessary, it is better to abandon the idea of outsourcing at this point, where the time and effort has been relatively small, than to invest further resources in the evaluation. However, if the outsourcing approach still appears feasible and cost-effective, it supports the decision to proceed to the next step, since the question is no longer "should we?" but "who should we use?"

8. *Prepare and distribute a Request for Proposal (RFP).* To many, the RFI and RFP are seen as interchangeable, but there are (or should be) major differences between them. Information that is included in the RFP will often appear in the final agreement negotiated between outsourcer and customer. And information that is excluded from the RFP will sometimes need to be included in the final agreement. Therefore, it behooves the RFP writer to think ahead about what terms and conditions will be requested during contract negotiation and to include such items, specified as wanted, in the RFP. It is not unusual to attach the proposal received in response to the RFP within, or appended to, the actual service agreement. Secondly, it is important to prescreen recipients of the RFP so that, if they respond with an appealing offering, you are not dealing with an unreliable provider, especially one with a bad reputation. Were one of the latter to respond with an attractive price and other good terms, it becomes most difficult to explain to superiors why that provider should not be chosen. On the other hand, it is important to send RFPs to a fairly large selection of vendors to get a good feel for what is being offered under what terms and conditions. The RFP should require that proposals be received by a specific time and date. This avoids stragglers and provides some

assurance that an early and prompt response represents an eager and responsible provider.

9. *Since the receipt of proposals is fraught with potential problems, it must be handled in a formal manner.* The date and time of receipt of the physical proposal, whether on paper, on other media or in electronic form, should be carefully logged, particularly for those proposals received at a time close to the suggested deadline. Heated arguments might occur if a provider is eliminated due to purported late submission, and so the decision should be made in advance as to what extenuating factors will and will not be acceptable. For example, a regional blackout may be an acceptable reason for delaying the deadline, whereas the provider claiming that their PC crashed and the document was lost may or may not be considered reasonable. In any event, some population of proposals will have been received and are then subject to analysis and evaluation.

10. *The customer should perform preliminary and in-depth evaluations of the proposals received.* An initial scan of the proposals might eliminate some outliers. Perhaps the charges are far in excess of other reputable bids or the proposal may lack key ingredients. Even the professionalism of the form of the proposal may indicate a questionable outsourcer, although one must beware of the impressive, elaborate, expensive proposal that contains little of substance. In other situations, the outsourcer may not have followed the guidelines for format and content and may have omitted key sections or ancillary documents, but instead submitted their own boilerplate. Again, the requestor has an opportunity to decide whether or not the submission is acceptable or should be rejected based on such differences. However, the requestor should consider being flexible enough to allow for bidders to make up moderate deficiencies within a specified time frame, so as not to disadvantage those who got the requirements right the first time. Ideally, all bidders will have submitted proposals exactly in conformance with the specified format, since this makes the analysis so much simpler. However, the requestor should realize that their RFP will not have considered everything, or that the format precluded the inclusion of important information, and adjust accordingly. In some cases, a provider might raise an important issue that was not included in the RFP, so that it then becomes necessary to request additional information from all bidders. The right balance between structure and flexibility must be achieved, but this is not easy to do.

11. *Having gone through each the proposals and eliminated some in an initial scan and others after more detailed analysis, the requestor should then select*

a short list of three or four top contenders. A polite note should be sent to those not making the short list, thanking them for their efforts, complimenting them on their submissions, regretting that they did not make the short list, and assuring them that they will be kept in mind for future projects. The note might indicate that, should the process not select among the remaining vendors, other applicants would be reconsidered—there is nothing to be gained in burning bridges. It has indeed happened that leading contenders have been eliminated for one reason or another, and that it has been necessary to revisit those outsourcers who did not make the short list initially. After all, it is apparent that, for many of the proposals, considerable effort and cost were expended, so that a brief thank-you note is warranted. It is important to note here that the RFP should contain language indicating that the requesting company will not be liable for any costs incurred by the bidder in responding the RFP. An organization does not want to be pressured by bidders because of their investment to date in the process.

12. *At this point, it is usual to review the proposals from the short list in greater detail.* This might involve investing in credit checks and other financial analyses, and calling or preferably visiting references,[1] having the bidders come on site to make presentations of their proposals and answer questions, and visiting the providers' own facilities or facilities they manage for others. The degree to which this is done depends very much on the magnitude of the deal and its criticality to the business. Clearly, for those on the short list, significant costs are incurred, and the requestor also incurs the cost of site visits. Consequently, this additional review should only be done for serious candidates, and it should be emphasized to them that their costs in responding will not be covered. An organization should make it a policy not to have service providers pay for visits by potential customers to their facilities or for other work done in regard to evaluating their proposals, as this can cause problems if the service provider is not chosen. The service provider might well apply pressure to an organization to select them based on such monies spent in the proposal stage.

13. *Ultimately and usually, only one outsourcer is selected as the preferred vendor.* This means having to notify the others that they were not chosen.

---

1. Even a visit to a customer site is no guarantee of an honest tour. I experienced a situation in which an employee of the vendor masqueraded as an employee of the reference company. Obviously, the opinion of the "customer" was a glowing one. It was only because I knew someone at the reference company and called him directly that the fraud was uncovered.

Here, it might be appropriate to make a personal call as well as send a thank-you note. The final contenders will have put even more effort and money into this effort. Showing appreciation is the right thing to do, and maintaining good relationships with the other vendors will be important if the deal with the number-one choice is not consummated or if proposals are sought from them in the future.

14. *By the time the selection has been made, many of the terms and conditions of the SLA should have been decided.* In fact, it might well be appropriate to begin discussions with those who are still under consideration on the agreement at the point the short list is named. However, it is not until the final selection is made that one can formally initiate serious negotiations of the SLA. This stage should not entail any surprises, but often does. Attention will not generally have been focused on this area, and when it is, new issues will surely arise.

15. *This is also the time to perform an in-depth due diligence of the selected outsourcer.* This is usually accomplished through one or more site visits; completion of questionnaires about such aspects as security posture and practices, network, and system architectures; typical processes for answering day-to-day questions; and procedures to respond to incidents (such as system outages or compromises). A very extensive and complete questionnaire, designed for U.S. financial institutions and called the "Expectations Matrix" is available on the BITS Web site at http://www.bitsinfo.org. The narrower the field of contestants, the more the analysis, so that with one choice to deal with, the effort to ensure that no problems will be uncovered later can be very large, depending again on magnitude and criticality of the project. It is important to remember here that these costs should have been anticipated and included in the original outsourcing analysis.

16. Once the appropriate due diligence and analysis have been done, and the terms and conditions of the contract with preferred service provider have been agreed to by everyone involved, *the contract is executed and work begins on setting up the newly agreed-upon relationship.*

17. *The transition or conversion period during which a service is cut over from an internal to external provider, from another provider, or from "scratch," must be carefully and closely managed to ensure that it goes smoothly and meets everyone's expectations.* This phase should be fully scripted in advance with individual tasks, accomplishments, and milestones specified in a project work plan. Progress should be reported against the plan, with mitigating actions being taken if gaps arise.

18. *Once the transition has taken place, it is necessary to manage the relationship.* This is accomplished in part by using metrics and scorecards to

monitor performance on an ongoing basis. Regular contact, through meetings and interchanges, is critical for any such relationships. Meetings require an agenda listing such items as reviews of performance measures, highlighting of exceptions, discussions as to which measures are resolved and which are in process, along with notations as to when pending items will be completed. It is also necessary to report any material changes in either party's condition, such as loss of key staff, mergers, acquisitions, and changes in business plan. Some changes might trigger actions as described in the agreement between the parties. For example, the acquisition of one or the other party by a third entity could activate an option to terminate the arrangement.[2]

19. *Under normal circumstances, the term of the service agreement is a specific time period, such as 1 year, 3 years, or even 10 years.* Often the agreement automatically renews for a specified period unless one party or another takes action. Sometimes terminating a contract early and paying a penalty makes sense rather than enduring inadequate service until an opportune end date. In any event, at some point in time, the parties must determine whether to renew or terminate the contract. This determination consists of revisiting each of the prior evaluation steps, since much in the environment may have changed during the life of the service arrangement.

20. *At this point, the parties to a contract must decide whether an automatic renewal or a renewal with minimal analysis will be instituted or whether the time is appropriate to reevaluate the whole arrangement in detail and consider other options.* A simple renewal continues virtually all aspects of the relationship, except possibly for an increase in price, which is generally tied to some economic inflation factor. If the market price of such services has dropped, due to, say, the competitive impact of offshore services, the specific price of this service might be reduced if other factors remain the same. Invoking the termination of the agreement activates the evaluation process again, with concomitant RFIs, RFPs, and proposals, unless the customer organization has decided to exit that particular business.

---

2. In some cases, the option to terminate an agreement may be exercised due to something within the control of the service provider, such as dissatisfaction with the quality of service. In other cases, the reason for termination may have nothing to do with service level or even relative cost. An acquiring party might have a similar service in-house to the one being outsourced and want to consolidate these particular services in-house; or the acquiring company might be a competitor of the outsourcer or of the outsourcer's parent company.

The evaluation of outsourcing opportunities has become a continuous process as new services become available, new sources of those services appear, and business takes on more of a global aspect. While the parameters will change and the answers will vary, the process remains the same. It behooves a nimble organization in a competitive market to keep its options open and its ability to evaluate choices finely tuned.

Appendix A:
Candidate Security Services for Outsourcing

The number of security services is expanding and so are the opportunities to outsource them. While organizations commonly use third-party physical security providers (e.g., for guard service), active debate exists on the appropriateness and cost-effectiveness of outsourcing many information security services, particularly if those services are provided from offshore locations.

In the following section, we shall look at the full range of security services and suggest whether they might be candidates for outsourcing and, if so, which factors should be considered prior to finalizing the decisions. In some cases, the security service providers offers expertise not generally or easily available, and in other situations, the tools or products needed for the job are prohibitively expensive for a small or medium-size organization, but viable when shared across a number of customers.

We now expand on the categories listed in Chapter 6, so as to represent more specifically the types of services offered in the marketplace.

Security policy:

- Policy;
- Standards;
- Baselines;
- Guidelines;
- Procedures;

- Awareness and training;
- Monitoring and enforcement;
- Response and disciplinary action.

Information security infrastructure:

- Firewalls, routers;
- Intrusion detection systems;
- Intrusion prevention systems.

Access control:

- Authentication;
- Authorization;
- Monitoring/reporting;
- Security administration;
- Help desk.

Personnel security:

- New-hire screening;
- Background checks;
- Regular verification;
- Ongoing attestations;
- Bodyguards, armored vehicles;
- Safety training and awareness.

Physical and environmental security:

- Physical authentication;
- Physical authorization;
- Intrusion detection;
- Alarms, notifications;
- Physical site protection (obscurity locks, gates, fences, metal bars);
- High-security area protection;
- Facility guards;

- Cameras, motion detectors, dogs;
- Training and awareness (e.g., fire drills).

Operations management:

- Operational responsibilities and procedures;
- Monitoring;
- Intrusion detection;
- Alerts;
- Incident response.

Protection against malicious software:

- Viruses, worms, Trojan horse protections;
- Denial of service avoidance and prevention;
- External attacks avoidance and prevention;
- Internal misconduct, negligence;
- Content management (screening) of e-mail;
- Web-site blocking and monitoring;
- Incident response plan and procedures;
- Forensics preparation and processing.

Network management:

- Monitoring;
- Intrusion detection and monitoring;
- Alerts processing;
- Incident response;
- Forensics.

Media and data handling:

- Acquisition of media;
- Use of media;
- Deletion of data;
- Disposal of media;

- Creation of data;
- Transmission of data;
- Storage of data.

System/application management:

- System planning and acceptance;
- Vulnerability management (patching);
- Monitoring;
- Intrusion detection;
- Alerts;
- Incident response;
- Forensics.

System/application development:

- Secure system development life cycle (SDLC);
- Secure programming standards;
- Secure coding and testing training;
- Security-oriented testing.

Business continuity and disaster recovery management:

- Business continuity planning;
- Disaster recovery planning;
- Contingency planning;
- Plan testing and correction;
- Regular plan updating.

Compliance with legal and regulatory requirements:

- Development of policies and procedures for compliance;
- Review of technical compliance;
- Awareness and enforcement;
- Auditing against policies and procedures.

For each of the above categories, we list some of the advantages and disadvantages of outsourcing and make comments and recommendations as to what to do in Table A.1.

Table A.1

Advantages and Disadvantages of Outsourcing

Category	Advantages of Outsourcing	Disadvantages of Outsourcing	Recommendations and Comments
Security policy, standards*	Access to experienced subject matter experts, particularly in the legal area, for development of policy, standards, and so on, and for training and awareness.	Relatively high cost of consulting for custom development of policy and implementation of automated delivery and distribution mechanisms.	At a minimum, adapt generally available boilerplate policy. Preferably, have security policy developed and certified by outside experts. Training is often better done by qualified trainers.
	Monitoring and enforcement might be better effected by third parties, such as private investigators. Disciplinary action might involve law enforcement and result in legal action, which is a recognized third-party activity.	Involving law enforcement might have unintended consequences, such as confiscation of critical systems.	
Information security infrastructure	Even if the information security function is managed in-house it is often beneficial for a third party to design, implement, and/or validate implementation of the infrastructure.	Third parties might over-engineer the solution and/or propose a solution that may be better suited to third-party implementation and management.	For the design, use a provider who is not in the managed security services business, and get a second opinion, if feasible.
	Such enterprise security assessments often provide certifications, which can be presented to customers, business partners, and regulators, to demonstrate a good security posture.	Use of external providers for firewall monitoring, intrusion detection, and so on might cause internal expertise to atrophy, unless some form of cosourcing is implemented.	Third-party certifications are recommended as they can bring with them a measure of credibility not usually attributed to assessments by in-house staff.
	Third parties generally have a broader view of threats and incidents, which they can bring to the evaluation of firewall monitoring and intrusion detection/prevention service setups.	Intrusion detection and intrusion prevention require knowledge of various applications, not generally known by third parties.	Concerns surround not knowing who might be looking at message traffic and the like, especially offshore.

Table A.1 (continued)

Category	Advantages of Outsourcing	Disadvantages of Outsourcing	Recommendations and Comments
Access control	The access control function is generally performed in-house, except for the help desk, which is often outsourced, sometimes offshore. Outsourced help desk services are usually better able to provide round-the-clock, around-the-globe services. Authentication services, such as those offered under outsourced versions of PKI, can handle the burdensome administrative overhead.	Some technical help desk services have come under criticism, especially offshore units, because of lack of training and expertise, and possibly due to cultural differences.	Access control is becoming more visible because of laws and regulations designed to protect individuals' personal information. It is therefore important to establish world-class management of access to systems and networks.
Personnel security	Much of the preliminary screening can be done by in-house staff except that, for critical roles dealing with highly confidential information, an outside agency can provide additional expertise. Personal security, such as that afforded to executives working in dangerous regions, needs particular knowledge and experience that is not usually available in-house.	Outsiders may not be sensitive to the particular needs of the organization or might miss the absence of essential attributes.	Many personal and personnel security tasks are better farmed out to specialists.
Physical security	Generally an organization will find it more economical and less burdensome to use third-party guard services to secure a facility and check identities and authorized destinations (i.e., who they came to visit) of those wanting access. It is common to have external parties provide intrusion detection systems linked up to third-party command centers to respond to alarms.	A significant amount of trust is put on these outside services, so that, when there is a problem (e.g., a guard with criminal intentions), it can be doubly dangerous because the outsider has insider access.	There has to be a tradeoff between bringing in specialists for physical security and trusting your critical facilities to an outsider. In general, it is cheaper and more effective to hire a security firm to secure your physical facilities.

Table A.1 (continued)

Category	Advantages of Outsourcing	Disadvantages of Outsourcing	Recommendations and Comments
Operations management	Certain operational functions, such as payroll processing, are specialty commodity services and are generally outsourced by all but the very smallest or largest organizations. It can be cost-effective to outsource operations and the management of those operations across a broad range of business processes and systems operations.	Loss of control is a considerable concern here, as is reduced flexibility.	The outsourcing of the management of operations is easy to justify for functions, such as payroll, that are important but not core to the business of the organization, whereas it is more difficult for core business and technical operations to be justified.
Protection against malicious software	Outside services generally have the size and scope to be able to provide a broader perspective. Also, they have an incentive to maintain their antivirus signatures very current and to screen out a high proportion of spam and similarly unauthorized messages. Development and maintenance of a workable incident response plan is better done by a third party that is in the business of preparing and testing such plans and advising on what to collect as evidence.	If there are false positives, it may be more difficult to retrieve quarantined e-mails from outsourcer. Third party may not be available at a time of crisis if they have to respond to many customers simultaneously.	Many organizations do not have adequate internal expertise for protecting against viruses and worms and for incident response and so it is usually advisable to seek outside help in these areas.
Network management	There have been quite a number of highly visible, large scale and successful outsourcing programs in which a third party is assigned full responsibility for managing large firms' networks. There are considerable savings and other benefits to be had, especially for 24/7 global networks.	High dependency on an outsourcer for such a critical area might lead to significant problems were the provider to go out of business.	It is common for part of an organization's network management to be outsourced, and for good reasons.

Table A.1 (continued)

Category	Advantages of Outsourcing	Disadvantages of Outsourcing	Recommendations and Comments
Media and data handling	Appropriate handling of media is often neglected by internal staff and therefore it is a good candidate for the discipline that often comes with outsourcing.	Having a third party work with the personal information of an organization's customers is very risky and can lead to unintended consequences in regard to unauthorized disclosure of information.	Handling of sensitive data is quite common in many third-party arrangements and, while required in order to use the services, suggests a higher level of due diligence and assurance that the data is being protected adequately.
Management of systems and applications	Although less common than outsourcing specific operations, computer applications, which were developed in-house, developed under contract or purchased off-the-shelf, can be managed by third parties. The latter will, due to their specializing in the area, be better equipped to ensure that patches have been applied and no intrusions have occurred, or if they do occur, to respond appropriately.	Often such applications and systems are the "crown jewels" of an organization, as opposed to commodity applications that are readily outsourced. Consequently, any compromise that is effected is that much more damaging.	Such a decision needs to be made carefully with all security concerns having been addressed before moving ahead with this type of service.
Development of systems and applications	Third-party expertise is valuable in helping establishing secure system development standards and practices. It is often preferable to have expert third parties train internal staff in the techniques of secure programming and testing and to regularly monitor that the staff is adhering to the standards.	In order to provide targeted methods and training, the third-party staff members will need to learn a great deal about the internal applications. This exposes these systems to the possibility of someone stealing intellectual property or introducing malware into the code.	On the whole, it is a good idea to bring in outside help, at least to establish a secure development environment and train the staff. Further involvement may be desirable based upon whether internal staff takes ownership of the process or not.

Table A.1 (continued)

Category	Advantages of Outsourcing	Disadvantages of Outsourcing	Recommendations and Comments
Business continuity and disaster recovery planning and management	Third parties have the expertise and experience to develop contingency plans for business units and computer systems and networks. They also introduce a level of discipline, which usually does not exist within an organization. Professionally developed plans are effective and are also readily accepted by business partners, customers, and so on, as a measure of the integrity and commitment to continuance by the organization.	Cost is generally higher than having in-house staff perform this function. Third parties may not have good business knowledge relating to the organization.	It is usually better to have one or more third parties work on the organization's contingency plans as they are likely to be more complete and will be maintained and tested.
Legal and regulatory compliance	Audits and recommendations by outside legal and accounting firms draw upon expertise and resources that are usually not available in-house. Such reviews sit well with regulators and auditors.	Cost is an issue here.	If used judiciously, such services can be well worth the cost.

* Many sample policy, standards, procedures, guidelines, and other boilerplates are available at little or no cost through publications or over the Internet. While these might serve as the basis for an organization's policies, there is a danger that they may lack appropriate legal, compliance, and personnel expertise and so should be reviewed by qualified professionals prior to distribution.

Appendix B:
A Brief History of IT Outsourcing

The Early Days

Electronic data processing systems were first developed in the mid-twentieth century essentially for military and scientific purposes. They began to see limited commercial use in the 1960s.[1] At that time, computers were physically large devices, typically being made up of dozens of single-function interconnected cabinets the size of large refrigerators. The computer equipment required special cooling, cabling, and power systems. Consequently, computers were confined to specially constructed rooms (or data centers). The operation of such machines required both physical access to them and particular technical knowledge.

To the extent that outsourcing took place at all, it was generally in the form of services from what are today referred to as applications service providers (ASPs). Not that an individual or organization had much choice in the matter. The few computers that existed were in the hands of the military or academic and scientific research organizations, so that everyone else with a need and the requisite funding had to request and buy time on someone else's computer, if available. Because computing power was such a rare commodity, applications were usually scientific and sophisticated in nature, and those persons requesting

---

1. Thomas Watson, Sr., who founded IBM Corporation in 1924, was said to have stated in 1953 that he believed that there was a market for only five computers worldwide. Apparently IBM believes he was commenting on orders for a particular model of computer, not the entire population.

computer time were knowledgeable in the technical aspects of computing machinery[2] and the software running on it.

In the early years of computing, organizations sprang up that offered to house and operate another company's computer systems. The offerer of this type of service was referred to as a "facilities manager." Today the term used for such an outsourcer is "hosting services provider" (HSP). One rarely, if ever, hears the term facilities management these days.

My first exposure to digital computers (as opposed to the analog computers with which I worked as an engineering student) was in an Algol 60 course taken during my electrical engineering studies at the University of Glasgow in the mid-1960s. The university's only digital computer was housed in the basement of the Chemistry Department and jealously guarded. The programming course took place solely in the classroom as the Chemistry Department would not allow lowly engineers, or anyone else for that matter, near their precious machine.

During that same time, I took a course in econometrics taught by someone who commuted from Edinburgh—a distance of about 50 miles. Students wrote data on coding sheets, which the professor carried back to Edinburgh. There the data was entered into a multiple correlation program running on a university computer. The results of the correlation and regression analysis were returned to students some two weeks later. Back then, turnaround times of days or weeks were not unusual. In today's vernacular, the computer facility in Edinburgh would have been called an ASP, since it offered the use of a statistical analysis application to "customers."

Imagine my surprise and delight when, in the late 1960s, I moved to the United States as a graduate student at Cornell University and took a course in which we actually wrote computer programs (in FORTRAN) and ran them. We used keypunch machines to perforate 80-column Hollerith cards with little rectangular holes, representing alphanumeric characters of our programs and data, and submitted the cards to run on a real computer. Submission of jobs was via a distant card reader, using remote job entry (RJE) technology. The modern computing era had arrived.

Remote Job Entry

This remote job entry (RJE) breakthrough in computing, which comprised the attaching of telecommunications networks via which the computer could be

---

2. When electronic computers first hit the marketplace they were called "computing machines," not computers. At that time, the term "computer" meant a person who did calculations on the various machines. The preeminent professional association in the computer industry is to this day called the Association of Computing Machinery.

accessed, enabled the power of large centrally located mainframe computers to be available to many programmers from remote locations. Initial applications of this nature involved the transmission of "batch jobs" over telephone lines. These jobs were loaded into a card reader, transmitted to the central computer, and run. Then the results were transmitted back to the original remote location (or possibly a different remote location) where they were printed on a unit also in contact with the central mainframe computer over communications lines. During this period, IBM dominated the world of mainframe computers, which was the only type of computing machine in common use.

This remote capability facilitated ASP relationships, since access no longer depended on geography and the need for direct physical access. For this type of outsourcing, a customer organization might use several third-party data centers accessible via communications lines from its own place of business. The seller of these services might have purchased the computers in order to sell time. On the other hand, an organization might have found itself with excess capacity during idle periods and recognized that incremental revenues might be gained by selling otherwise wasted capacity.[3]

As students at Cornell University, during peak periods of demand, we sometimes waited days or more than a week, for the results of a single computer run. When we received the results, we would often discover that simple errors meant that jobs had to be resubmitted, which subjected us to additional days or weeks of delay. It could take a month or more to complete a single project, which today can be done in a matter of hours, or even minutes. This system became particularly frustrating towards the end of a semester when students, faculty, and outside contractors were trying to complete their work by the end-of-semester deadline and were competing for the limited available resources.

During that time, I happened to work on a project with outside funding. Outside funds, or "hard money," bought the highest priorities. Jobs would be returned within minutes, whereas students running similar work waited days for output. It occurred to me that the intrinsic value of the work had much less to do with the priority of service than the source of funds (i.e., internal, grant, hard money) and the identity of the person submitting the job (e.g., student, faculty member, consultant). My observation of this approach to assigning computer resources led to a dissertation topic on the effective allocation of computing resources, later to be published in book form [1, 2].

---

3. I recall being on a consulting engagement in the early 1970s where we had to run a very large multiple regression analyses. While we had used several smaller machines in the Greater New York City area, the only machines with adequate speed and capacity that were available for purchasing of time-sharing belonged to aircraft manufacturers. We ended up using a computer in Canada, connecting via an RJE link from Manhattan.

Time-Sharing

When it became technically feasible for an individual to run jobs on a central computer system from a terminal, usually situated at a remote location, we saw the next major breakthrough in the use of computers, which was called *time-sharing*. Time-sharing, which had its heyday in the 1970s, became the model for future directions in computer use, with the latest incarnation being Web services, which is time-sharing taken to the extreme.

The idea behind time-sharing was that each person sitting at a terminal (these days we call such a device a "dumb" terminal, as opposed to an "intelligent" workstation or personal computer) had access to a specific set of computer resources. These resources (e.g., processing time, storage space, and input and output capabilities) were under that person's direct control. The magic of such a system was its ability to schedule numerous requests for services in such a manner that, to the person sitting at the terminal, the resources appeared to be dedicated, while in fact they were shared.

This use of computer technology gave rise to considerable interest in scheduling algorithms and priority setting. A number of time-sharing service providers sprang up. Again, some were dedicated solely to providing the "plain vanilla" use of computer resources to customers. Other companies, which were not in the primary business of selling computer time but found themselves with excess capacity, offered these unused resources on a time-shared basis, often at prices well below market. These providers were able to do this because their internal use covered most, if not all, of the fixed costs of the system, so that any revenues above the fixed cost were profit except for the relatively small cost directly attributable to providing the services.

Many time-sharing customers saw cost and operational benefits in using third-party services as opposed to building or expanding capacity in-house. This was particularly true when specific short-term requirements existed or if the outsourcer could provide certain capabilities not available internally. Such capabilities might include the ability to write programs in a particular computer language or to support specific commercially available applications or operating systems. In today's terminology, a time-sharing company would be called an HSP if it provided raw computer power along with system and communications software and little else. If the company provided use of certain applications, it would be equivalent to an ASP.

My first time-sharing experience was in the 1960s when working for the summer at IBM World Trade Corporation. I used an internal time-sharing service and wrote programs in APL (A Programming Language)[4] on the system.

---

4. APL is a relatively obscure language that takes the form of strings of operators represented mostly by Greek characters. A special keyboard is needed. The language is interpretive rather

Besides being very slow by today's standards, the system would abruptly terminate sessions and disconnect terminals after ten minutes of use—ready or not. Users developed a strategy of saving their work every minute or two, to avoid its being lost due to summary disconnection, and immediately upon being cut off madly dialing back to reconnect before someone else could jump in and take control. With demand much greater for access ports than the supply available, capturing scarce resources and maintaining some semblance of continuity became something of a game.

My second experience with time-sharing, this time provided by a third party, was in the early 1970s. Access was via an ancient Teletype machine, much like the ones used at the time for sending and receiving telegrams. The Teletype terminal was painfully slow and noisy, chugging away as the type head rotated and applied each character painstakingly to the paper. However, the service was relatively inexpensive compared to other services, with a flat hourly charge for unlimited use. Unfortunately, only 8,000 bytes of memory were available to each user session, so that much time was spent transferring data to and from higher capacity, but slower, disk storage. Nevertheless, the luxury of having unlimited, apparently dedicated resources available at a reasonable cost was a delight and outweighed the inconveniences.

Time-sharing evolved from the provision of raw computer power, with which one could write and run programs, to making applications available, such as early spreadsheet, database, and statistical analysis programs. This was the transition from HSP to ASP.

Distributed Systems

During this same era of time-sharing in the early 1970s, the architecture of computer systems was changing from large centralized mainframes to include smaller departmental minicomputers, popularized by such defunct brands as Digital Equipment Corporation (DEC), Perkin-Elmer, Prime, and Data General (DG). Minicomputers could run standalone as "departmental computers," or act as "front ends" to mainframes. At that time, departments that had previously insourced their computer processing to centralized corporate mainframes or outsourced to third parties could now take control of their own computer needs. Accordingly, the industry saw smaller organizational units owning and operating their own minicomputers.

---

than being compiled, which means that each time a change is made to the source code it is automatically reflected in machine language, or "object," form.

It was not clear at the time how the introduction of minicomputers would affect IT outsourcing. To some extent, one expected that departments would reduce their outsourcing activities because they would now be able to bring in a computer solely to suit their needs and thereby control their own systems. However, the other factors favoring outsourcing, such as inadequate or unqualified internal staff, tended to push departments towards outsourcing anyway. Often departments discovered that running a computer was a big headache distracting them from their main line of business, so they would return to the centralized model with services provided internally or externally. This trend towards spreading computer capabilities to the departmental level grew with the appearance on the scene of the personal computer and the more highly powered desktop workstation discussed in the next section.

In a parallel trend, the minicomputer evolved into the modern-day "server." Typically, today, large organizations run hundreds and even thousands of servers networked together in a server farm, where once they may have had a couple of mainframes. Surprisingly, the mainframe computer's demise was greatly exaggerated, and mainframe and server still coexist in many organizations. With servers' increasing power and capabilities, it is becoming more difficult to distinguish between the two—the main distinction being the different system software they run (i.e., Unix, Microsoft Windows, and Linux on servers, and IBM's operating systems on mainframes).

Personal Computers and Workstations

The initial versions of personal computers (PCs) were standalone units with much of the power of mainframes from a previous generation. Early PCs did not generally have communications capabilities and were often purchased by departments as "office equipment," even though they had significant computational power. In this way, they easily infiltrated into the workplace with little attention paid to the policy, standards, and practices that mostly governed mainframes, minicomputers, and servers.[5] The PCs of the early 1980s were frequently used in the workplace for word-processing and spreadsheet analysis, and these applications tended to replace typewritten documents and hand-written spreadsheets.

---

5. This "infiltration" without appropriate controls is often seen when significant new technologies are introduced. It happened again in the early to mid-1990s with the Internet, which individuals had implemented at home often well before corporations got control of the technology. It is happening today with wireless networks, where organizations are struggling with the security implications of the technology, whereas individuals have installed the networks at home, are using them in Internet cafés, and may have sneaked unauthorized wireless devices into the corporate environment.

Early PCs were generally not used for off-loading work from departmental mini-computers and central mainframes.

Another view of PCs, mostly held by mainframe manufacturers and other likeminded proponents, was that they functioned in much the same role as their dumb terminal predecessors. With this model, there would be little need to change the overall architecture whereby processing power and control would remain under the purview of the mainframe owners. This centralized configuration did not allow for partial outsourcing—it was all or nothing, for the most part.

How wrong they were.[6] This model was incomplete and quite misleading. Workstations and PCs were and still are used to access legacy mainframe applications. But over time more and more PC interactions were directed towards server applications and to outside networks, particularly to the Internet, with the PC acting as a "client." This trend has made the outsourcing of individual applications, services, and functions relatively simple to do, although many control and security issues have arisen.

However, a major use of PCs is the running of computer software—variously called standalone applications, end-user computing, or desktop applications—by the person authorized to use a particular dedicated PC. These stand-alone programs may run independently of connections to other computers or may require that data or programs be downloaded from other computer sources. These PC-based programs also supply information to other receiving computers. There is a whole range of control and security issues with standalone end-user supported programs, as well as concerns about the potentially damaging interactions between these and other systems.

In any case, the advent of the PC and workstation did not change the outsourcing model that much from the one where dumb terminals were used, except that the sharing of work between the clients' PCs and the outsourcers' servers or mainframes became much more flexible.

The Advent of Big-Time Outsourcing

In the late 1980s, around the same time that we witnessed the proliferation of PCs and the emergence of servers in the workplace, an IT outsourcing

6. It is really quite remarkable that mainframe-oriented IBM became a pioneer in the PC arena, considering the shakeout among the manufacturers of older technologies that this new technology caused. Minicomputer manufacturers, with the exception of Hewlett Packard (HP), missed the boat entirely. Ken Olsen, the founder of DEC, considered the PC a toy and did not take it seriously. Years later, DEC (then called Digital) was purchased by portable PC pioneer Compaq Corporation, which in turn was bought by the Hewlett-Packard Company.

revolution took place. It is a testament to the stability and measurability of their computer and network operational functions that companies felt more comfortable in having a third party manage the computer and network "factories" that had evolved in the prior two decades.

In October 1989, Kodak signed a 10-year, $250 million outsourcing deal with the IBM Corporation, Digital Equipment Corporation, and Businessland Inc. (the latter two of which are no longer in business) to operate its data centers and support its PCs. In an article published 10 years later, in October 1999, Tom Field looked back to explain why Kodak is credited with having been the originator of the large-scale IT outsourcing deal, even though Enron Corporation had executed a deal of three times the value that same year. Field credits the fact that Kodak was the first well-known, Dow Jones Industrial Index company to have engaged in this type of outsourcing [3].

Previously, the equivalent of outsourcing (i.e., facilities management) was viewed negatively as something companies used if they were unable to run their own operation properly. This view was still pervasive in 1989. However, Kodak was not seen as badly managed at that time.

In the 15 years since 1989, we have seen the Kodak deal dwarfed by outsourcing megadeals such as the J. P. Morgan's $2 billion outsourcing arrangement with Pinnacle Alliance, a consortium consisting of CSC (Computer Sciences Corp.), Andersen Consulting (now Accenture), AT&T Solutions, and Bell Atlantic Network Integration (BANI), which was signed in 1996. In January 2003, the consolidated J. P. Morgan Chase bank decided not to renew the Pinnacle Alliance contract but instead signed a $5 billion 7-year outsourcing deal with IBM Corporation.

Many domestic IT professionals were affected directly by these outsourcing arrangements. However, all in all, it was really a "zero sum" situation whereby groups of IT professionals at outsourcers were, for the most part, substituted for the customer organizations' staff. In fact, in many arrangements staff was transferred from the customer organization to the outsourcer. For example, in the Kodak arrangement, 300 Kodak employees transferred to IBM and another 400 to Digital and Businessland. This could be done because, in many cases, although the infrastructure changed ownership, it was not moved physically. Customer organizations were able to reduce capital expenditures, save costs, and increase shareholder value [4].

The Move Offshore

The use of contract programmers and consultants is not new. For decades, companies and government agencies have hired specialized programmers to develop projects beyond the technical skills of internal staff, or for one-time projects for which it was not worth hiring internal staff that would be unneeded once the project was over. For example, fixing programs to prevent a Y2K meltdown was the ultimate one-time project.

This need for Y2K remediation programmers did much to promote the extension of outsourcing beyond computer operations and network management to software development. It also created a huge demand for programming work in the developed countries, since they had the bulk of older programs, in which demand for expertise greatly exceeded the domestic supply. This resulted in a global search for programming talent—and countries such as Russia, Ireland, and India were only too ready to oblige.

But once the need for Y2K remediation was over, the supply of programming talent soon exceeded the demand, especially with the dot-com bursting bubble jettisoning hundreds of thousands of programmers into the marketplace. At the same time, technical schools and universities, particularly in Asia, had geared up to satisfy the surge in demand towards the end of the twentieth century. Large numbers of newly minted graduates were joining the many who had been displaced, to generate a huge pool of programmers just as the demand had fallen off.

With improved global telecommunications and the portability of design and development work, the outsourcing of application development, help-desk functions, and business processing can now move quickly and somewhat seamlessly from continent to continent. No longer is outsourcing tethered to particular locations, as it was when operational functions and physical facilities were being outsourced. With the technical limitations of going offshore eliminated and communications costs much reduced, the pricing difference of labor has become a determining factor in many cases. This price differential will stay in force into the foreseeable future so that, barring major political and economic changes, the rapid growth in offshore application development and business process outsourcing will continue.

And Now to Security

In this book, we have discussed the appearance and establishment of managed security services providers. This area has generally seen small-scale arrangements, in which a third party might manage firewalls or intrusion detection systems (IDS). This business is projected by the Gartner Group to grow from $548 million in 2002 to $1.2 billion in 2006, which is the fastest-growing service type across all vertical markets.

As part of this growth, Merrill Lynch has again been a pioneer in the scale of its May 2003 deal with VeriSign, where the latter is to manage more than 300 firewall and IDS devices [5]. This agreement clearly relates to the Internet, and therefore we will now go back a little in time to see other aspects of its impact.

Networked Systems and the Internet

That ubiquitous public communications highway, the Internet, with its myriad of information and transactional sites is called the World Wide Web. It arose from an exclusive means of communications that was originally developed by academics under the sponsorship of the Defense Advanced Research Projects Agency (DARPA). The resulting ARPAnet facilitated reliable and resilient computer communications among academics and government scientists. The network architecture was designed to be redundant in order to survive major outages affecting large segments of the network. It was developed as a means of ensuring that messages could be exchanged even if there was major damage to the communications infrastructure.

Prior to the Internet, setting up communications links between two distant entities involved a costly and lengthy coordination effort in which lines were ordered, installed, tested, and operated at costs in the hundreds and thousands of dollars per month. Each network connection had to be dealt with separately. Since much of IT outsourcing did (and still does) involve extensive communications linkages between entities, the costs and inconvenience of installing lines inhibited the expansion of remote-access outsourcing.

Suddenly, we were confronted with the Internet and its protocols, which operate on a whole range of operating systems and hardware platforms and across many types of communications links. Thus, a major impediment to communications between entities and with individuals' computers disappeared. The freedom of choice of implementation environment and the capability for rapid deployment were major factors behind the explosive growth of the Internet in the late 1990s and early 2000s. The more individuals and entities attached to the Internet, the more valuable the Internet became as a means to connect with business partners, customers, and service providers.

In no time at all, a whole compendium of service providers sprang up. Some were merely spruced-up old-style service bureaus with Internet access and Web sites bolted on the front. However, others were truly new forms of enterprise made possible through the universal access provided by the Internet and World Wide Web. Along with the new format came a new term, the service provider (SP), as in XSP, where X stands for the letters as A (application), B (business), H (hosting), I (Internet), M (managed), MS (managed security), and MSM (managed security monitoring). To add to the confusion, the same letter can have different meanings in different contexts (e.g., "A" can stand for application or authentication).

The Brave New World of Service Providers

This plethora of service providers has, as stated above, all sorts of names and abbreviations. Perhaps best known are application service providers (ASPs), which offer customers the use of particular applications, such as human resource services (payroll, benefits), customer relationship management (CRM), and enterprise resource management (ERM). These applications can be either homegrown by the ASP or purchased, or even supplied by the customer, although in this case the customer may be dealing with a hosting service provider (HSP). In the case of an HSP, the customer's staff can access resources and facilities, often over the Internet, which are located and managed on the service providers' premises.

There are also arrangements in which facilities remain in-house at the customer's site, and the service providers' employees access some of these in-house facilities, usually from their own locations. Examples of this might include off-hours help-desk services and some MSM services, which could fall under cosourcing.

For the most part, such services have existed for many years, even when communications choices were limited and took the form of dedicated lines and switched circuit services. However, what is different today with the Internet is the ease of setting up access and low cost of entry. Such arrangements often depend on the ability of the parties to ensure secure transmissions, storage, and use of each other's information assets. Still, the low cost of Internet access made many services economically feasible that were not so under the costly dedicated communications line alternative.

The extension of services across the Internet characterizes the recent advent of Web services. Here the overall application can be broken down into discrete functions that can be acquired from a number of different providers specializing in subcomponents of the application. This is expanded upon later.

The Electronic Commerce Model

It might appear that we may have glossed over what is surely the primary commercial use of the Internet, namely electronic commerce, or e-commerce. E-commerce is essentially the use of architectures consisting of Web servers and supporting services for the purposes of transacting business.

During the dot-com era at the close of the twentieth century and the beginning of the twenty-first century, many e-commerce activities included only the informational broadcast of the Web site and corresponding transactional services. Such organizations often did not have any product on hand in warehouses and used third parties to actually store and ship product or provide services. In a certain sense this might be considered the reverse of the IT outsourcing model, where organizations retain the IT function, since IT is their primary added value, and they have others stock products, pick them in response to orders, and ship them directly to the customer. Whether, in this case, the warehousers and shippers could be considered as having outsourced the marketing and sales functions is an interesting question.

Taking another view, many organizations do not develop their own Web sites. Instead, they arrange for specialist firms to design and implement customized Web sites. This is not outsourcing per se. However, in some cases, one company will host the Web site for another firm, which is considered outsourcing according to our definition, since the service provider manages and operates the site. Although the distinguishing line is fuzzy, we can differentiate between consulting services and outsourcing services by considering the former to apply to finite development and implementation projects and the latter to refer to ongoing operations.

At this point in time, the shakedown in dot-com firms is mostly over and those Web-based sites remaining have matured and reduced their ambitions and expectations to realistic levels. This has not, however, stymied the inventiveness and creativity of leading-edge technologists and we are seeing continuing development in capabilities offered over the Web.

Portals, Aggregation, and Web Services

A Web site typically supports a single application or service, albeit a complex one. In such cases, managers of Web sites provide and support the form and content of Web sites, even if the sites contain information supplied by third parties.

Over time it was realized that, in certain situations, it might be very convenient for someone accessing a particular Web site to be able to get to a number of applications or services through that single Web site, rather than having to log on to each application separately. In response to this, along came the portal. Portals are single points of entry into a portfolio of services. The services may be internal to an organization, external, or a combination of both. Likewise, those using the portal may be employees (in which case it is termed an "enterprise portal"), customers, or some combination of internal employees and external customers.

Portals can in fact encourage outsourcing since they provide ready access to numerous applications, whether those applications reside within the organization hosting the portal or not. Thus, management of the portal may be outsourced and so can the applications accessed via the portal. It is readily seen that portal technology facilitates sharing and can blur pure ownership and branding, making for a potentially promiscuous business environment.

Whereas portals provide gateways through which access to applications is gained, aggregation is a different concept. With aggregation, for example, information about a particular customer can be gathered together from a number of sources and displayed on a single screen. For instance, a customer may want to have current information from his or her bank checking and savings accounts, brokerage accounts, credit card accounts, and mortgage status, all displayed on or immediately accessible from a single screen. The aggregation application program links to various Web sites that have access to each such piece of information, logs on to that site on the customer's behalf, and downloads the required information.

Often, the development and operation of the aggregation site is outsourced to a third party. Sometimes this is at the behest of a financial institution, which provides some of the data itself. However, it may also be implemented for another party, such as a Web portal company, that is not responsible for any particular piece of information displayed.

Aggregation Web sites are very similar to Web portals in appearance and operation as far as the customer is concerned. Both aggregation sites and portals offer single sign-on, in that a customer only need log on to the hosting site once, and connections to other facilities, whether they be applications (in the case of portals) or information (for aggregators), are made "under the covers."

As it turns out, aggregation has not been particularly well received by retail customers, and may not be successful in the long run. Apparently, customers are not comfortable, from privacy and confidentiality points of view, with having so much data about themselves collected and available in one place. After all, if someone were to compromise that site, a person's entire financial position might be accessible and misused.

Portals, on the other hand, have seen some success and will likely be the predominant way to access systems, whether from the Web or internally, in the future. The first rush of companies wanting to supply organizations with portal development, implementation, operation, and support has been tempered by the complexity of implementation. However, over time, this will improve, and many organizations will likely not have direct control of the way in which their own applications and data are accessed, but will depend on one or more service providers to take care of the intricacies.

A related upcoming facility, which is receiving a great deal of press, is the "Web services" initiative. Web services are defined as a "standardized way of integrating Web-based applications using open standards ..." [6]. In a sense, this technology provides an aggregation of applications, versus aggregation of data, as described earlier.

Straight-Through Processing (STP) and Grid Computing

Traditional data processing took place in what was called "batch mode." That is to say, even when transactions were done and recorded in real time, the bulk of the processing was done, and is still done in may cases, by means of a nightly batch run. Computer jobs are assembled together and run in a predetermined sequence, accounting for interdependencies of processes and data modification requirements.

In the financial services industry, in particular, there has been a push towards instantaneous processing of transactions so as to eliminate the batch cycles and to achieve global access and reporting of such transactions 24 hours a day and 7 days per week. This is resulting in a major redesign of the architectures of business processes and the systems that support them.

The demands of real-time instantaneous processing of transactions across financial entities, such as banks and securities firms, will produce a need for high-security, high-availability logical and physical links and interdependencies between the various components and phases in the processing cycle. Thus, STP initiatives will have major security implications for outsourcing from the perspectives of both the buyers and providers of services.

Relationships between organizations and service providers will increasingly be more like partnerships rather than buyer-seller relationships. The interdependencies will be so great as to require exceptional understanding of each other's businesses, well beyond the requirements of today. Any failure on any party's behalf will likely have an immediate impact across the entire process.

An even newer concept is grid computing. In one sense, grid computing can be thought of as a massively parallel version of STP, which follows a sequential processing paradigm. In grid computing, a particular process or calculation is split into many small parts, each of which is run on a different computer. The results are then combined. This process is more often insourced, since it is easier to arrange for the use of hundreds or thousands of computers if they are under a single organization's control. However, there have been outsourcing examples of requesting access to the processing power of many hundreds or even thousands of computers across the World Wide Web. In one case, computers were used to perform an enormous number of calculations to assist in the search for extraterrestrial life.

Mobile Computing

Mobile computing is really just another way of communicating between computers. But mobile computing operates over the ether rather than across wires or optical fiber. However, it does have some specific requirements that favor outsourcing, such as the need to receive and transmit signals across a wide area. With mobile computing there is significant concern over threats to the integrity and confidentiality of customers' information due to the relative ease of intercepting signals. With wireless one does not have to tap into a physical circuit, but can scan for signals in the proximity of the source. Consequently, the relatively new, but rapidly growing, area of mobile computing only exacerbates the risks and fears that already exist with wire or fiber-based communications.

Here again, the nature of the technology makes the outsourcing of the technology and its support viable for many organizations. The ubiquity and ability to communicate from practically anywhere serves well the outsourcing model since the person on the sending end may not even be aware of who is handling the signals at the receiving end.

References

[1]   Axelrod, C. W., "The Allocation of Computer Resources Among Semi-Autonomous Users," Ph.D. Dissertation, Cornell University, 1971.

[2]   Axelrod, C. W., *Computer Effectiveness: Bridging the Management-Technology Gap*, Washington, D.C.: Information Resources Press, 1979.

[3]   Field, T., "Outsourcing: 10 Years that Shook IT," *CIO Magazine*, October 1, 1999, http://www.cio.com.

[4]   Glassman, D., "IT Outsourcing and Shareholder Value," *EVAluation*, New York: Stern Stewart Research, 2000.

[5]   Hulme, G. V., "Merrill Lynch Hands Off Network Security to VeriSign," *Information-Week*, May 21, 2003.

[6]   Hall, M., "Web Services Open Portal Doors," *Computerworld*, Vol. 36, No. 26, June 24, 2002, pp. 28–29.

Appendix C:
A Brief History of Information Security

As expected, the history of security parallels or, to be more accurate, follows that of computing. It is regrettable—but largely unavoidable—that security is practically always trying to catch up with threats and repair vulnerabilities. Warnings of impending attacks seldom are given the attention they deserve and require. When something does raise concerns, such as the dire predictions of adverse Y2K scenarios, the mitigation strategies, when successful, turn the threatened attack into a nonevent. As a result, credibility can be lost and subsequent warnings are not taken seriously enough. In such cases it is difficult to recover from the resulting sense of invincibility, until the next incident.[1]

We now trace the development of information security through the various generations of information technology, as outlined in Appendix B.

The Mainframe Era

Isolated Data Centers

In the early days, when mainframe computers were physically isolated in their own data centers and were not accessible via network connections from the outside, the protection of systems, applications, and data was accomplished through

---

1. Stanley "Stash" Jarocki, former vice president of Morgan Stanley and former chairman of the FS/ISAC, noted that the half-life of management's concern following a security event (such as a virus or denial of service attack) is about 3 months.

physically securing the site. At least initially, logical access to a computer system required that the person actually be within the walls of the data center. At that time, knowledge of the systems and access to the systems was held by those few knowledgeable "high priests" who ruled within their "glass temples."

Computers of that time lent themselves to this form of public display since control panels boasted rows of blinking lights, tape drives had whirling reels, and printers chattered away, spitting out box upon box of sprocket-holed fan-fold paper. Later, this visual openness was not considered good practice since anyone with evil intentions could readily reconnoiter the facility through the glass walls. Today the norm is to have data centers and network control centers hidden away in windowless internally located rooms within unmarked and inconspicuous buildings.

Remote Access

When remote access to central computers became generally available, through the use of remote job submission and remote printing in the 1960s and hard-wired dumb terminals in the 1970s, the concept of protected physical areas still prevailed. Restricted physical access to facilities, whether they contained computer equipment or data-entry terminals, remained the dominant form of security.

However, in the 1970s, we saw the arrival of time-sharing, usually enabled through remotely connected terminals. Then, the physical security of an area in which the terminals were located was not assured. At that point, it became necessary to identify the person using the terminal, and then to verify that person's identity. This was achieved by giving those with authorized access to various computer applications an ID, or identifier, which displayed such features as the person's name, department, and company, and was linked to a password presumed to be known only by the specific owner of that identity. The password verified that the ID holder was the authorized person. While it is widely recognized that this combination of ID and password is among the easiest authentication methods to compromise, it is still by far the most popular, as it is simpler and cheaper to implement than most other forms of authentication.[2]

Over time, technologies for remote access advanced dramatically. Today they are readily available, at reasonable cost, to virtually anyone with access to a

---

2. Today there are a large number of authentication technologies from which to choose. They include magnetic cards (i.e., with a magnetic stripe running across the surface), smart cards (i.e., with a microchip embedded in the card), biometrics (e.g., fingerprint, iris, face, and voice recognition), and tokens (that automatically generate one-time passwords).

personal computer and a telecommunications link. This makes fraud that much easier.[3]

Along with the greatly expanded access came more stringent requirements for authenticating the person, process, or system being granted that access. Also, it became more critical to be effective at authorizing use of specific functions of one or more applications and access to specific data. No longer could one rely on physical restrictions to preserve the security of a remote access node.

The basic "law" of authentication is that a person, in particular, can be authenticated by "what they have," "what they know," and/or "what they are." In today's terms, these requirements can be realized as follows:

- *What you have:* This is usually in the form of a piece of paper or card (e.g., a driver's license or passport) or a magnetic or smart card, a security "token," or even a key, either physical or electronic.

- *What you know:* This is usually a password or personal identification number (PIN), but can also be a lock or safe combination. It often also includes the knowledge of an identifier.

- *What you are:* This refers to some physical characteristic as would be used with biometrics, such as a fingerprint, voice print, face structure, or iris.

It is generally held that at least two of these factor classes are needed in order to achieve "strong authentication." Therefore, a combination of a magnetic card and a PIN (which is often used for ATM cash machines) is considered strong authentication. Similarly a smart card and a fingerprint reader, or a token and a PIN, are also acceptably strong methods of authentication. It is not usual to have two factors in the same category used for authentication, such as a magnetic card and a key. However, such a combination is still strong authentication. On the other hand, authentication via two things that you know, such as ID and password, is not generally considered strong, since IDs usually follow some

---

3. The transition during the 1980s from the "dumb" terminal or CRT (which stands for the "Cathode Ray Tube") to the "intelligent" multipurpose PC, provided tremendous capability and flexibility to the person using the PC and at the same time, increased the security risks by orders of magnitude. The main culprit of the increased risk exposure was the standard installation of a disk drive to write to, and read from, a removable floppy disk. Suddenly, what was a relatively difficult and inconvenient task of removing significant amounts of information from what was previously a closed system, became as easy as copying a file to the floppy disk and sneaking it off the premises. Newer technologies, such as memory cards and USB memory sticks, make the task even harder to detect.

easily learned rule and passwords can be easily cracked by someone with access to password files and readily available software tools.

In addition to determining who or what should be able to access which systems and applications (and functions and data within applications)—which is the authorization challenge—there arose the need to protect messages or traffic traversing communications lines. With earlier technologies, most access was over dedicated or shared telephone lines that were isolated physically from ready access. It was held that, in order to gain access to the information being transmitted over these lines, there was a need to have physical access and specialized monitoring equipment. These requirements formed a barrier that was adequate for most purposes, other than very high security situations, in which case encryption of the messages might be used.

Distributed Systems

Minicomputers

As computer system architectures moved from mainframes with local, and then remote, access to minicomputers front-ending mainframes, then operating independently, to client-server in all its many varieties (two-tier, three-tier, thin client, fat client), so did security needs and solutions.

Mainframe architectures advanced from one-program-at-a-time, sequential processing to multiprocessing (a number of processors, each running application programs within the same "box") and multiprogramming (a number of programs running simultaneously on one processor). As a consequence, the need increased to protect each program and its related data from other applications and data running on the same machine, and from others who had access to that machine. This resulted in the appearance of mainframe security access programs such as RACF (pronounced "rack-eff") from IBM, and ACF2 and Top Secret from Computer Associates.

When minicomputers came on the scene, they often reverted to single-use platforms. In general, the security of such systems was similar to that of single-processing mainframes, and, as a result, security software was lacking—there just didn't seem to be the same need. Also, minicomputers were touted as requiring far fewer support staff than mainframes, so that there generally was not as many, if any, dedicated resources focusing on security matters, as was more usual in the mainframe world.

As minicomputers became larger and faster, and demands on them became greater, they began to take on many of the same multiprocessing attributes and multiprogramming applications, some of which were business critical, so the need for access security increased commensurately. Also, minicomputers were designed, as a matter competitive advantage—versus proprietary mainframe designs—to be compatible with other systems and networks, with their manufacturers subscribing to open systems designs. Minicomputers were able to interface with many communications protocols. However, this very openness increased the risk of compromise, and consequently the need for stronger security tools. Ironically, capable minicomputer security products did not have time to mature before the minicomputer was eclipsed by the client-server world, and is still not up to par for servers.

In the late 1980s and early 1990s, it was a difficult task to find access administration software that could run on minicomputers. The requirement to implement such a security system would often come from internal auditors familiar with the tightly controlled mainframe environment. The auditors would extend mainframe security concepts to minicomputers, which appeared on the surface to be a perfectly reasonable assumption. However, comparable security tools were just not as available at the time for minicomputers. In a less-than-good example of timing, a number of security products were launched just about the time of the general demise of minicomputers, as they were replaced with powerful workstations, intelligent client machines, and high-powered servers.

Client-Server Architecture

Unfortunately, because the early versions of client-server systems often came out of research and development academic arenas (the Unix operating system, for example, was created at Bell Labs), access security was not given much of a priority.[4] The various types of Unix, the first credible Unix challenger, Microsoft Windows, and the recent Windows and Unix challenger, Linux, were all notorious for their lack of security. They were, and still are, known to grant overriding priority access to administrators without having to go through reasonable checks and balances.

Adding to this weakness has been the accepted design, development, and operational environments of the client-server world. As with minicomputers, many smaller "shops" and some that weren't so small, embarked on the construction of client-server systems without much thought to security. Often the pressure to show dramatic improvements in price-performance caused nice-to-have features (among which security was often inappropriately included) to be

---

4. Even today, the academic world is known for its lax security practices. Such freedom of use has facilitated a number of distributed denial-of-service attacks, such as those experienced in February 2000, as university-owned machines were compromised and used as "zombies" (i.e., launching pads) for such attacks. The research laboratories, particularly those involved in highly classified government work, have purportedly strengthened the security of their systems following a number of embarrassing incidents.

neglected. Security was, and largely still is, an afterthought (when someone does indeed think of it) to be bolted onto a system after the fact, with mostly inadequate results. Without security having been part of each stage of the system development life cycle, from design through development and testing and on to implementation and operation, any postimplementation ideas as to how the system might be made more secure are generally too little and too late.

While there were some notable instances where vendors did introduce security aspects into client-server and database products, the norm was to ignore it. Scott McNealy, founder and CEO of Sun Microsystems, made the comment in January 1999, "You have zero privacy anyway—get over it." In mid-2001, McNealy came out with: "...absolute privacy is a disaster waiting to happen."

It took until January 2002 for Bill Gates, cofounder and chairman of Microsoft, to make security an official priority for his company with the Trustworthy Computing Initiative. Although many question Gate's level of commitment based on Microsoft's prior performance in the security arena as a whole, it remains to be seen whether or not this is a bona fide commitment.

The Wild World of the Web

The major driving force behind the realization that security mattered in the 1990s and into the second millennium was the rapidly increasing number of applications and services dependent on the Internet. In order to meet the public's and businesses' growing demands to be able to act unencumbered, an environment was needed that would protect personal and confidential information and ensure that no unauthorized persons or systems could access, change, or destroy critical information.

The challenge of maintaining such a secure environment increased by orders of magnitude when the World Wide Web became available over the Internet and personal and corporate use of the Web exploded. The Internet itself was designed for reliability and availability, in particular if significant segments of the interconnecting networks were to break or become nonoperational. The Internet was built originally to facilitate the sharing of information among an exclusive and self-policing population of military personnel and academics. There was little or no consideration of having to protect system use or the transmission of information from one person or system to another.

Initially, security concerns about misuse and misappropriation of information on the Internet were few because the Internet was shared among a relatively small cohort of knowledgeable military personnel, professors, and graduate students. As the Internet became popular with other groups (e.g., business and the general public), not only were the best and the worst elements of society introduced, but renegades showed up even in the academic world. Academic institutions frequently became spawning grounds for hackers as well as breeding environments for viruses and launch pads for distributed denial of service (DDoS) attacks. The *laissez faire* attitude of the select group of early Internet users, which was really successful in furthering knowledge, became a severe handicap as the Internet extended itself into the world at large.

The task to secure the Web became particularly difficult and burdensome precisely because security was given such short shrift during its creation and expansion. The inadequacy of security continues, in part, because the image of the playful geek hacker persists, rather than the recognition that hackers are destructive criminals. In reality, there are many malevolent individuals or groups crawling the Internet for easy, valuable pickings or to create as much havoc as they know how. We see one vulnerability after another being exposed and exploited. We learn of new threats practically every day. And although there are many reported events, the vast majority of such incidents never appear in the public arena.

The information security scene of today was virtually unknown as late as the mid-1990s. Then, the firewall, which has become ubiquitous in commercial, government, and academic networks today, was not known outside the military.[5] In fact, former Israeli military personnel developed the first widely used commercial firewall, produced by Checkpoint. A number of other popular security products have similar military origins.

The proliferation of information security products was, of course, related to both real and perceived risks. During the Cold War, there was major concern that the other side would get hold of military secrets stored on computers. The most feared security events were inside jobs, such as those perpetrated by spies infiltrating internal operations or capturing or luring key knowledgeable personnel, since physical presence was paramount in those early days.[6]

The first real jolt to that reality that communications networks could be compromised and through them the computer systems could be taken down or searched, was the Morris worm in 1988. For the first time it was realized that an

---

5. As reported in [1], a survey of 1,716 IT security professionals by the Information System Security Association (ISSA) and Business Software Alliance (BSA), 97% had firewalls deployed as of the third quarter of 2003 and 1% plan to deploy firewalls over the following 12 months.

6. Back in the 1970s, a colleague, who had in-depth knowledge of certain mainframe computer systems' "internals," told me that he belonged to a group of similarly expert individuals, who were so concerned about their being kidnapped by foreign governments that they set up a calling chain to keep track of one another. He told of one situation in which a group member was contacted and asked to fly somewhere. When he activated his calling chain from the airport, his colleagues appealed to him not to board the plane as they did not recognize the names or affiliation of his contacts.

attack could occur from the outside, and that a piece of programming code could replicate across an extensive network and infect thousands and, today, millions of computers attached to that network.

In the 1980s, paralleling the growth in the number of PCs deployed but not yet attached to networks, we saw computer viruses spread through the exchange of removable media, such as "floppy disks" or "diskettes." Transmission of these wicked programs was slow compared to today, because of their reliance on the "sneaker net" for spreading. Nevertheless, practically everyone experienced them, which was indicative of the promiscuous sharing of floppies at that time. This latter "vector" has been replaced, as the dominant means of spreading viruses, worms, and other forms of attack, by networks, in particular the Internet. The current most popular spreading mechanism is via macros (or programmed routines) in documents and by executables attached to e-mails. Some viruses are spread through access to Web sites. Because of the lightning speed at which huge volumes of messages are shared over the Internet, the rate of proliferation of viruses and other malware has been reduced from weeks and days to hours and minutes.

Another form of security breach that can be much more damaging, but which is far less dramatic, is the unauthorized access of wrongly (or rightly) authenticated individuals, often employed by the organization, to information assets that they are not entitled to access. A refinement of this is type of breach occurs when someone, who is authorized to access a specific application with limited powers, discovers that he or she can access information beyond their proscribed limits. For example, they may be able to modify information that a person, with their particular role, should only be able to view and not change.

This bypass of a restriction of function within a legitimately accessed application is often due to a failure in the access administration process to apply the appropriate constraints or it could be due to a "hole" in the application. There is a difference between someone having been given inappropriate access to a system and actually using it. Those discovering that they can see data that they should not be able to, or operate functions that they should not have the capability of doing, have a choice. They can report the error to management or they can exploit it. In the latter case they will be subject to disciplinary action if they are caught.[7]

The Web has provided many opportunities for exploitation and misuse. It is not inherent in the systems. It is due to the fact that prevention of such

---

7. It was reported in [2] that the director of admissions at Princeton University had hacked into the Yale admissions site and accessed students' statuses regarding their Yale applications. He had used personal information of students, to which he had access through Princeton's application process. While the Yale admissions department could be faulted for having weak security on its Web site, that is not an excuse for a competitor to take advantage of the vulnerability.

misdeeds can be complex and expensive and require a high level of expertise not readily available to an organization.

The Wireless Revolution

Just when security professionals thought that they were getting a handle on Internet security, along came wireless. The ubiquity of wireless communications can be traced back to the growth in use of cellular telephones. Until then, the average member of the public did not have the capability for two-way communication over the ether. There were Citizens Band (CB) radios, radio communications, and beepers. But these were generally available to a select few for whom the high cost and difficulty of use could be justified. Once the cellular telephone became palm-size and the cost of the equipment itself dropped dramatically, the acceptance rate became very high.

Initially there was justifiable concern that cellular phone conversations could be intercepted using a simple scanner, as several very embarrassing high-profile personal conversations have been made public. Analog communications could be relatively easily listened to, so there was a push toward digital cellular telephone service, which is much more difficult, although not impossible, to intercept and interpret.

The next trend was the combination of the pager, cellular phone, and personal digital assistant (PDA). For example, the ubiquitous Blackberry pager device allows for the receipt and sending of electronic mail messages. However, as the features and capabilities of these units advanced, so did the risk related to the interception of these messages. Regrettably, as with many other technologies, the security of wireless networks lags woefully behind their rapid adoption.

Where IT Outsourcing and Security Meet

As we look back over the relatively brief history of IT outsourcing—and the even shorter time for which information security has become an issue for the public at large (it was always an issue for the military and the intelligence agencies)—it is clear that security professionals have been playing catch-up. That is, security attacks have outpaced defenses except (arguably) for a very short time in their early history during which computers were locked away in glass houses and the protection of information assets was under direct physical control.

Minicomputers were intrinsically secure as long as they were cloistered and isolated and they followed the mainframe model. However, it was their deployment across many areas and their interconnectivity that created the risk of compromise at an unguarded location. Even then, however, security was at least somewhat controllable. Although adequate auditing, monitoring, and reporting tools were not readily available, the limited population with access and restrictions of access did mitigate some of the security problems. However, "superuser" status, which gave the system administrator universal access, required many controls and not a little trust. This trust was not always warranted.

It was the introduction of the PC in the early 1980s, however, that really let the cat out of the bag. At first security risks came through the exchange of floppy disks, spreading viruses at what was then an alarming rate, but which appears decidedly sluggish by today's standards. But it was only a short time before many of these PCs were connected to networks and the spread of malware jumped at an accelerating rate as viruses, worms, Trojan horses, and denials of service passed across the network at lightening speed.

The fact that security has, and still is, lagging compared to the creation of new threats has important and far-reaching implications for IT outsourcing. One must be concerned about the level of security at the outsourcer and on the security of communications links between the outsourcer and its customers. Not only has one to be reassured that one's own information is being protected, but the concern must carry over to how well the protective mechanisms have been applied throughout the outsourcer's customer base.

Customers' confidential and secret information has been made available from the genesis of IT outsourcing, as in the case of payroll services. Again, in the early stages, physical security prevailed and was sufficient to meet the security needs as they were.

Even when distributed processing and time-sharing became popular, outsourcers could maintain security by physically isolating services and having information transmitted over secured links from known and protected sources. There were breaches, of course, but many of these were due to "human error," where an operator would not follow set procedures fully or where an error was made in defining the destination of a printout, for example. That is, most breaches were by insiders using authorized or unauthorized access, either intentionally or accidentally.

Over the past 5 years or so, we have seen the growth and change in nature of IT outsourcing. With the advent of the Internet, outsourcers have taken advantage of the low cost and rapidity of deployment that this ubiquitous network allows. At first, the Internet was used as a quick, cheap method of making connections, where all that was needed at the client end was a PC, modem (or other network connection), and browser software. However, such ease of setup and access also meant that evildoers could also easily and cheaply set up means for access. This brought the technologies of strong authentication and encryption to the "common man" where, in the past, it had been restricted to very high-security networks and applications. This raising of the bar, meant that outsourcing relationships had to consider additional security factors, not previously included, in the due diligence performed by customers and in the service agreements negotiated between the corporate parties and with the public.

The outsourcing of Web site development, management, and operations has brought with it a whole new set of issues in regard to the preservation and protection of customers' image and reputation. And, as these Web sites evolve into aggregation sites and corporate and customer portals, the need for protection against damage and misuse is taking another leap upward.

The latest development, that of Web services, has intensified the relationship between customer and outsourcers, where many sources in combination must be relied upon to provide secure processing environments. This spreading out of responsibility for maintaining security across multiple applications, platforms, and networks confronts security professionals with what is by far their greatest challenge to date. Given that our tools, processes, and practices can barely manage the current environment from a security perspective, how are we to handle the next phase?

References

[1]   Verton, D., "IT Security Pros Confident of Defenses," *Computerworld*, Vol. 37, No. 49, December 8, 2003, p. 16.

[2]   Arenson, K. W., "Princeton Pries into Web Site for Yale Applicants," *The New York Times*, Vol. CLI, No. 52,191, July 26, 2002, p. A1.

Selected Bibliography

Annotated References and Resources

This selected bibliography is in the form of lists of books and magazines, articles and papers, conferences and seminars, and on-line (Web) references. These are intended to bridge your way to further research and inquiry on the topics of outsourcing, security, or, more specifically, outsourcing information security.

Because we are cutting across two disciplines, we generally find only a few references specific to outsourcing security and securing outsourcing. We have to go to IT outsourcing references and filter through to find specific mention of security. We can plough though the security literature and select references to outsourcing. However, in the latter case we are more likely to find a focus on the outsourcing of security services, as in engaging MSSPs.

I have attempted to differentiate among three categories, namely:

- Security referenced in outsourcing sources;
- Outsourcing referenced in security sources;
- Specific references to third party security services.

Now a disclaimer: The scope of each category is broad and rapidly expanding in reach and in depth. We are seeing many players, or professed players, jumping on the bandwagon and considerable reportage, increasingly appearing in the popular press, particularly in regard to offshore IT outsourcing and the domestic loss of well-paying, white-collar jobs. The rate of change is so fast that it is well nigh impossible to keep up—the best one can hope to do is to just continue to read, learn, and expand one's horizons as an independent researcher.

So please consider this bibliography as a jumping-off point, not as all-inclusive, and continue to scan publications, conferences, and the Web for new developments, trends, and insights.

Books

Butler, J., *Winning the Outsourcing Game: Making the Best Deals and Making Them Work*, Boca Raton, FL: Auerbach, 2000.

This book provides a framework for developing an outsourcing strategy, choosing what to outsource, and managing the risks of using third-party contractors.

Kuong, J., (ed.), *Security and Privacy for Application Service Provisioning (ASP)—Best Practices and SLAs for ASP Providers and Outsourcers*, Wellesley Hills, MA: Management Advisory Publications, 2001.

This report primarily covers security as it relates to application service providers. This is more targeted to our topic, but limited to one particular category of outsourcer, namely, the ASP.

McCarthy, L., *IT Security: Risking the Corporation*, Upper Saddle River, NJ: Prentice Hall, 2002.

Chapter 9 of this book is entitled "Outsourcing Security" and it illustrates the importance of thoroughly checking the security of third-party providers as well as the customer's security as it relates to the outsourcer.

In order to achieve a satisfactory overall security posture, the author recommends the following:

- Conduct security assessments using commonly available security auditing tools.

- Develop detailed procedures for the audits themselves.

- Perform such audits on a regular basis and when a new system is introduced.

- Ensure that the problems found are in fact resolved.

Purser, S., *A Practical Guide to Managing Information Security*, Norwood, MA: Artech House, 2004.

This book provides a complete guide to how information should be secured and how the information security function should be managed. It is typical of many information security books in that it merely touches upon outsourcing as one aspect of risk related to information security management. However, as pointed out in this book, it is necessary to get a good grounding in the security issues, which this book provides.

Stees, J. D., *Outsourcing Security: A Guide for Contracting Services*, Boston, MA: Butterworth-Heinemann, 1998.

This book provides a guide for contracting services, especially those relating to protective organizations. It is aimed at helping security and facility managers in planning, evaluation of proposals, and contract negotiation. The focus is physical security rather than information security. However, as the worlds of IT and physical security converge, it serves each group to understand the other.

Verton, D., *Black Ice: The Invisible Threat of Cyber-Terrorism*, New York: McGraw-Hill/Osborne, 2003.

Dan Verton examines issues specifically relating to cyber-terrorism and does not discuss outsourcing per se. However, some have voiced concerns that cyber-terrorists will take advantage of their access to source code and production systems to effect cyberattacks, possibly through the introduction of Trojan horse code or just in the knowledge of critical systems and their weaknesses. Verton suggests that, while such acts are feasible, there is no evidence that this has been done.

Williams, O. D., *Outsourcing: A CIO's Perspective*, Boca Raton, FL: St. Lucie Press, 1998.

This book addressed frequently asked questions regarding IT outsourcing and reviews the advantages and disadvantages of it. It does not focus on the security aspects of outsourcing.

Newspapers, Journals, and Magazines

Computer-Related Publications

Understandably, many IT-related publications report negatively about offshore IT outsourcing since it is the jobs of their readership that are most threatened by the trend. Given the obvious bias, there are some important lessons to be learned from the adverse experiences of others as depicted in a number of the following articles. Interestingly, when the outsourcing is domestic, with the transfer of many employees from the customer to the provider, it is seen in a much more positive light.

Anonymous, "Why Outsourcing Won't Work," *CSO Magazine*, Vol. 2, No. 3, March 2003, pp. 58–60.

This article was apparently written by an embittered security officer, whose function is being outsourced, although seemingly not offshore. It criticizes the "number-crunchers" for their not having taken into account in the ROI analysis such intangible, difficult-to-measure factors as loyalty, dedication, and willingness to go the extra mile.

Bertch, W., "Why Offshore Outsourcing Failed Us," *Network Computing*, Vol. 14, No. 21, October 16, 2003, pp. 65–70.

Weslet Bertch describes the experiences of Life Time Fitness when they outsourced the development of a relatively small Web application to a "Tier 1 Indian vendor." The causes for failure were given as inexperienced labor, overemphasis on process, and performance metrics that masked problems.

A sidebar to the article quotes a Deloitte Consulting report stating that the 80% lower wages in India, as compared to the United States, are eaten up by a number of factors, with the actual resulting labor cost saving being in the 10% to 15% range.

Boardman, B., "The Handoff," *Network Computing*, Vol. 14, No. 14, July 24, 2003, pp. 34–38.

This article examines the factors underlying the network and systems management outsourcing decision, be they cost savings, expertise, or degree of control. Particularly interesting is the variation in the types of network problems typically encountered with the size of the company. While cost containment is fairly standard across the board, smaller companies outsource defensively to make up for lack of in-house skills, whereas larger companies are looking to support mobile and wireless connections, obtain international coverage, and offload legacy technologies.

Coffee, P., "Epicenters: Offshore Coding Myth," *eWeek*, May 3, 2004, p. 60.

The subtitle of Peter Coffee's column is "Setting the Record Straight on Programming Quality." He backtracks from his prior siding with a panel of "software security experts," which asserted that the programmers in India do better quality work than those in the United States. He writes that he came upon a report, published in June 2003, which showed that the defect rate of U.S. programmers was better than for those in India, but much worse than than produced by Japanese programmers.

Collett, S., "Losing Control," *Computerworld*, Vol. 38, No. 11, March 15, 2004, p. 38.

With increased legislation and regulation relating to protecting personal sensitive data, in particular, there is a need to ensure that such data is safe. The article provides some very useful tips to how this can be accomplished, including:

- Visit the outsourcing site.
- Require a security audit by a reputable third party.
- Conduct remote vulnerability scans.
- Provide partial information about customers.
- Limit subcontracting in the contract.
- Limit employee turnover at outsourcer contractually.
- Have vendor provide a paperless clean-room environment.
- Keep centralized databases at home site.

Datz, T., "Outsourcing World Tour," *CIO Magazine*, Vol. 17, No. 19, July 15, 2004, pp. 42–48.

Todd Datz's article gives very useful country-by-country ratings for geopolitical risk, English proficiency, and average programmer salary, as well as pros, cons, and an insider tip for each country for countries in Asia, Europe, and the Americas.

Ferranti, M., "Going Abroad," *InfoWorld*, Vol. 26, Issue 6, March 8, 2004, pp. 39–43.

Marc Ferranti's lengthy article provides good insights into the offshore outsourcing decision. He quotes Forrester Research regarding the top outsourcing concerns expressed in a survey of 45 IT executives, ranked in order from the highest, as follows:

- Security concerns about moving work to the provider's county;
- Long-term viability of vendor;
- Resistance from IT staff or business executives;
- Overhead costs of managing offshore projects and services;
- Cultural and language differences;
- Lack of internal management skills.

The article also quotes the Giga Information Group, which was purchased by Forrester Research, as listing the "six steps to offshore success" as follows:

1. Understand why you are outsourcing.

2. Focus on management.

3. Include senior executives.

4. Use project management tools.

5. Institute pilot projects.

6. Send appropriate projects offshore.

Field, T., "Outsourcing 10 Years that Shook IT," *CIO Magazine*, October 1, 1999.

Field describes the major historic IT outsourcing deal initiated by Katherine Hudson of Kodak in 1989. This is viewed as a watershed event, which, while not the first or the largest at the time, had the most impact because Kodak was such a prominent company. This tenth anniversary look back provided some lessons learned and things that Kodak might have done differently in hindsight, such as contract for 5 years rather than 10.

Hayes, M., "Taboo," *InformationWeek*, Issue 949, July 28, 2003, pp. 32–38.

In the first of a two-part series, Mary Hayes describes how many companies are uncomfortable about discussing their offshore outsourcing decisions for fear of a backlash from employees, customers, IT workers, politicians, and the press.

Hayes, M., and E. Chabrow, "Foreign Policy: Should Government Pursue Offshore Outsourcing If It Means U.S. Jobs?" *InformationWeek*, Issue 931, March 17, 2003, pp. 20–22.

As the title suggests, U.S. government agencies are looking to reduce costs through offshore outsourcing. Some politicians appear to support such a trend, whereas others are looking to have businesses and government agencies look to local vendors.

Hayes, M., and P. McDougall, "Gaining Ground," *InformationWeek*, Issue 933, March 31, 2003, pp. 34–42.

This article describes how competition from China, Eastern Europe, and the Philippines in the software development arena is pushing Indian outsourcers to offer higher-end services such as consulting and systems architecture work.

In a sidebar with the title "Foreign Intrigue: Continuity Is a Legitimate Concern," Mary Hayes discusses concerns customers have about offshore IT service companies having confidential data and intellectual property in countries with different regulations and ownership laws. These concerns extend to the business continuity plans such service providers have in place. In another sidebar entitled "Made in the U.S.A.: Small Firms Tout Cheap Native Talent," John

Soat mentions domestic firms that have lowered their charges so as to compete effectively with offshore providers.

Hoffman, T., and P. Thibodeau, "Exporting IT Jobs," *Computerworld*, Vol. 37, No. 17, April 28, 2003, pp. 39–42.

The authors play upon the fear of U.S. IT workers who are concerned that their jobs may be transferred to outsourcing firms in foreign countries. They quote a Forrester Research study that predicts about 473,000 IT and mathematics jobs will go offshore by 2015. In a sidebar, called "There's More to Consider Than Cheaper Labor," Hoffman and Thibodeau discuss political risks, additional indirect project and program management costs, including travel costs and productivity losses during the time away from the office, project requirements "creep" (when it occurs), and the potential loss of intellectual property and trade secrets. The latter two can occur under any outsourcing conditions. The implication is that the risk is greater offshore.

Horwitt, E., "Outsourcing Grows Up," *Microsoft Executive Circle*, Vol. 2, No. 4, Winter 2003, pp. 28–31.

The author states that the cost-cutting benefits of outsourcing are taken as given and that emphasis should be placed on agility and time to market. The article provides a very useful categorization of functions and applications that are most suited to outsourcing, namely:

- Generic, nonbusiness-specific applications;
- Underlying infrastructures;
- Stable applications that are in production;
- Managed hosting of Web-based applications and platforms;
- Strategic applications and services that need to be deployed quickly.

Those candidate applications and services less suited to outsourcing include:

- Business-specific applications;
- Applications and functions that involve sensitive and competitive information;
- Applications still under development;
- Applications that require customized configurations;
- Legacy applications with established support infrastructures.

Hulme, G., "Security's Best Friend?" *InformationWeek*, Issue 846, July 16, 2001, pp. 38–44.

This article describes the growing use of MSSPs, with an estimate by the Yankee Group of $1.7 billion in security services by 2005, as well as the concerns voiced by some security officers and the satisfaction expressed by others. A sidebar with the title "Use Caution When Choosing a Managed Security Vendor" warns of the risk related to the viability of MSSPs, of which the Gartner Group predicts a 60% failure or acquisition rate.

Johnson, M., "Indian Outsourcer Taps Skills of U.S. IT Workers," *Computerworld*, Vol. 37, No. 30, July 28, 2003, p. 14.

In an interview with Kumar Mahadeva, CEO of Cognizant Technology Solutions Corp., a rapidly growing Indian outsourcer, Maryfran Johnson, editor-in-chief of *Computerworld*, highlights the fact that Cognizant, during the latter part of 2003, was hiring about a quarter of new staff locally in the United States for senior-level positions in particular.

King, J., "Damage Control," *Computerworld*, Vol. 38, No. 28, July 12, 2004, pp. 31-32.

In this article, suggestions are provided as to how to guard against the anticipated backlash of offshore outsourcing from employees and customers. Preventive measures when dealing with employees include:

- Centralizing communications and delivering previously agreed-upon key messages;
- Including all stakeholders in the decision-making process;
- Reinvesting some of the savings in the management of the arrangement.

With regard to customers, the article suggests:

- Minimizing the movement offshore of customer-facing applications;
- Guaranteeing service levels to customers;
- Stating benefits in terms of customer value rather than cost savings.

Krishna, S., S. Sahay, and G. Walsham, "Managing Cross-Cultural Issues in Global Software Outsourcing," *Communications of the ACM*, Vol. 47, No. 4, April 2004, pp. 62–66.

The focus of this article is on cross-cultural issues as they relate to choosing appropriate projects to outsource offshore, managing the relationship, selecting the right mix of staff, and cultural training for employees prior to being assigned to a project.

Levinson, M., "Life After Outsourcing," *CIO Magazine*, Vol. 17, No. 15, May 15, 2004, pp. 36–43.

This article takes a very positive look at the impact of three major outsourcing agreements, which Nextel executed with Amdocs, IBM, and EDS during the 2000–2002 period for some $2.2 billion. The contracts were for terms ranging from 5 to 9 years. Levinson reports on interviews with Nextel's CIO, a senior operations manager, a business unit vice-president, and an employee who was among about 4,800 employees who transferred to the outsourcers. The general tenor of the article is upbeat with descriptions of real operational and business benefits derived from these arrangements.

Lynch, R., "Outsourcing Leadership: Hands On, Hands Off," *CIO Magazine*, August 15, 2000; http://www.cio.com.

This article discusses what it takes to manage outsourcing relationship successfully and asks whether one person, namely, the CIO, can handle both high-level and detailed aspects. The article points to the importance of setting up a sustaining structure and direction, building processes and monitoring the day-to-day relationship. It also describes how successful outsourcing relationships optimize the skills of the leader supplemented by those of persons delegated operational responsibilities.

Mearian, L., "Merrill Lynch Hands over SAN Management," *Computerworld*, August 20, 2001; http://www.computerworld.com.

Merrill Lynch is again shown to be a pioneer in outsourcing. This time it is with storage area networks. The focus is on control and costs. Security issues or protection of customer information is not mentioned in the article. Considering that securing customer data under the control of a third party has become a major regulatory requirement for U.S. financial firms, one would hope that adequate due diligence was done on protecting customer data in a SAN environment.

Overby, S., "Lost in Translation," *CIO Magazine*, Vol. 17, No. 19, July 15, 2004, pp. 50–56.

Stephanie Overby addresses the issue of knowledge transfer to offshore vendors—what makes it successful, what to expect, which projects are favorable, and which are not.

Rae-Dupree, J., "Offshore Winds," *CIO Insight*, Number 38, April 2004, pp. 50–56.

While the article does not address security specifically, it does touch on risks due to political, economic, and social uncertainty. According to a *CIO Insight* survey, conducted in February 2004, only 3% of respondents considered these risks to be the most significant management issue. One interesting item is the comparison of the actual hourly software development rate and the risk-adjusted rate. Using such a comparison, China's risk-adjusted rate is half, or less than half, of that of any other country considered, which includes Canada, Ireland, Mexico, Poland, India, and Israel. This is despite it having one of the highest ratios between risk-adjusted rates to regular rates.

> Rothfeder, J., "The Road Less Traveled," *CIO Insight*, No. 37, March 2004, pp. 42–52.

Merrill Lynch's human resources (HR) management determined that they could reduce costs by more than double were they to streamline their in-house HR call center rather than outsource to a third party.

> Solomon, M., "Outsourcing Overhauls," *Computerworld*, Vol. 34, No. 35, September 2, 2002, pp. 40–41.

The subtitle of this article is "How to Renegotiate Troubled Relationships and Live Happily Until a Contract's End," which referred to an IT outsourcing contract farmed out by Johns Manville to (I)Structure Inc. The article describes how a troubled relationship was renegotiated and brought back into line. Such real-life articles are extremely valuable, since they provide readers with a suggested roadmap for repairing unhappy outsourcing relationships.

> Tas, J., and S. Sunder, "Financial Services Business Process Outsourcing," *Communications of the ACM*, Vol. 47, No. 5, May 2004, pp. 50–52.

Tas and Sunder extend the concept of business process outsourcing in manufacturing to workflow processes in financial services in the belief that the latter will soon follow the pattern of the former. Driving factors for offshore outsourcing include the increasing sophistication of software and other technologies, the falling cost of infrastructure, and the increasing availability of communications lower-priced bandwidth.

> Thibodeau, P., "Another State Looks Offshore," *Computerworld*, Vol. 37, No. 51, December 22, 2003, pp. 1 and 49

In response to Washington State Health Care Authority's problems in regard to an offshore outsourcing contract, State Representative Zack Hudgins was planning to introduce a bill in the Washington State Legislature blocking the state from sending work offshore.

> Thibodeau, P., "Banks Plan Offshore Sharing," *Computerworld*, Vol. 38, No. 8, February 23, 2004, pp. 1 and 14.

A meeting, organized by the Financial Services Technology Consortium (FSTC) of financial services firms, including J.P. Morgan Chase, Citibank, and Wells Fargo, was arranged to develop best practices for offshore outsourcing operations related to basic services, such as business continuity planning, where the firms are not competing. They were to consider sharing information on political and environmental risks in foreign countries. Baseline practices were to be considered in physical, information, and personnel security, protecting intellectual property, software change management, and so on.

Thibodeau, P., and S. Lemon, "R&D Starts to Move Offshore," *Computerworld*, Vol. 38, No. 9, March 1, 2004, pp. 1 and 16.

The reporters describe a trend for U.S. companies to send more sophisticated IT work, such as research and development, to facilities in India, for example.

Verton, D., "Offshore Coding Work Raises Security Concerns," *Computerworld*, Vol. 37, No. 18, May 5, 2003, pp. 1 and 16.

Reporting on a Techno-Security Conference in Myrtle Beach, South Carolina, Dan Verton voices the concerns, which were expressed by a panel of corporate security officers, regarding the risks related to outsourcing critical software development to countries, particularly China, which already is claimed to have "a significant economic espionage program that targets U.S. technology."

Vijayan, J., "Premier 100 IT Leaders 2004: Outsourcing," *Computerworld*, Vol. 38, No. 1, January 5, 2004, pp. 30–32.

Of course, it is better to avoid outsourcing problems than to have to fix them. CNA Financial Corp. pulled the plug on a $20 million software application upgrade project gone wrong, which had been outsourced to a provider in India. The article provides advice and how to avoid the problems encountered by CNA.

Security Publications

Ollman, G., "Third Party or Third Rate?" *SC Magazine*, May 2004, p. 29.

As a security consultant, his more security-savvy customers occasionally ask Ollmann to perform security assessments of third-party service providers. Among other things required of providers, he suggests examining reports by any third-party security reviewers and finding out which of the recommended changes have been implemented and whether resources are shared with other customers. He also says that the customer, in demanding that an assessment be done, may be able to split the costs with the provider, who also benefits.

Schneier, B., "Outsourcing Security," *Password: The ISSA Magazine*, February 2002, pp. 4–6.

As the CTO and founder of Counterpane Internet Security, Inc., a managed security services provider, Bruce Schneier is clearly biased in favor of organizations using third parties to take on certain information security functions, such as vulnerability scanning, monitoring, consulting, and forensics. He suggests that the customer retain management of its own security. His arguments in favor of outsourcing include cost-effectiveness, around-the-clock coverage by specialists, aggregation of expertise, a broader view of the Internet, and frequent exposure to attacks.

Business and Business/Technology Publications

Ante, S. E., with Hof, R. D., "Look Who's Going Offshore," *BusinessWeek*, May 17, 2004, pp. 64–65.

This is one of an increasing number of articles appearing in newspapers and magazines which point to what is viewed as a new trend, namely, technology start-ups looking to set up research centers offshore. There is also an interest by venture capitalists in funding such start-ups since they believe that the lower costs thereby incurred will increase the chances of success for a given investment. The article does not mention such aspects as the theft of intellectual property or industrial sabotage, yet these should be real concerns when such leading-edge functions are set up in other countries.

Axelrod, C. W., "The Risks of Outsourcing," *Securities Industry Management*, Vol. 2, No. 1, February/March 1994, pp. 50–51.

Written in the wake of major IT outsourcing arrangements by Kodak, Merrill Lynch, and Salomon Brothers, this article is somewhat negative towards management who engaged in such ventures. Certain areas were seen to be suitable for outsourcing, if conducted subject to specific factors.

Daly, R., "Navigating the Offshoring Seas," *Waters*, February 2004, pp. 22–26.

The article describes investment bank Lehman Brothers' experiences with outsourcing software development and help-desk support to four centers in India in order to reduce costs. Lehman partnered with Tata Consultancy Services (TCS) and Wipro Technologies. At the end of the article, Lehman acknowledged that there were problems with some of the relationships and that it was discontinuing its arrangement with Wipro's Sprectramind unit because of service-level problems with help desk support. A Lehman spokesperson recommended not sending services requiring 24-hour, 7-day support and client interaction offshore, but keeping them in the United States or Canada, if they are to be outsourced.

Dobbs, L., "Is Nothing Private Anymore?" *The Dobbs Report, U.S. News & World Report,* Vol. 136, No. 17, May 17, 2004, p. 57.

This column raises the issue of the transfer abroad of proprietary information, intellectual property, and business intelligence. In particular, personal financial information and private medical records are being shipped offshore to meet processing requirements. Legislators are active at the national and state level proposing bills to protect such information from unauthorized use and abuse.

Einhorn, B., and M. Kripalani, "China: Move Over, India," *Business Week,* August 11, 2003, pp. 42–43.

The article quotes a Gartner Dataquest prediction that China will have practically caught up with India in its revenues from software and computer services by 2006, fueled in part by India's companies seeking cheaper skilled labor in China.

Hulme, G., "Security Handoff: More Large Companies Are Turning to Service Providers to Handle Their Security," *Wall Street & Technology,* July 2003, pp. 26–28.

George Hulme, who is also a senior editor at *Information Week,* quotes from executives at financial services companies, such as Merrill Lynch and Raymond James Financial, who have outsourced security services.

Marlin, S., "The Right Fit," *Bank Systems & Technology,* June 2002, pp. 27–30, and 46.

The article describes how major outsourcing deals fall into categories defined by Gartner Dataquest. Dataquest distinguishes between the extent to which the outsourcer provides shared or dedicated services and to whether the primary benefit is value or efficiency.

Marlin, S., "Opening Gambit," *Bank Systems & Technology,* February 2003, pp. 22–25, and 37.

As with many business-oriented, rather than computer-related, publications, Marlin's article is favorable to outsourcing and describes a series of major outsourcing deals to providers, such as IBM and EDS, from financial institutions including JP Morgan Chase, Bank of America, ABN Ambro, Deutsche Bank, American Express, and CIBC. The first four deals alone totaled $13.3 billion.

Ramsaran, C., "Special Report: Outsourcing Obstacles," *Bank Systems & Technology,* June 2004, pp. 38–39.

Cynthia Ramsaran maintains that, despite political pressure and concerns about security, U.S. financial institutions can establish and benefit from safe off-shore outsourcing relationships if goals are realistic and strict legal guidelines are defined in advance. The "rules of the game" are given as follows:

- Know the company with whom you are dealing.
- Know your overseas staff.
- Find out the company's technology infrastructure.
- Don't fall into the legal trap.
- Prepare for more downstream outsourcing.

The last item refers to further subcontracting by an offshore outsourcer to another country.

Safire, W., "On Language: Outsourcing—And the Urge to Insource," *New York Times Magazine*, March 21, 2004, Section 6, p. 30.

William Safire gives interesting origins, histories, and definitions of words such as "outsourcing," "insourcing," and "intersourcing."

Schmerken, I., "Offshore Outsourcing: Is Your Data Safe?" *Wall Street & Technology*, May 2004, pp. 14–20.

Ivy Schmerken's article is one of the few to date that actually is directed at the security of outsourcing. Ivy, whom I have known for many years, called me early in the writing of the article and I was able to assist with background information only (no quotes), as I did not have permission for attribution. The article provides a good summary of the threats and risks related to offshore outsourcing.

"Business Keeps Getting Better for Offshore-Outsourcing Vendors," *Wall Street & Technology*, June 2003, p. 10.

This brief, one-page summary quotes from industry analysis firm The TowerGroup, which lists major clients of firms such as I-flex, Infosys, and Wipro and describes the nature of the providers' services. It also lists the securities industry activities outsourced to Indian vendors and their extent of use of those activities.

Web-Based Resources

The Web is an incredible resource. Research that once took weeks or months to complete can now be accomplished in a matter of minutes. The vast amount of information available at little or no cost on the millions of Web sites, each of which can be accessed in seconds, combined with extremely fast search engines, such as Google, makes for rapid convergence upon needed information. Combined with hot links that bring you immediately to other referenced Web sites, this makes for highly efficient searches and very effective narrowing down to relevant sources.

Nevertheless, there are some downsides to the Web, which bring a measure of caution to providing and following up on Web references, as follows:

- Much of the information available on the Web has not been subjected to a reviewer or referee's scrutiny, so that its validity or accuracy may be questionable. Sometimes the source of the information is sufficiently well respected to itself validate the quality of a reference.

- With the shenanigans of hackers on the Internet, it is possible for information on a Web site to have been tampered with and therefore a reader might be tricked into assuming that something is from a respected and trusted source when it is not.

- Site owners can withdraw information, in the form of reports, articles, news items, and the like, from Web sites at any time. Consequently, one might provide a Web address as a source and that information may no longer be available. Sometimes, a search engine, such as Google, might cache the information. In such a case, clicking on "cache" might retrieve the noncurrent version of a reference.

  In his popular book *Secrets & Lies: Digital Security in a Networked World* (New York: John Wiley & Sons, 2000, p. 399), Bruce Schneier states the following in a preamble to his "Resources" section:

  All URLs [Web site addresses] are guaranteed as of ... [date]. Some Internet pundits have decried the Web as useless for scholarly archives, claiming that URL's move and disappear regularly. Consider this list to be an ongoing experiment to prove or disprove that thesis.

  I accessed the Web site addresses mentioned here and throughout the book in the April–August 2004 period, and referenced documents were available at that time. As I mentioned elsewhere, in the event that a particular reference is not available, it can often be obtained by contacting the owner of the Web site or the author(s) of the document.

- Some references may not have ever been posted to a Web site, possibly due to their having been created prior to the setup of a particular Web site or even prior to the Internet itself in its current ubiquitous form. Here again, the Web-site owner or author(s) may be willing to oblige with a copy of the document(s).

Despite all the above disclaimers, the Web remains the primary source of current information and thinking and, when used judiciously, supplies invaluable information often at a very low cost. Here is a small sample of Web sites relevant to our topics:

http://www.aspnews.com

News headlines related to ASPs, news articles, discussion forums, analysis, and articles on industry trends are provided at this Web site. There is also an ASP Industry Directory, which listed about 1,800 ASPs and 200 products as of May 2004. Articles available at the Web site are well written and informative.

http://www.aspstreet.com

There is an ASP directory at this site, which lists a variety of ASP organizations.

http://www.bitpipe.com

Bitpipe provides access to many IT-related reports and papers produced by vendors, which are generally free, and by research groups, for which there is generally a charge that can be quite high.

http://www.outsourcing.com and http://www.outsourcing institute.com

The Outsourcing Institute touts itself as "the first and only global professional association dedicated solely to outsourcing." Be that as it may, the Web site has separate categories for buyers, service providers and industry "influencers." While clearly marketing oriented, the site does provide access to a number of publications and issues an "Annual Outsourcing Index," which contains articles of interest to the various constituencies, mostly the providers.

http://www.outsourcing-center.com

The OutsourcingCenter (run by the Everest Group) is a very extensive resource containing a wide variety of publications and other material. It is a commercial site, clearly funded by those in the outsourcing business or supporting outsourcing (such as consultants and law firms), and it is often necessary to give up contact information in order to obtain referenced information. However, the richness and scope of the information make it well worth a visit. There is an on-line magazine called *Outsourcing Journal*, which includes write-ups of major outsourcing deals and has an annual awards program. There is a research area where "sponsored research" is available. With the warning that content is clearly biased in favor of outsourcing, the site provides interesting insights and keeps the reader up to date with outsourcing activity throughout the world.

Web-Based Resources Related to Specific Publications

Some publications have really good research or resource centers on the Web, which specialize in outsourcing and security. Here are some examples.

Computerworld has an excellent site called the "Outsourcing Knowledge Center" at http://www.computerworld.com/managementtopics/outsourcing. The site contains a special report entitled *Outsourcing: Offshore Buyer's Guide*, which includes such on-line articles as Mark Willoughby's "Offshore Security: Considering the Risks" and "Hidden Malware in Offshore Products Raises Concerns" (*Computerworld*, September 15, 2003), which specifically deal with security issues relating to outsourcing. While these particular articles focus on offshore outsourcing, they apply for the most part to all forms of IT outsourcing. *Computerworld*'s "Outsourcing Knowledge Center" also very useful links to other sources, obtained by clicking on the word "Resources" on the home page.

CIO Magazine has so-called research centers for outsourcing as well as security and privacy available at http://www.cio.com/research/outsourcing and http://www.cio.com/research/security respectively. *CIO Magazine* also has a section of its Web site called "Executive Summaries," of which one is devoted to outsourcing at http://www.cio.com/summaries/outsorcing. Of particular interest are the subsections on ASPs and SLAs. In the ASP subsection, there is a checklist that includes the following pieces of useful advice:

- Keep the contract term as short as possible.

- Benchmark through vendor competition by getting bids from a number of vendors.

- Establish one or two simple metrics to track growing use, number of users, or number of transactions processed.

- Create really effective performance penalties, which motivate good service.

- Arrange for cost-free termination in the case of underperformance.

The site also provides a number of good resources, some of which are given in the next section.

NetworkWorld magazine has a very informative Web site called NetworkWorldFusion at http://www.nwfusion.com. Of interest are the Outsourcing Research Center, in particular, and the Security Research Center, which provide news items, breaking news, case studies, special reports, white papers, and articles.

Conferences and Seminars

While the conferences listed have already taken place, they are often annual events. Consequently, you can check the various Web sites mentioned for upcoming conferences, seminars, and the like. Also, it might be possible to obtain copies of presentations, not currently available on the Web sites, from conference organizers or directly from presenters.

"Managing Risk for Service Provider Relationships," *BITS/American Banker Financial Services Outsourcing Conference*, Washington, D.C., November 14–15, 2002.

As spelled out in the conference title, the presentations addressed issues facing financial services firms in regard to outsourcing IT and business processes. Specific security-related presentations included the following: "Outsourcing Security: Shifting the Function but Never the Responsibility" by Susan M. Koski, Mellon Financial Corporation, "SAS 70, Systrust and WebTrust: The Third-Party Assurance Shootout" by Everett C. Johnson, Deloitte & Touche, LLP, and "Outsourcing Managed Security Services" by Dr. Carol Sledge, Software Engineering Institute, Carnegie Mellon University, and "BITS IT Service Provider Security Assessments Framework" by Lari Sue Taylor, Fleet Bank. At the same conference, I was on a panel on "Cross-Border Outsourcing: Tales from the Front" which was moderated by Stephanie Moore, Giga Information Group. Presentations are no longer available on the Web.

"Critical and Emerging Outsourcing Issues and Trends," *Second Annual BITS/American Banker Financial Services Outsourcing Conference*, Washington, D.C., November 6–7, 2003.

Continuing from the previous year's successful meeting, the 2003 conference provided updates from regulators and industry practitioners. Laura Berger of the Federal Trade Commission presented "Service Provider Requirements under the Safeguards Rule," relating to the information security programs that financial institutions must develop, including oversight of service providers. Many of the presentations, including the above, are available at http://www.tfconferences.com/conferences/Archives/FSO03/presentations.html.

"The Offshore IT Outsourcing Forum," *Outsourcing Strategies 2004 Conference*, Las Vegas, NV, March 3–5, 2004.

This conference consisted of keynote presentations, thought-leader roundtables, sessions, and case studies covering such topics as:

- RFP Outsourcing Due Diligence Strategies;
- Offshore Outsourcing to China: A Case Study in Software Development;

- Offshore Outsourcing Backlash.

High-level descriptions of the sessions are available at http://www.out-sourcingstrategies.biz/live/25/.

Second Annual Cyber Security in the Financial Services Sector Executive Summit, New York, October 9–10, 2003.

Security-oriented, this conference had a couple of sessions relating to outsourcing. One was entitled "International Network Complexities" and touched on the following items:

- Offshore outsourcing;
- International privacy regulations;
- Security concerns with international third parties;
- Internal system exposures of non-U.S. subsidiaries and branches;
- Considering country risk;
- Regulatory and audit requirements.

Another session had the title "The Outsourcing Lifecycle: Keys to Successfully Managing the RFP/Selection/Vendor Management/Service Level Agreement Lifecycle" and addressed the following topics, among others:

- Is outsourcing the future of cyber security?
- Offshore outsourcing: can you be sure that it is safe?
- Assessing your potential outsourcers: keys to successful due diligence;
- Monitoring service providers;
- Third-party assessments.

The third annual conference was scheduled for October 27–28, 2004. Information regarding theses conferences can be found at http://www.imn.org.

The 2004 India Outsourcing Summit, Bangalore, India, October 12–14, 2004.

This is an annual conference, which is organized by TFCI (Trade Fairs & Conferences International), that covers the outsourcing business from the perspective of Indian vendors.

Publications from Professional Associations and Academic Institutions

Basel Committee on Banking Supervision, Bank for International Settlements (BIS), "The Joint Forum: Outsourcing in Financial Services," August 2004; http://www.bis.org/publ/joint09.pdf.

The BIS is an influential international organization, which serves to maintain global monetary and financial stability through fostering cooperation among central banks and international organizations. This paper presents a set of principles designed to mitigate the risk aspects of outsourcing that are particularly relevant to the banking, securities, and insurance sectors and from which more focused guidance is to be developed by each sector. The report emphasizes that, when outsourcing, financial institutions transfer risk, management and compliance to third parties. The Committee expressed particular concern in regard to possible over-reliance on outsourcers for critical activities affecting the viability of a financial institution and the institution's obligations to its customers.

BITS IT Service Provider Working Group, *BITS Framework for Managing Technology Risk for IT Service Provider Relationships, Version 2*, Washington, D.C.: Banking Industry Technology Secretariat (BITS), November 2003; http://www.bitsinfo.org.

This report provides a detailed framework for evaluating proposals from IT service providers. It includes advice on developing a request for proposal, performing due diligence, negotiating service level agreements, implementing services and managing ongoing relationships with both U.S. onshore (domestic) and offshore providers. This is one of the best and most comprehensive publicly available guides to selecting IT service providers and represents the combined intelligence and experience of practitioners from some 75 of the largest U.S. financial institutions. And it's free!

Network Systems Survivability Program, *Outsourcing Managed Security Services*, Pittsburgh, PA: Software Engineering Institute, Carnegie Mellon University, 2003, http://www.fedcirc.gov.

The report deals with the process for evaluating and implementing an outsourcing relationship with an MSSP. While it emanates from academia, the researchers took pains to consult with practitioners and created a document that follows a particular framework that the Software Engineering Institute has developed and used throughout a series of reports. Yet the report is also valuable as a guide for the practitioner. In fact, members of the BITS IT Service Provider Working Group, mentioned earlier, participated in the writing and editing of this report.

Research Groups

The reports referenced in this section are not generally available without first subscribing to the information services of the respective research groups. The information provided by the groups with which I am familiar, is well worth the cost as it is not in the public domain and often gives a view of the outsourcing and security industries, which is not accessible elsewhere. For any organization expecting to invest heavily in these outsourced services, being aware of the industry dynamics and the experiences of other companies, as well as benefiting from the subject matter expertise of the analysts, can easily justify the expenditure.

Forrester Research

> Rasmussen, M., "Securing Business Partner and Outsourcing Relationships," Forrester Research "ForrTel," March 4, 2004.

Mike Rasumussen, who wrote the foreword to this book, is a director at Forrester Research. Forrester conducts periodic teleconferences, accompanied by simultaneous slide presentations accessible from their Web site, which they call "ForrTels." This particular ForrTel discussed "securing the extended business," meaning that it necessary to assure oneself that business partners are secure and comply with many of the same requirements as the customer organization. The discussion covered the components of due diligence as well as specifically addressing general security, security management, personnel security, access control, system development and maintenance, network security, and disaster recovery/business continuity.

Gartner

The Gartner Group, at http://www.gartner.com, provides a range of information technology research and papers on their Web site at no charge. There is a specific focus area with the title "IT Services and Outsourcing" and another on "Security and Privacy." Gartner offers a free *Outsourcing Handbook* and a special report with the title "India Offshore Sourcing Options." Gartner also held an *Outsourcing Summit* in May 2004 in Las Vegas and was planning *Gartner Summit India 2004* for August 2004 in Mumbai (formerly Bombay) in India.

Government Sources: Legal and Regulatory

> FDIC, *Offshore Outsourcing of Data Services by Insured Institutions and Associated Consumer Privacy Risks*, June 2004. Available at http://www.fdic.gov/regulations/examinations/offshore/offshore_outsourcing_06-04-04.pdf.

The FDIC (Federal Deposit Insurance Corporation), which is an independent agency created by the U.S. Congress in 1933 to supervise banks and insure deposits, issued this report. The report contains findings of a study of risks associated with offshore outsourcing with emphasis on threats to the privacy of customers. It provides an excellent listing of risks, including country risk, operations/transaction risk, compliance risk, strategic risk, and credit risk. The main recommendations from the study is that financial institutions should:

- Encourage identification of undisclosed third-party contracting arrangements.
- Consider enhancing Bank Service Company Act (BSCA) retention procedures through the creation of a central database.

FFIEC, *IT Examination Handbook: Supervision of Technology Service Providers*, March 2003.

As indicated on their Web site (http://www.ffiec.gov), the U.S. Federal Financial Institutions Examination Council (FFIEC) is a formal interagency body empowered to prescribe uniform principles, standards, and report forms for the federal examination of financial institutions. FFIEC members are the Board of Governors of the Federal Reserve System, the Federal Deposit Insurance Corporation, the National Credit Union Administration, the Office of the Comptroller of the Currency, and the Office of Thrift Supervision. The FFIEC also makes recommendations to promote uniformity in the supervision of financial institutions.

The FFIEC has published a series of booklets that provide guidance to the examiners. When completed, the booklets will replace the *1996 FFIEC Information Systems Examination Handbook*.

In the current series of booklets, the FFIEC published "The Supervision of Technology Service Providers (TSPs)" in March 2003 (http://www.ffiec.gov/ffiecinfobase/booklets/tsp/tech_ser_provider.pdf), which provides excellent guidance in managing risks related to financial institutions' engaging IT service providers.

The FFIEC issued a booklet in June 2004 on "Outsourcing Technology Services (OT)," which "provides guidance and examination procedures to assist examiners and bankers in evaluating a financial institution's risk management processes to establish, manage, and monitor IT outsourcing relationships." This booklet is available at http://www.ffiec.gov/ffiecinfobase/booklets/outsourcing/Outsourcing_Booklet.pdf.

Another booklet, namely, "Development and Acquisition," published in April 2004, addresses risk issues related to the management of software development outsourcing. It is available at http://www.ffiec.gov/ffiecinfobase/booklets/d_a/d_and_a.pdf.

Outsourcing risk management is also addressed in the "Management," booklet, published in June 2004 and available at http://www.ffiec.gov/ffiecinfo-base/booklets//mang/mang.pdf

On page 32 of the booklet, institutions are advised to consider the following factors:

- Ensuring that the institution's overall objectives and strategic plans are supported by each outsourcing arrangement;
- Performing evaluations of outsourcers with regard to the scope and criticality of the services to be outsourced;
- Developing a degree of monitoring justified by the initial and continuing risks related to the outsourcing arrangement.

Office of the Comptroller of the Currency, *OCC Bulletin: Third-Party Relationships*, OCC 2001-47, November 1, 2001.

Office of the Comptroller of the Currency, *OCC Bulletin: Bank Use of Foreign-Based Third-Party Service Providers*, OCC 2002-16, May 1, 2002.

The Office of the Comptroller of the Currency (OCC) issues bulletins to provide guidance to national U.S. banks for managing risks. The above two bulletins, OCC 2001-47 and OCC 2002-16, deal specifically with business relationships with third parties and with outsourcing relationships with foreign-based third-party service providers respectively. The bulletins are available at http://www.occ.treas.gov/ftp/bulletin/2001-47.doc and http://www.occ.treas.gov/ftp/bulletin/2002-16.doc.

United States General Accounting Office, *Information Technology: Leading Commercial Practices for Outsourcing of Services*, GAO-02-214, November 2001. Available at no charge at http://www.gao.gov.

The General Accounting Office (GAO) is the investigative arm of Congress and, as such, analyses, recommends and otherwise provides assistance to support Congress in its oversight responsibilities. In order to address concerns relating to the acquisition of IT services, particularly with respect to the Department of Defense, the GAO identified what they considered to be leading commercial practices for acquiring IT services. This report provides an excellent overview of best practices for IT outsourcing.

Vendors and Service Providers

As part of their marketing and public relations efforts, many vendors and IT service providers, and their associations and lobby groups, offer an abundance of marketing brochures, white papers, and other forms of informational literature. Of course, these are heavily biased in favor of outsourcing and using MSSPs, but they can provide additional perspectives and some useful information for when a justification has to be made.

Counterpane Internet Security, Inc.

Perhaps the most outspoken proponent of the MSSP concept is Bruce Schneier, founder and chief technology officer of Counterpane, which pioneered the MSSP marketplace and continues to be a leader in its field. On May 19, 2004, Counterpane announced that it had received a 2004 Red Herring 100 award.

Counterpane's Web site, at http://www.counterpane.com, contains a number of essays, white papers, and presentations by Bruce Schneier presenting a strong justification for the use of MSSPs.

Wipro Technologies

Wipro is a major offshore outsourcing company based in India. The company's Web site, which is at http://www.wipro.com, contains many interesting and informative white papers and presentations, which they sponsor. For example, the carry a white paper by S. M. Torto and R. Yesner of the research group, IDC, with the title "The Role and Benefits of Quality in Delivering Offshore IT Services." This paper addresses many of the items mentioned in this book, although the bias is very much towards the more positive aspects of offshore IT services.

Similarly, a Wipro white paper, entitled "Outsourcing Total Cost of Management Benefits," looks at all the costs and cost savings and shows significant benefits for offshore outsourcing versus internal operations. Most of the benefits derive from invisible or hidden costs, particularly productivity and revenue losses due to down time.

Education and Certification

Kenneth van Wyk, noted expert and author on secure application programming, mentioned in May 2004 that his nephew had just obtained an undergraduate computer science degree from a respected institution of higher education without once touching on the subject of how to write secure code. This appears to be the norm, rather than the exception. Some information security or security-related courses are appearing in certain information technology graduate programs, however. In 2001 the U.S. government initiated a program called Federal Cyber Service Scholarship for Service (SFS), under which students obtain scholarships if they commit to working for a certain period of time in government. Whereas the latter is meant to address the shortage of security professionals, it appears that the graduates of the government program had difficulty in placing graduates into suitable employment within government.

Leading U.S. business schools have recently added outsourcing courses to their curricula, as described in the *New York Times* article "Executive Life: Outsourcing Joins the M.B.A. Curriculum" (March 28, 2004, Section 3, p. 11).

Currently, the main sources of education are the several security-related certifications offered by organizations such as (ISC)^2 or IISSCC (International Information Systems Security Certification Consortium), ISACA (Information Systems Audit and Control Association), and the SANS (SysAdmin, Audit, Network, Security) Institute. The (ISC)^2 offers the Certified Information Systems Security Professional (CISSP); ISACA has the Certified Information Security Manager (CISM) and SANS has the more technical Global Information Assurance Certification (GIAC) program. You can learn more about these at http://www.isc2.org, http://www.isaca.org, and http://www.sans.org, respectively.

About the Author

C. Warren Axelrod is a director of Pershing LLC, a BNY Securities Group Co., with global responsibility for information security. He develops and enforces corporate security policies, standards, and architectures for Pershing. He has worked in many areas of the securities industry, at firms such as SIAC and HSBC Securities, and is involved at both industry and national levels with security and critical infrastructure protection issues.

Dr. Axelrod was honored with a *Computerworld* Premier 100 IT Leaders Award for 2003 and his department's implementation of an intrusion detection system earned a Best in Class award.

He represented financial services security interests at the Y2K command center in Washington over the century date rollover. He also served two terms on the Board of Managers of the Financial Services Information Sharing and Analysis Center (FS/ISAC), which is a public-private collaborative effort to share information on security threats, vulnerabilities, and incidents among members.

Dr. Axelrod testified at a Congressional Hearing on November 15, 2001, on the subject of cyber security and contributed a section on physical security to the Banking and Finance Sector's "National Strategy for Critical Infrastructure Assurance," which was published in May 2002.

He is on the editorial advisory board of *The ISSA Journal*, and is also chairman of the Generally Accepted Information Security Principles (GAISP) Information Security Policy Principles Working Group. The latter group is charged with developing a set of detailed global principles relating to information security policy, standards, guidelines, and practices.

Dr. Axelrod has chaired and participated in many professional and industry conferences throughout the United States, Europe, and Asia. He has published two previous books on computer management and more than 50 articles on many aspects of information technology, including computer and network security, contingency planning, and computer-related risks. He has chaired and presented at about 60 conferences for the financial services industry and for computer management, technology, and security professionals.

Dr. Axelrod holds a Ph.D. in managerial economics from the Johnson Graduate School of Management at Cornell University in Ithaca, New York. He also earned a B.A. in electrical engineering and an M.A. in economics and statistics, both from the University of Glasgow, Scotland. He is certified as a CISSP and CISM.

Index

Role-Based Access Controls, David F. Ferraiolo, D. Richard Kuhn, and Ramaswamy Chandramouli

Secure Messaging with PGP and S/MIME, Rolf Oppliger

Security Fundamentals for E-Commerce, Vesna Hassler

Security Technologies for the World Wide Web, Second Edition, Rolf Oppliger

Techniques and Applications of Digital Watermarking and Content Protection, Michael Arnold, Martin Schmucker, and Stephen D. Wolthusen

For further information on these and other Artech House titles, including previously considered out-of-print books now available through our In-Print-Forever® (IPF®) program, contact:

Artech House
685 Canton Street
Norwood, MA 02062
Phone: 781-769-9750
Fax: 781-769-6334
e-mail: artech@artechhouse.com

Artech House
46 Gillingham Street
London SW1V 1AH UK
Phone: +44 (0)20 7596-8750
Fax: +44 (0)20 7630-0166
e-mail: artech-uk@artechhouse.com

Find us on the World Wide Web at:
www.artechhouse.com